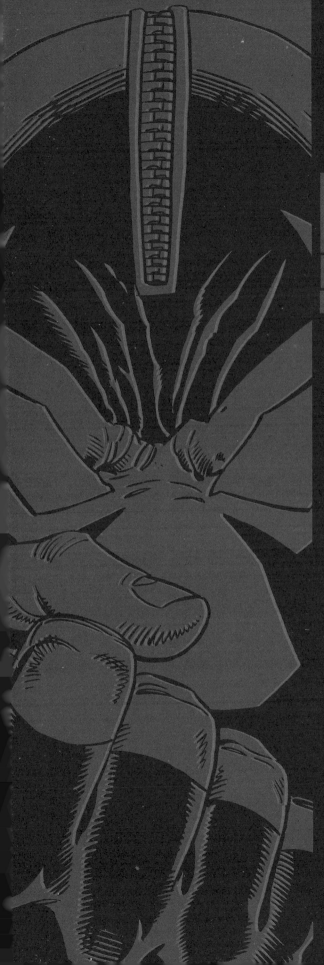

BATMAN
KNIGHTFALL
PART ONE: BROKEN BAT

BATMAN

KNIGHTFALL

PART ONE: BROKEN BAT

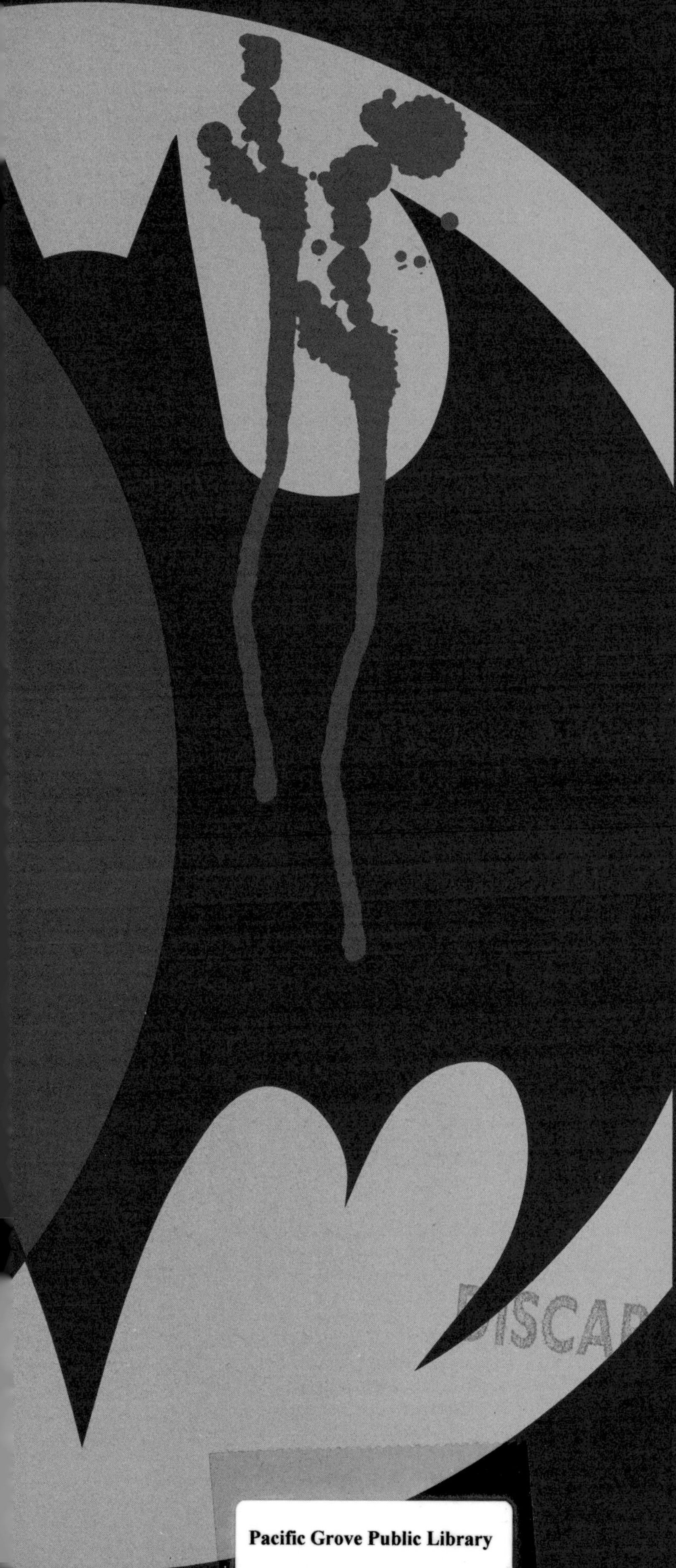

DOUG MOENCH
CHUCK DIXON
WRITERS

JIM APARO
NORM BREYFOGLE
GRAHAM NOLAN
JIM BALENT
PENCILLERS

SCOTT HANNA
NORM BREYFOGLE
JIM APARO
TOM MANDRAKE
BOB WIACEK
JOSEF RUBINSTEIN
DICK GIORDANO
INKERS

ADRIENNE ROY
COLORIST

RICHARD STARKINGS
JOHN COSTANZA
TIM HARKINS
LETTERERS

BATMAN CREAT
BY BOB KANE

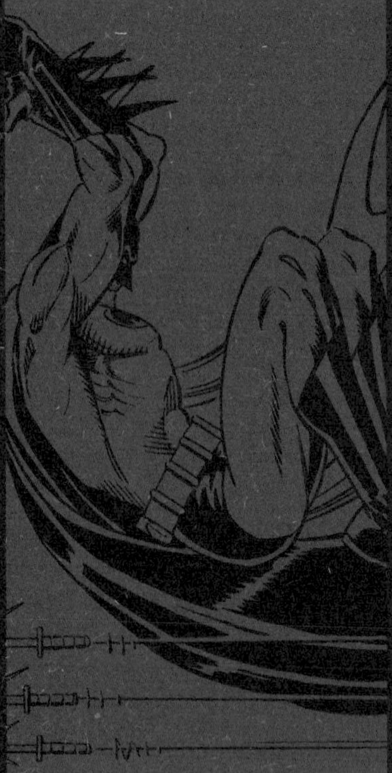

Dan DiDio	VP-Executive Editor
Dennis O'Neil and Scott Peterson	Editors-original series
Dale Crain	Editor-collected edition
Jordan B. Gorfinkel	Assistant Editor-original series
Michael Wright	Assistant Editor-collected edition
Robbin Brosterman	Senior Art Director
Paul Levitz	President & Publisher
Georg Brewer	VP-Design & DC Direct Creative
Richard Bruning	Senior VP-Creative Director
Patrick Caldon	Senior VP-Finance & Operations
Chris Caramalis	VP-Finance
Terri Cunningham	VP-Managing Editor
Stephanie Fierman	Senior VP-Sales & Marketing
Alison Gill	VP-Manufacturing
Rich Johnson	VP-Book Trade Sales
Hank Kanalz	VP-General Manager, WildStorm
Lillian Laserson	Senior VP & General Counsel
Jim Lee	Editorial Director-WildStorm
Paula Lowitt	Senior VP-Business & Legal Affairs
David McKillips	VP-Advertising & Custom Publishing
John Nee	VP-Business Development
Gregory Noveck	Senior VP-Creative Affairs
Cheryl Rubin	Senior VP-Brand Management
Jeff Trojan	VP-Business Development, DC Direct
Bob Wayne	VP-Sales

BATMAN: KNIGHTFALL PART ONE: BROKEN BAT
Published by DC Comics. Cover and design pages © 2000.
Compilation copyright © 1993 DC Comics. All Rights Reserved.
Originally published in single magazine form as BATMAN 491-497
and DETECTIVE COMICS 659-663. Copyright © 1993 DC Comics.
All Rights Reserved. All characters, their distinctive likenesses
and related elements featured in this publication are trademarks of
DC Comics. The stories, characters and incidents featured in this
publication are entirely fictional. DC Comics does not read or accept
unsolicited submissions of ideas, stories or artwork.
DC Comics, 1700 Broadway, New York, NY 10019
A Warner Bros. Entertainment Company
Printed in Canada. Fifth Printing.
ISBN: 1-56389-142-5.
Cover illustration by Mike Deodato.
Cover color by Lee Loughridge.
Publication design by Louis Prandi.

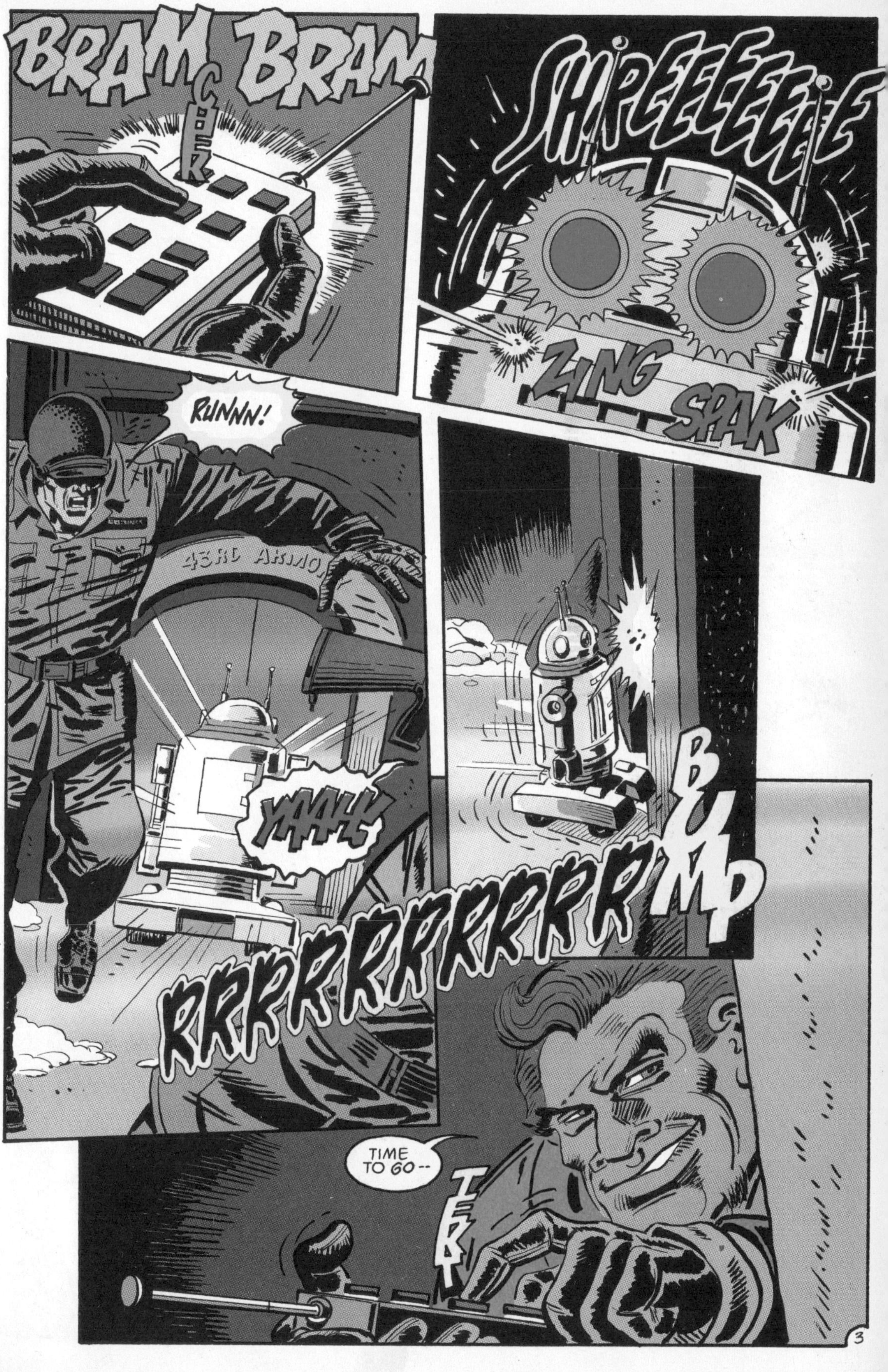
BRAM BRAM
CHEK
SHREEEEEEEE
ZING
SPAK
RUNNN!
43RD ARMO
YAAAH!
BUMP
RRRRRRRRRRRRRRRM
TIME TO GO --
3

POLICE H.Q:

IT'S LIKE AN *ORDNANCE INVENTORY FOR WORLD WAR THREE,* COMMISH...

AUTOMATIC ASSAULT RIFLES, ANTI-PERSONNEL MINES, MORTARS, HEAVY MACHINEGUNS, FRAGMENTATION GRENADES...

...AN' EVEN A FEW CRATES O' *SHOULDER-LAUNCHED STINGER MISSILES.*

PIZZA KITCHEN

AND THE ONLY *BRIGHT SIDE* IS THAT NO ONE WAS *HURT...*

NOT AFTER THE ARMORY GUARDS *RAN AWAY* FROM THEIR *U.F.O. MONSTER...* BUT SOMETHING TELLS ME THERE'S STILL A *BODY COUNT* TO COME.

THEN YOU THINK THOSE MUNITIONS WERE STOLEN FOR *DOMESTIC USE,* MONTOYA?

WITH *THAT M.O.,* COMMISSIONER, I DON'T KNOW *WHAT* TO THINK...

MY GUESS IS *NICARAGUA* -- ROGUE C.I.A. ELEMENTS.

...BUT *ONE* THING'S READY FOR THE BANK -- THAT WAS A WHOLE *TRUCKLOAD* OF MIGHTY *EXOTIC WEAPONRY...*

...AND RIGHT NOW IT'S LOOSE ON *OUR STREETS!*

YES...

...BUT IN *WHOSE* HANDS?

5

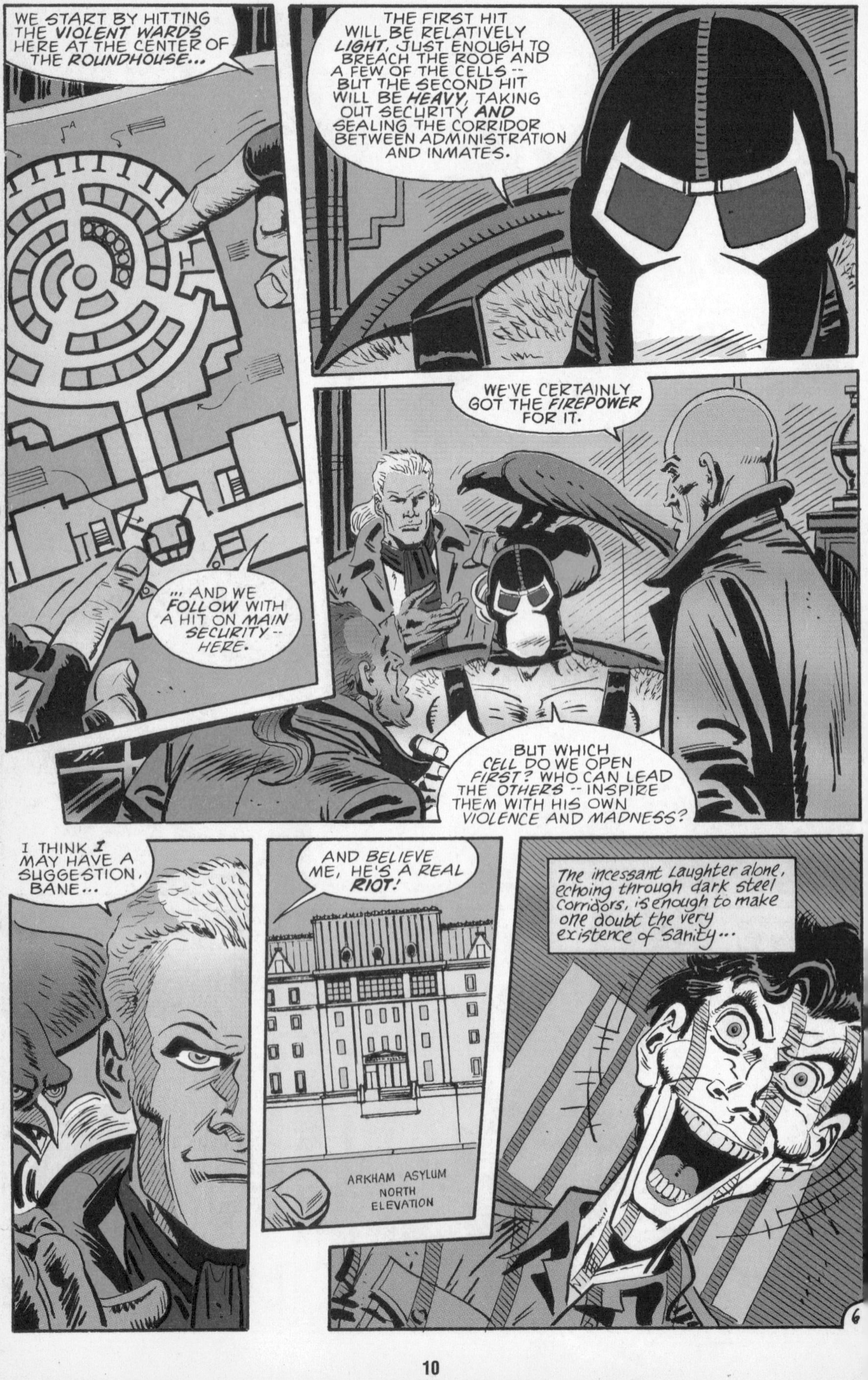
WE START BY HITTING THE VIOLENT WARDS HERE AT THE CENTER OF THE ROUNDHOUSE...
THE FIRST HIT WILL BE RELATIVELY LIGHT, JUST ENOUGH TO BREACH THE ROOF AND A FEW OF THE CELLS -- BUT THE SECOND HIT WILL BE HEAVY, TAKING OUT SECURITY AND SEALING THE CORRIDOR BETWEEN ADMINISTRATION AND INMATES.
...AND WE FOLLOW WITH A HIT ON MAIN SECURITY -- HERE.
WE'VE CERTAINLY GOT THE FIREPOWER FOR IT.
BUT WHICH CELL DO WE OPEN FIRST? WHO CAN LEAD THE OTHERS -- INSPIRE THEM WITH HIS OWN VIOLENCE AND MADNESS?
I THINK I MAY HAVE A SUGGESTION, BANE...
AND BELIEVE ME, HE'S A REAL RIOT!
ARKHAM ASYLUM NORTH ELEVATION
The incessant Laughter alone, echoing through dark steel corridors, is enough to make one doubt the very existence of sanity...
6

Add to that all the shrieks and whimpers, the snarls and whispers, all the cunning drool-garbled incantations of paranoia and revenge, and one sees that this is NOT, in fact, an ASYLUM.

ARKHAM ASYLUM
FOR THE CRIMINALLY INSANE

It is, simply and unarguably, a MADHOUSE.

NOT, in fact, an ASYLUM.

It is, simply and unarguably, a MADHOUSE.

And if one is the keeper and controller of such a place, does that make one SANE -- or merely the KING of the MAD?

Indeed, one won—

Indeed, one wonders if madness might not be INFECTIOUS in a certain sense, a contagion by virtue of its omnipresent influence, so much more vivid and strident than the mundane, smothering cloak of so-called normalcy.

They have become my world, echoing down steel corridors to enter my MIND -- where they echo, now, even LOUDER...

REAL SHORT?

I WANT IT OFF -- OUT OF THE WAY.

YOU GOT IT.

NO, I DON'T, NOT YET. BUT I WILL GET IT.

SHKKT

If so, then surely I have been infected by now, for the laughter and shrieks, the canny gasps from the gloom, are the voices with which I live, here in Arkham, here in the madhouse of my making.

...clamoring to get out.

7

11

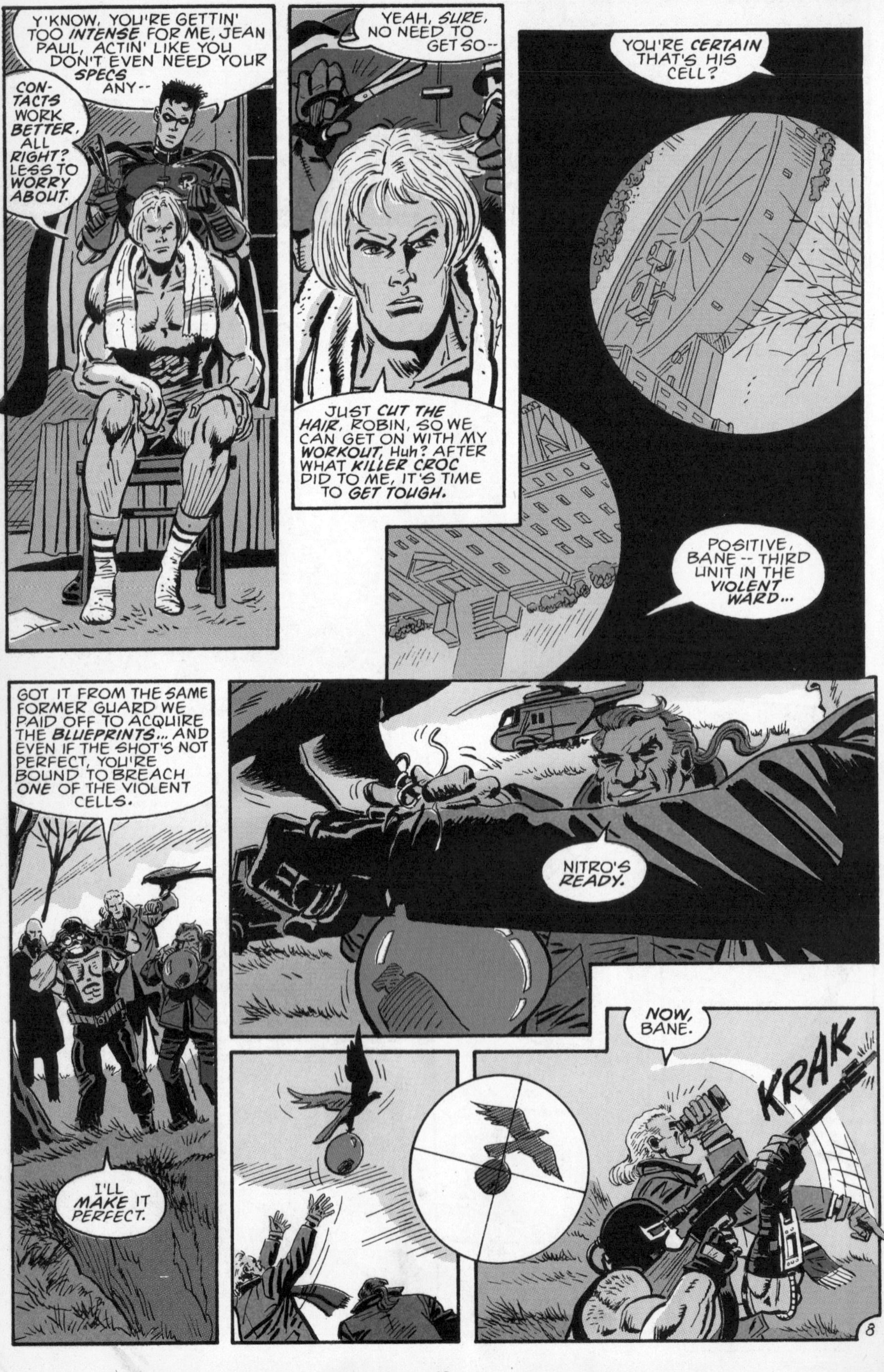
Y'KNOW, YOU'RE GETTIN' TOO INTENSE FOR ME, JEAN PAUL, ACTIN' LIKE YOU DON'T EVEN NEED YOUR SPECS ANY--
CONTACTS WORK BETTER, ALL RIGHT? LESS TO WORRY ABOUT.
YEAH, SURE, NO NEED TO GET SO--
JUST CUT THE HAIR, ROBIN, SO WE CAN GET ON WITH MY WORKOUT, Huh? AFTER WHAT KILLER CROC DID TO ME, IT'S TIME TO GET TOUGH.
YOU'RE CERTAIN THAT'S HIS CELL?
POSITIVE, BANE -- THIRD UNIT IN THE VIOLENT WARD...
GOT IT FROM THE SAME FORMER GUARD WE PAID OFF TO ACQUIRE THE BLUEPRINTS... AND EVEN IF THE SHOT'S NOT PERFECT, YOU'RE BOUND TO BREACH ONE OF THE VIOLENT CELLS.
I'LL MAKE IT PERFECT.
NITRO'S READY.
NOW, BANE.
KRAK
8

13

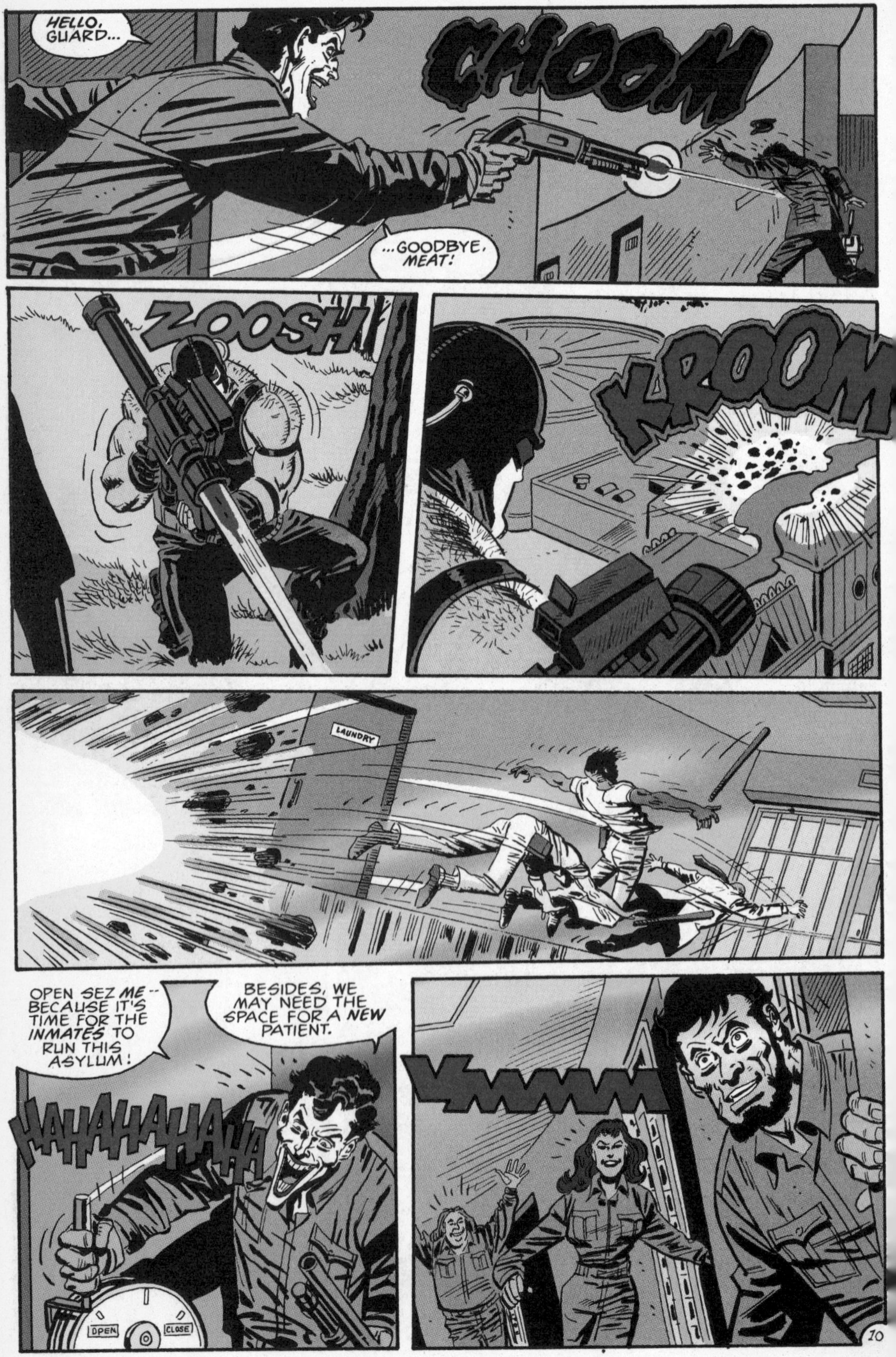
HELLO, GUARD...
CHOOM
...GOODBYE, MEAT!
ZOOSH
KROOM
LAUNDRY
OPEN SEZ *ME* -- BECAUSE IT'S TIME FOR THE *INMATES* TO RUN THIS ASYLUM!
BESIDES, WE MAY NEED THE SPACE FOR A *NEW* PATIENT.
HAHAHAHAHA
OPEN
CLOSE
VMMMM
10

15

...EIGHTY-TWO... EIGHTY-THREE...

ROBIN HERE. WHAT'S--

I'M UPSTATE-- ALMOST AT ARKHAM. YOU STAY IN GOTHAM.

ARKHAM? BUT... IF YOU'RE STILL SICK -- SO OUT OF IT YOU CAN BARELY GET OUT OF BED...

...MAYBE YOU SHOULD HAVE SOME HEL--

OVER AND OUT.

MORE PUSHUPS--

YEAH -- AND YET ANOTHER PUT-DOWN.

SO WHEN DO WE GET TO RETURN FIRE?

MAYBE NEVER -- AS LONG AS THEY'VE GOT HOSTAGES IN THERE.

14

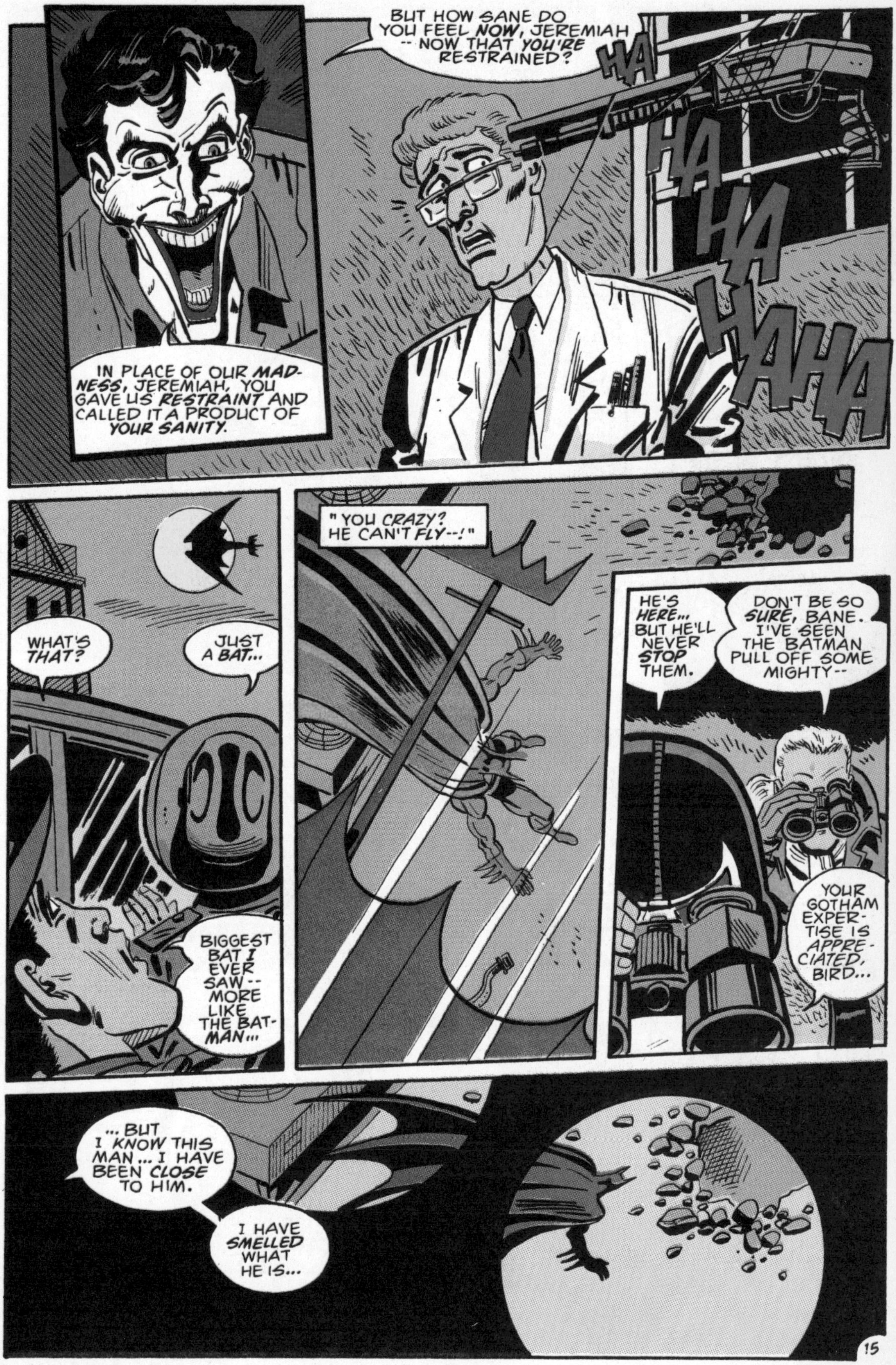
IN PLACE OF OUR MADNESS, JEREMIAH, YOU GAVE US RESTRAINT AND CALLED IT A PRODUCT OF YOUR SANITY.
BUT HOW SANE DO YOU FEEL NOW, JEREMIAH -- NOW THAT YOU'RE RESTRAINED?
HA HA HA HA HAHA HA
WHAT'S THAT?
JUST A BAT...
BIGGEST BAT I EVER SAW -- MORE LIKE THE BATMAN...
"YOU CRAZY? HE CAN'T FLY--!"
HE'S HERE... BUT HE'LL NEVER STOP THEM.
DON'T BE SO SURE, BANE. I'VE SEEN THE BATMAN PULL OFF SOME MIGHTY--
YOUR GOTHAM EXPERTISE IS APPRECIATED, BIRD...
...BUT I KNOW THIS MAN... I HAVE BEEN CLOSE TO HIM.
I HAVE SMELLED WHAT HE IS...
15

HOW'D THEY GET OUT INTO THE *YARD?* WHAT HAPPENED TO THE *WALL?*

NEAR AS WE CAN FIGURE... SOME KIND OF *SMART MISSILES.*

MISSILES? BUT *WHO* THE--?

"WE DON'T KNOW... BUT OBVIOUSLY SOMEONE A *LOT* BETTER EQUIPPED THAN *SADDAM HUSSEIN.*"

BRAKA CHOOM BLAM BLAM

--ALREADY DISPATCHED FIVE OF OUR *TACTICAL* UNITS, MR. MAYOR, TO ASSIST THE STATE POLICE ON THE *SCENE...*

...BUT WITH THE *HOSTAGE SITUATION,* I DON'T KNOW WHAT ANY COP COULD --

I CERTAINLY HOPE THEY'VE BEEN TOLD TO SHOOT TO *KILL.*

IT DOESN'T *WORK* THAT WAY, MAYOR KROL. MY MEN DISCHARGE THEIR FIREARMS ONLY TO *DEFEND* THEMSELVES -- OR *OTHERS.*

THEN YOU'RE GOING TO HAVE A LOT OF *DEAD MEN,* GORDON -- SOMETHING I DO *NOT* WANT DURING MY *ADMINISTRATION.*

I RAN ON A *LAW AND ORDER* PLATFORM -- AND NOW THAT I'VE BEEN *ELECTED,* I'M NOT ABOUT TO ABANDON EVERYTHING I *STAND* FOR.

YOU RAN *UNOPPOSED.*

EVEN MORE PROOF OF MY *MANDATE!*

PROOF OF YOUR *MACHINE...*

17

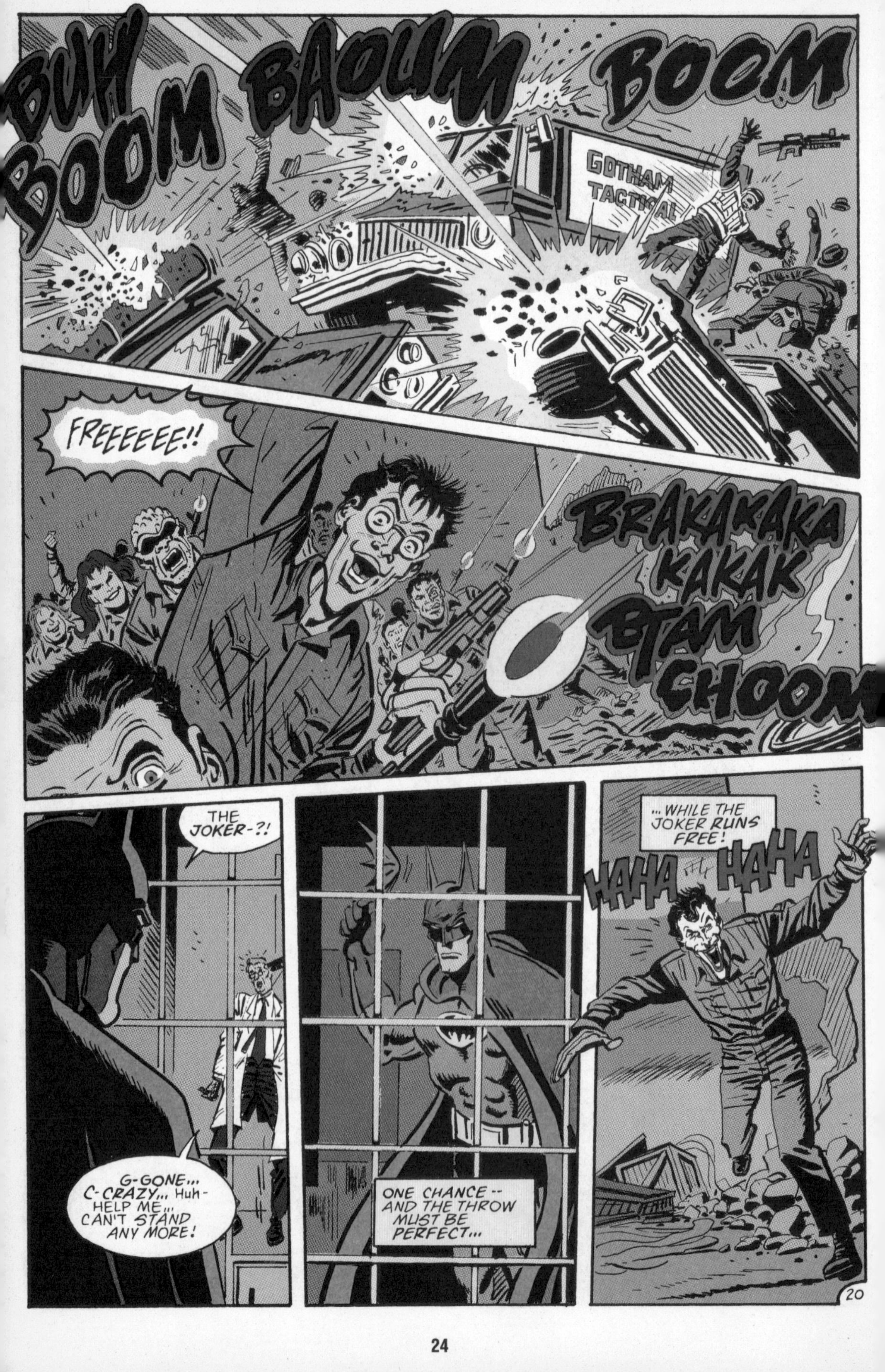
BUH BOOM
BAOUM
BOOM
GOTHAM TACTICAL
FREEEEEE!!
BRAKAKAKA KAKAK BTAM CHOOM
THE JOKER-?!
G-GONE... C-CRAZY... Huh- HELP ME... CAN'T STAND ANY MORE!
ONE CHANCE -- AND THE THROW MUST BE PERFECT...
...WHILE THE JOKER RUNS FREE!
HAHA HAHA
20

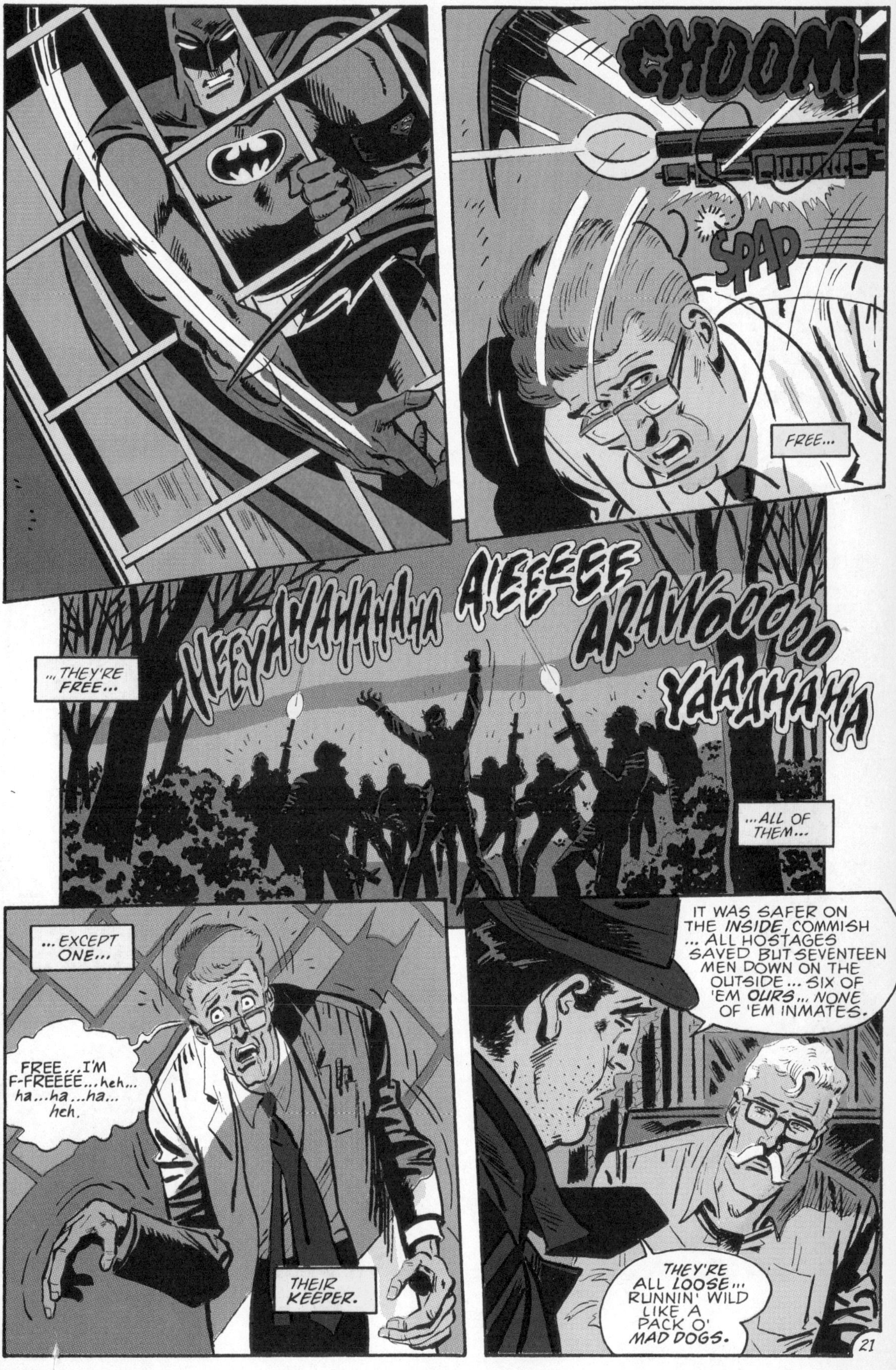
CHOOM
SPAP
FREE...
HEEYAHAHAHAHA
AIEEEEE
ARAWOOOOOO
YAAAHAHA
...THEY'RE FREE...
...ALL OF THEM...
...EXCEPT ONE...
FREE...I'M F-FREEEE...heh... ha...ha...ha... heh.
THEIR KEEPER.
IT WAS SAFER ON THE INSIDE, COMMISH ... ALL HOSTAGES SAVED BUT SEVENTEEN MEN DOWN ON THE OUTSIDE... SIX OF 'EM OURS... NONE OF 'EM INMATES.
THEY'RE ALL LOOSE... RUNNIN' WILD LIKE A PACK O' MAD DOGS.
21

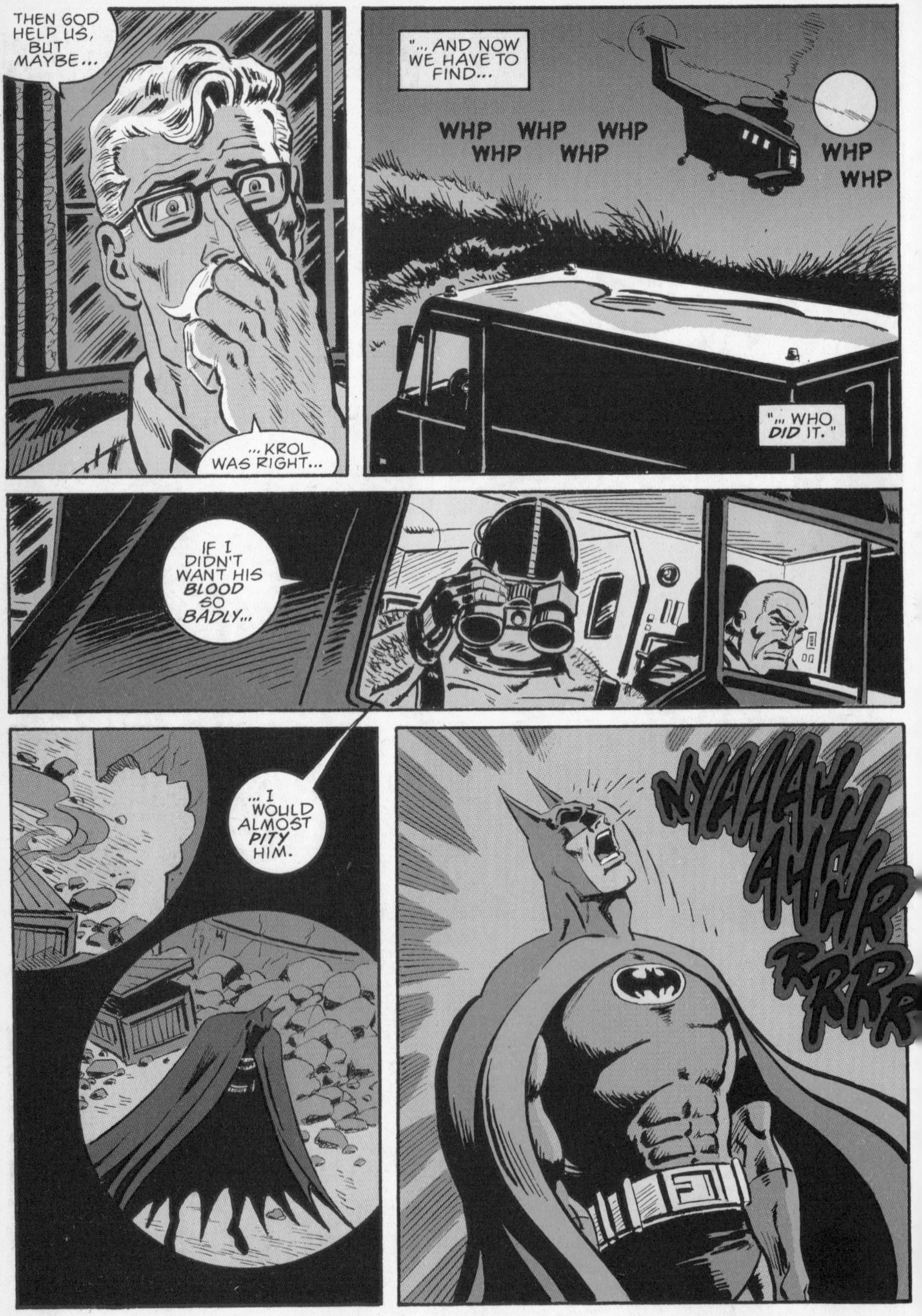
THEN GOD HELP US, BUT MAYBE...
...KROL WAS RIGHT...
"...AND NOW WE HAVE TO FIND...
WHP WHP WHP
WHP WHP
WHP
WHP
"...WHO DID IT."
IF I DIDN'T WANT HIS BLOOD SO BADLY...
...I WOULD ALMOST PITY HIM.

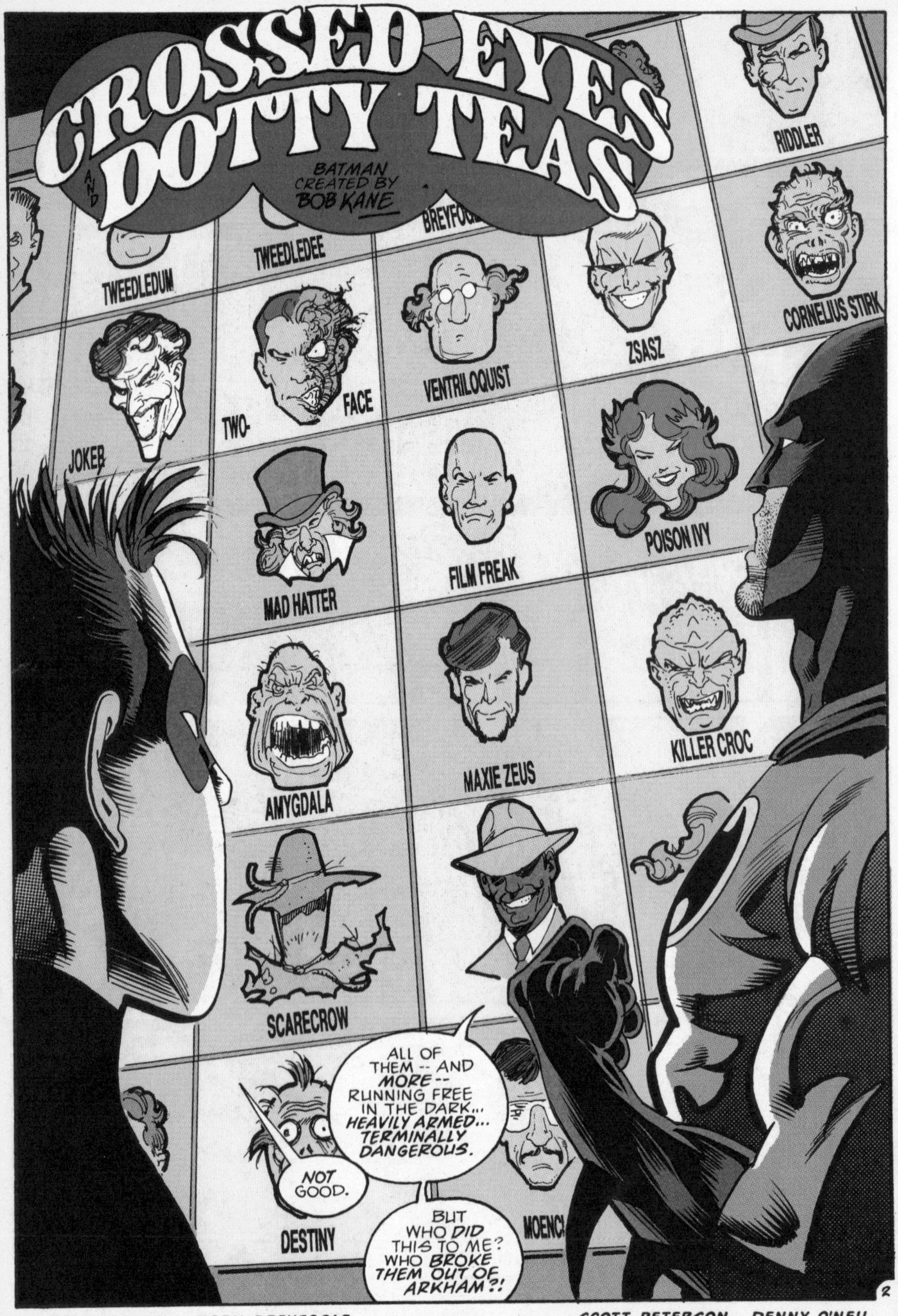
CROSSED EYES AND DOTTY TEAS
BATMAN CREATED BY BOB KANE
RIDDLER
TWEEDLEDUM
TWEEDLEDEE
CORNELIUS STIRK
ZSASZ
VENTRILOQUIST
TWO-FACE
JOKER
POISON IVY
FILM FREAK
MAD HATTER
KILLER CROC
MAXIE ZEUS
AMYGDALA
SCARECROW
DESTINY
ALL OF THEM -- AND MORE -- RUNNING FREE IN THE DARK... HEAVILY ARMED... TERMINALLY DANGEROUS.
NOT GOOD.
BUT WHO DID THIS TO ME? WHO BROKE THEM OUT OF ARKHAM?!
2

DOUG MOENCH WRITER · NORM BREYFOGLE ARTIST · ADRIENNE ROY COLORIST · RICHARD STARKINGS LETTERER · SCOTT PETERSON, JORDAN B. GORFINKEL ASST EDITORS · DENNY O'NEIL EDITOR

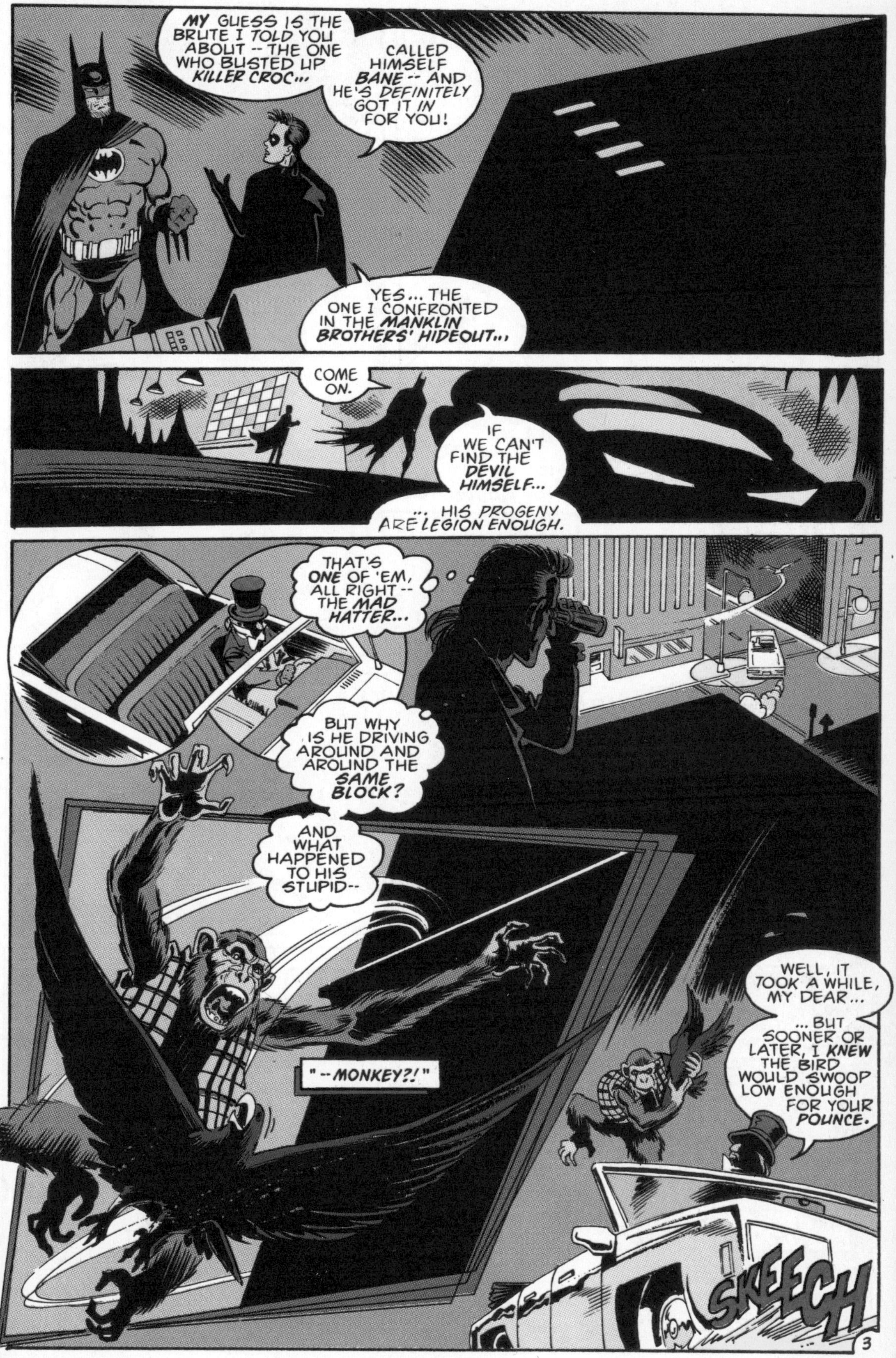
MY GUESS IS THE BRUTE I TOLD YOU ABOUT -- THE ONE WHO BUSTED UP KILLER CROC...
CALLED HIMSELF BANE -- AND HE'S DEFINITELY GOT IT IN FOR YOU!
YES... THE ONE I CONFRONTED IN THE MANKLIN BROTHERS' HIDEOUT...
COME ON.
IF WE CAN'T FIND THE DEVIL HIMSELF...
... HIS PROGENY ARE LEGION ENOUGH.
THAT'S ONE OF 'EM, ALL RIGHT -- THE MAD HATTER...
BUT WHY IS HE DRIVING AROUND AND AROUND THE SAME BLOCK?
AND WHAT HAPPENED TO HIS STUPID--
"--MONKEY?!"
WELL, IT TOOK A WHILE, MY DEAR...
... BUT SOONER OR LATER, I KNEW THE BIRD WOULD SWOOP LOW ENOUGH FOR YOUR POUNCE.
SKEECH
3

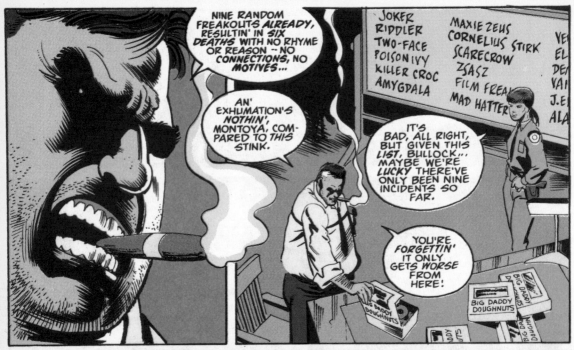

NINE RANDOM FREAKOUTS *ALREADY*, RESULTIN' IN *SIX DEATHS* WITH NO RHYME OR REASON -- NO CONNECTIONS, NO *MOTIVES*...

AN' EXHUMATION'S *NOTHIN'*, MONTOYA, COMPARED TO *THIS* STINK.

JOKER
RIDDLER
TWO-FACE
POISON IVY
KILLER CROC
AMYGDALA
MAXIE ZEUS
CORNELIUS STIRK
SCARECROW
ZSASZ
FILM FREAK
MAD HATTER

YE
EL
DE
VAI
J.E
ALA

IT'S BAD, ALL RIGHT, BUT GIVEN THIS LIST, BULLOCK... MAYBE WE'RE *LUCKY* THERE'VE ONLY BEEN NINE INCIDENTS SO FAR.

YOU'RE *FORGETTIN'* IT ONLY GETS *WORSE* FROM HERE!

BIG DADDY DOUGHNUTS

THE COMMISH IS *ALREADY* UNDER HEAVY PRESSURE FROM *MAYOR KROL* TO WRAP THE WHOLE THING UP LIKE A *TIDY MIRACLE*.

SPLUT

YESTERDAY.

BUT, YA KNOW, IF WE COULD FIGURE OUT *WHO* BUSTED 'EM FROM ARKHAM AN' *WHY*... MAYBE WE *COULD* COLLAR 'EM ALL AT ONCE.

BUT WHAT KINDA *PLAN* OR *CRIME* WOULD REQUIRE THE ESCAPE OF SO MANY LUNA--

MAYBE THERE *IS* NO PLAN, BULLOCK.

MONTOYA

YOU'RE THINKIN' SOMEONE SPRUNG 'EM FOR THE SHEER *HELL* OF IT, MONTOYA?

OR, AT MOST, A *SMOKE-SCREEN* -- TO DISTRACT US WHILE SOMETHING *ELSE* GOES DOWN.

THEN THIS'S *BAD*, BABE, *WICKED BAD*...

...CUZ EITHER WAY IT'D MEAN DEALIN' WITH *RANDOM LUNACY* -- THE KINDA STUFF DETECTIVE SCHOOL CAN'T *TEACH*, CRIMES WITHOUT MOTIVE, CRIMES NO COP CAN *ANTICIPATE*...

...AN' *ALMOST IMPOSSIBLE* TO CRACK.

CAN'T BE HILL STREET *EVERY* DAY.

6

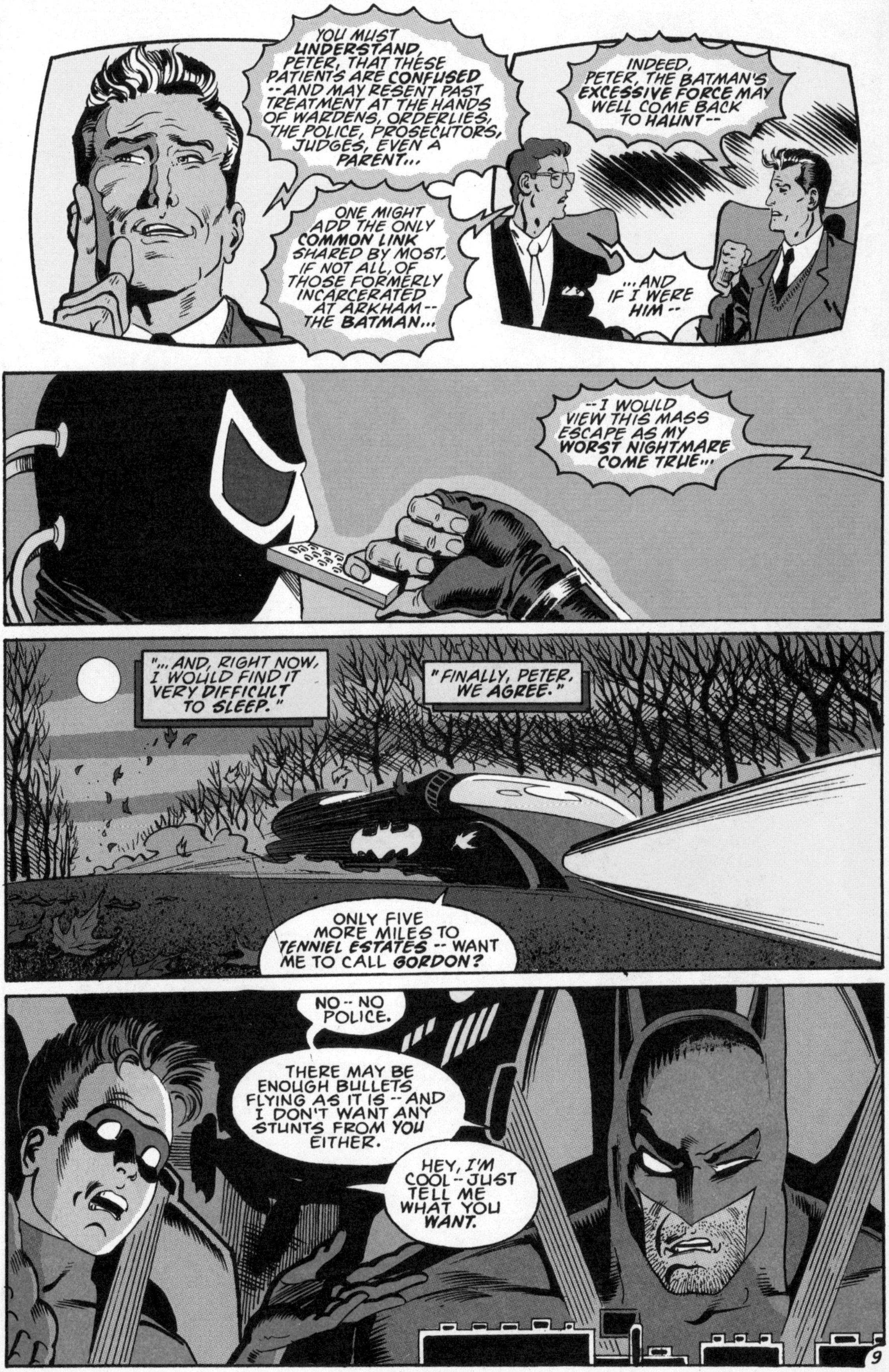
YOU MUST UNDERSTAND, PETER, THAT THESE PATIENTS ARE CONFUSED --AND MAY RESENT PAST TREATMENT AT THE HANDS OF WARDENS, ORDERLIES, THE POLICE, PROSECUTORS, JUDGES, EVEN A PARENT...
ONE MIGHT ADD THE ONLY COMMON LINK SHARED BY MOST, IF NOT ALL, OF THOSE FORMERLY INCARCERATED AT ARKHAM -- THE BATMAN...
INDEED, PETER, THE BATMAN'S EXCESSIVE FORCE MAY WELL COME BACK TO HAUNT --
...AND IF I WERE HIM --
-- I WOULD VIEW THIS MASS ESCAPE AS MY WORST NIGHTMARE COME TRUE...
"...AND, RIGHT NOW, I WOULD FIND IT VERY DIFFICULT TO SLEEP."
"FINALLY, PETER, WE AGREE."
ONLY FIVE MORE MILES TO TENNIEL ESTATES -- WANT ME TO CALL GORDON?
NO -- NO POLICE.
THERE MAY BE ENOUGH BULLETS FLYING AS IT IS -- AND I DON'T WANT ANY STUNTS FROM YOU EITHER.
HEY, I'M COOL -- JUST TELL ME WHAT YOU WANT.
9

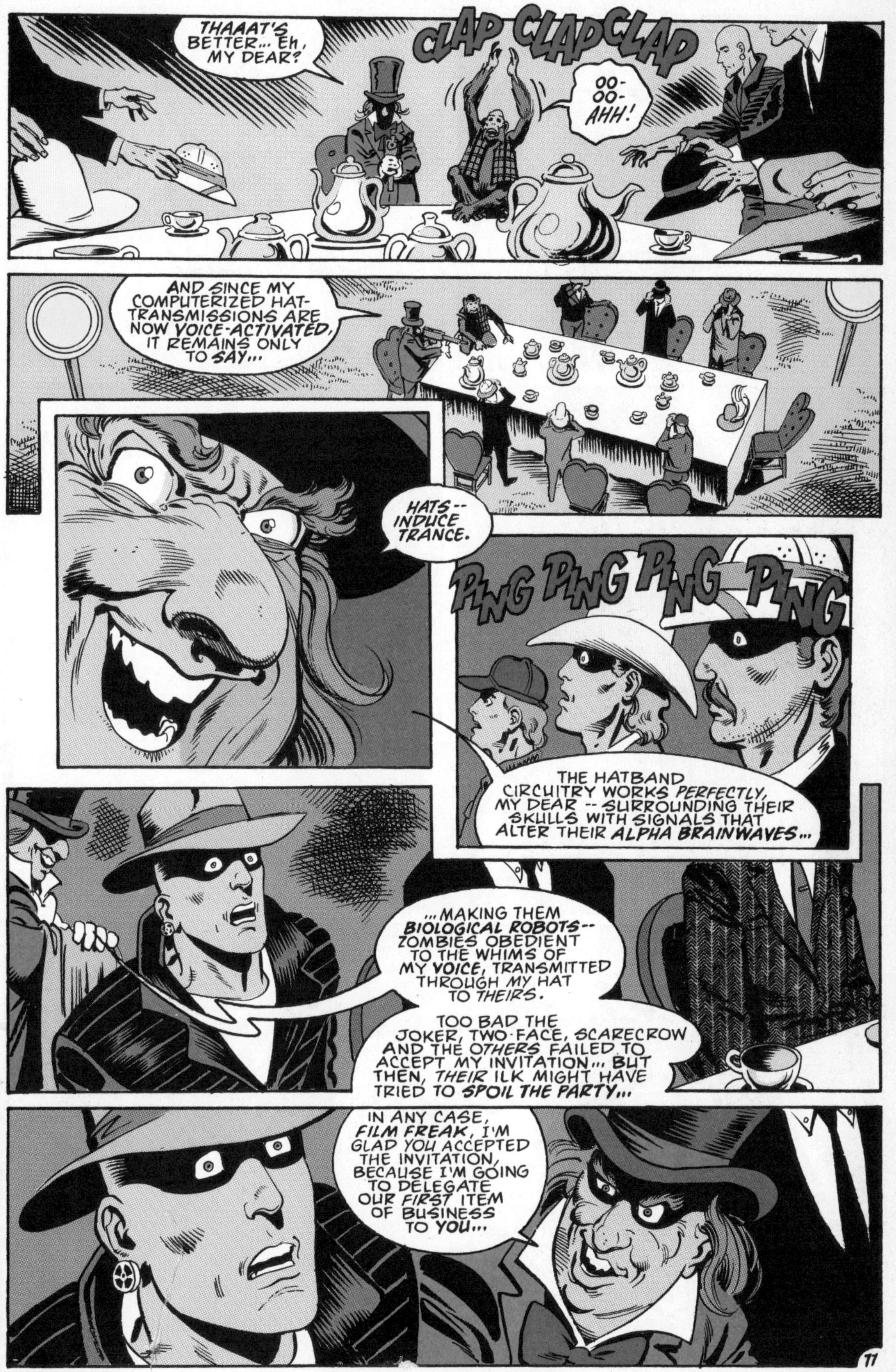
THAAAT'S BETTER... Eh, MY DEAR?
CLAP CLAP CLAP
OO-OO-AHH!
AND SINCE MY COMPUTERIZED HAT-TRANSMISSIONS ARE NOW VOICE-ACTIVATED, IT REMAINS ONLY TO SAY...
HATS -- INDUCE TRANCE.
PING PING PING PING
THE HATBAND CIRCUITRY WORKS PERFECTLY, MY DEAR -- SURROUNDING THEIR SKULLS WITH SIGNALS THAT ALTER THEIR ALPHA BRAINWAVES...
...MAKING THEM BIOLOGICAL ROBOTS -- ZOMBIES OBEDIENT TO THE WHIMS OF MY VOICE, TRANSMITTED THROUGH MY HAT TO THEIRS.
TOO BAD THE JOKER, TWO-FACE, SCARECROW AND THE OTHERS FAILED TO ACCEPT MY INVITATION... BUT THEN, THEIR ILK MIGHT HAVE TRIED TO SPOIL THE PARTY...
IN ANY CASE, FILM FREAK, I'M GLAD YOU ACCEPTED THE INVITATION, BECAUSE I'M GOING TO DELEGATE OUR FIRST ITEM OF BUSINESS TO YOU...
11

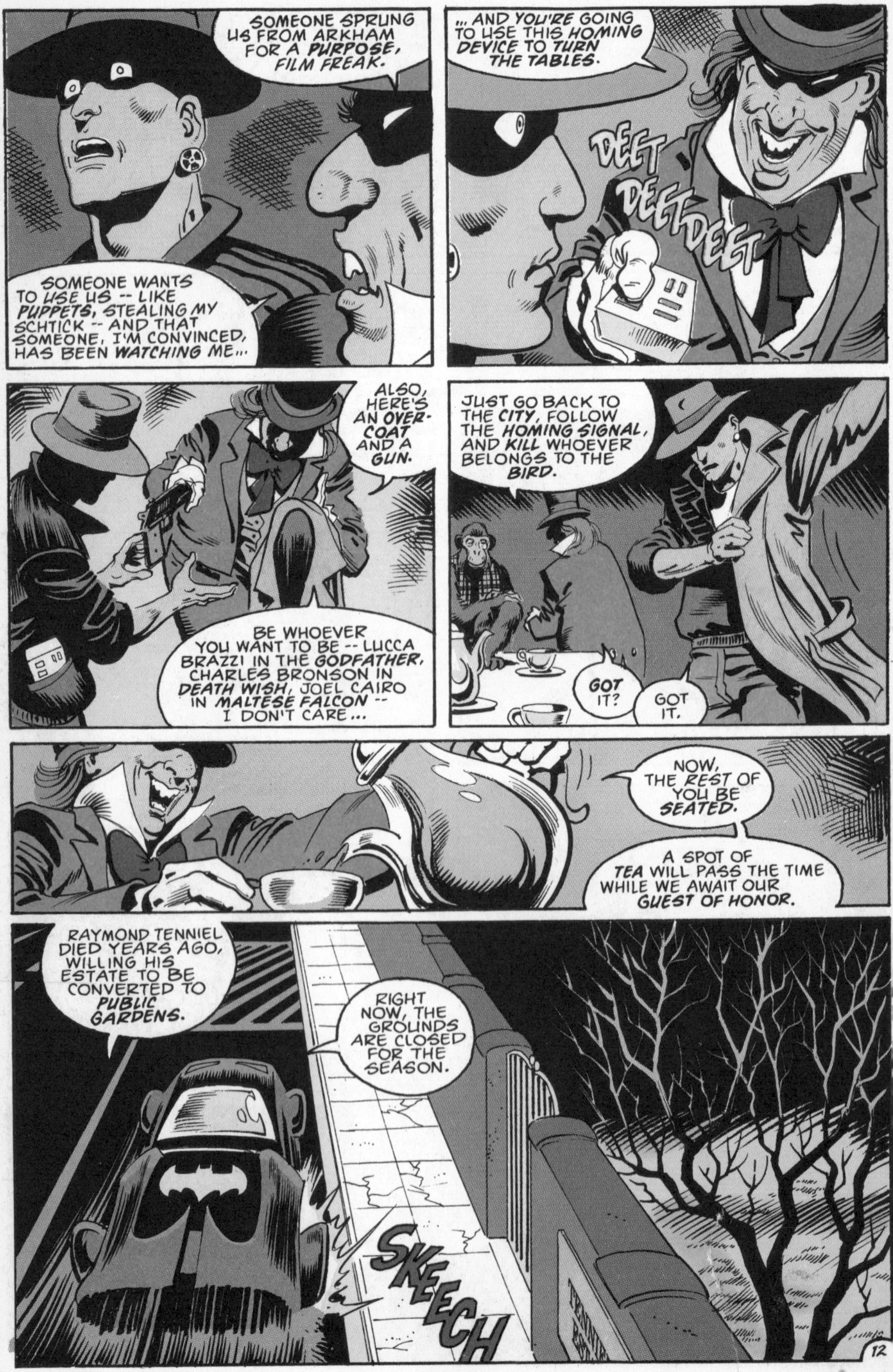
SOMEONE SPRUNG US FROM ARKHAM FOR A PURPOSE, FILM FREAK.
SOMEONE WANTS TO USE US -- LIKE PUPPETS, STEALING MY SCHTICK -- AND THAT SOMEONE, I'M CONVINCED, HAS BEEN WATCHING ME...
...AND YOU'RE GOING TO USE THIS HOMING DEVICE TO TURN THE TABLES.
DEET DEET DEET DEET
ALSO, HERE'S AN OVER-COAT AND A GUN.
BE WHOEVER YOU WANT TO BE -- LUCCA BRAZZI IN THE GODFATHER, CHARLES BRONSON IN DEATH WISH, JOEL CAIRO IN MALTESE FALCON -- I DON'T CARE...
JUST GO BACK TO THE CITY, FOLLOW THE HOMING SIGNAL, AND KILL WHOEVER BELONGS TO THE BIRD.
GOT IT?
GOT IT.
NOW, THE REST OF YOU BE SEATED.
A SPOT OF TEA WILL PASS THE TIME WHILE WE AWAIT OUR GUEST OF HONOR.
RAYMOND TENNIEL DIED YEARS AGO, WILLING HIS ESTATE TO BE CONVERTED TO PUBLIC GARDENS.
RIGHT NOW, THE GROUNDS ARE CLOSED FOR THE SEASON.
SKEECH
12

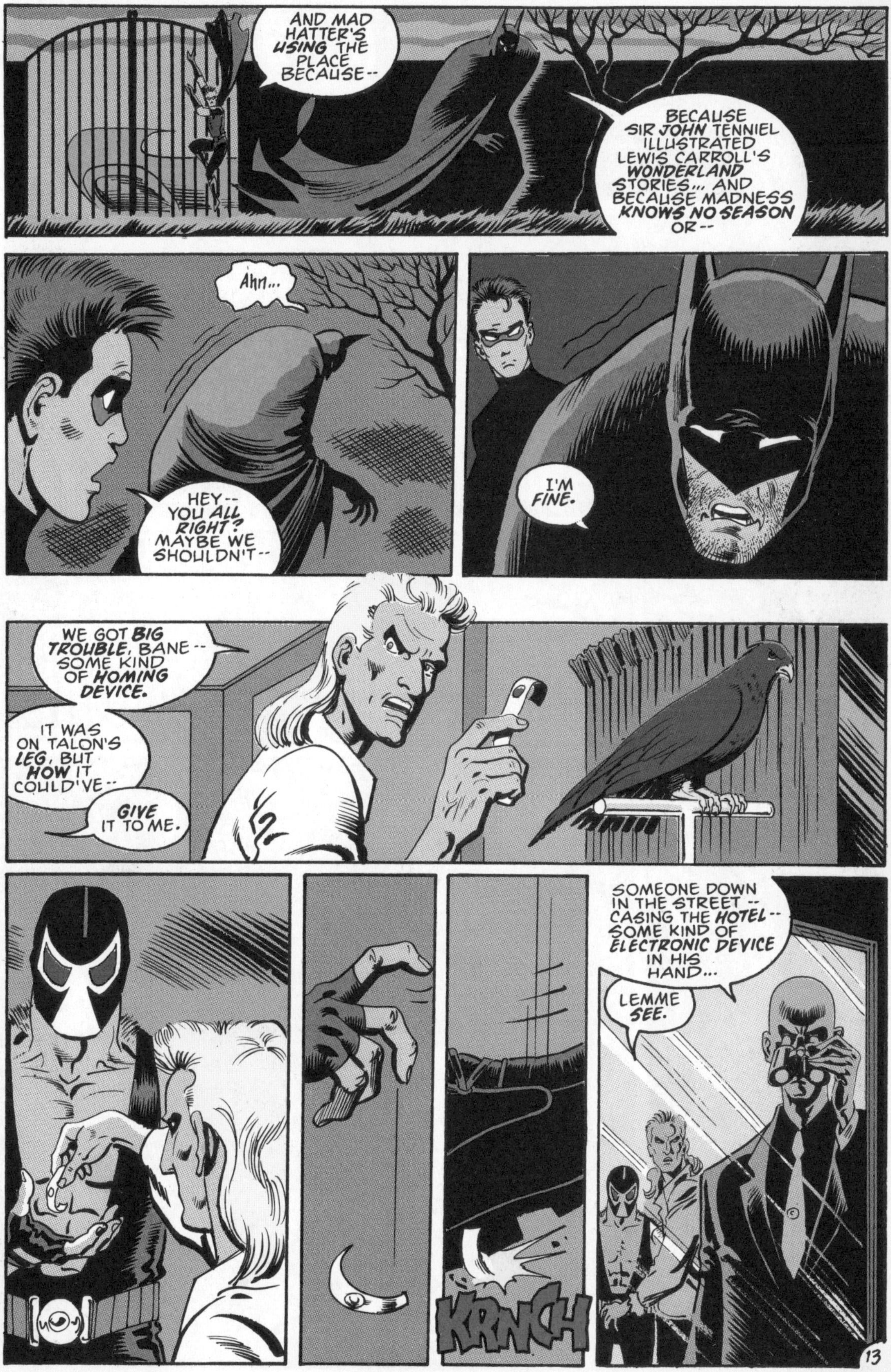
AND MAD HATTER'S USING THE PLACE BECAUSE--
BECAUSE SIR JOHN TENNIEL ILLUSTRATED LEWIS CARROLL'S WONDERLAND STORIES... AND BECAUSE MADNESS KNOWS NO SEASON OR--
Ahn...
HEY-- YOU ALL RIGHT? MAYBE WE SHOULDN'T--
I'M FINE.
WE GOT BIG TROUBLE, BANE-- SOME KIND OF HOMING DEVICE.
IT WAS ON TALON'S LEG, BUT HOW IT COULD'VE--
GIVE IT TO ME.
KRNCH
SOMEONE DOWN IN THE STREET -- CASING THE HOTEL-- SOME KIND OF ELECTRONIC DEVICE IN HIS HAND...
LEMME SEE.
13

40

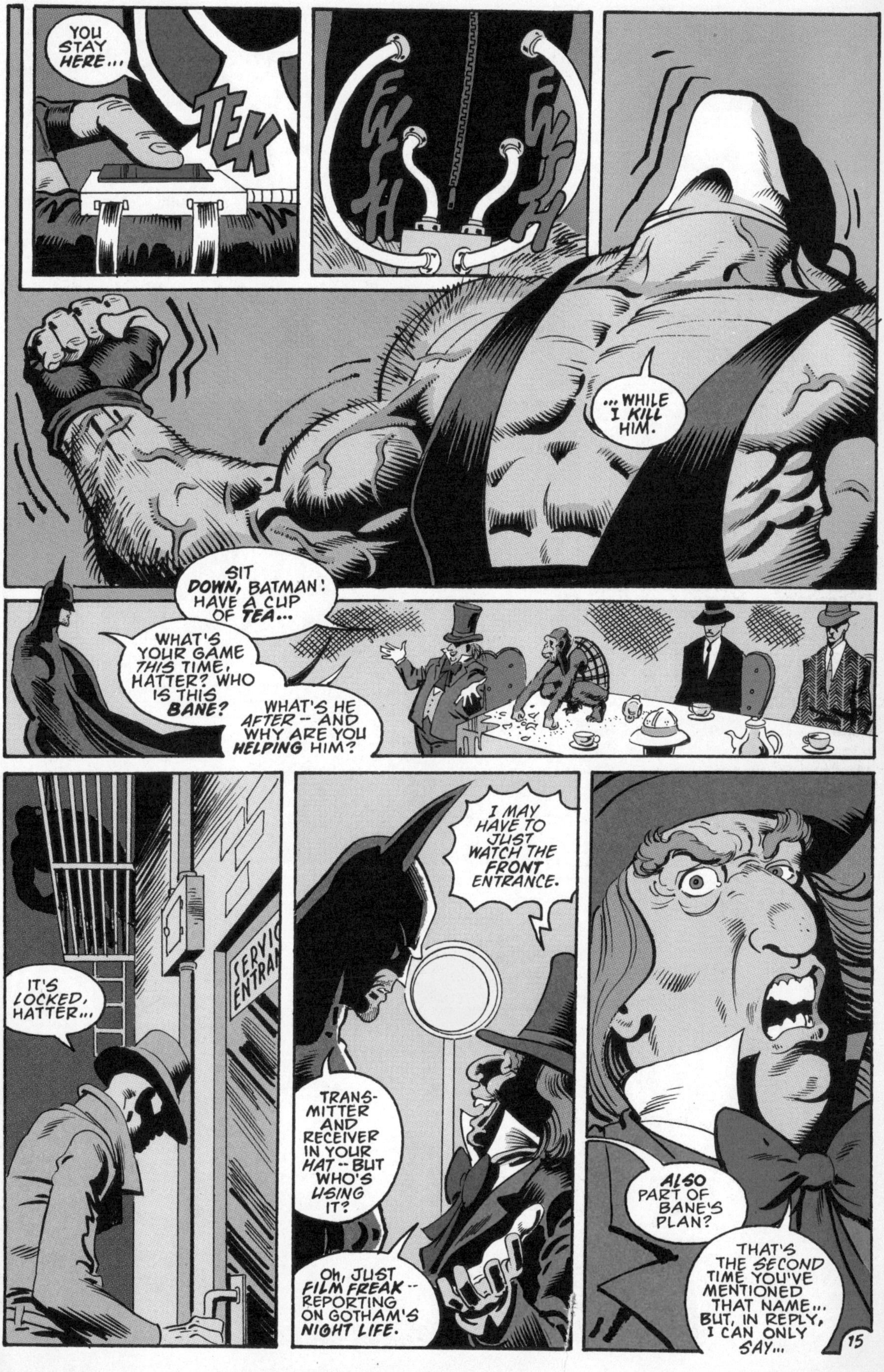
YOU STAY HERE...
TEK
FWSH
FWSH
...WHILE I KILL HIM.
SIT DOWN, BATMAN! HAVE A CUP OF TEA...
WHAT'S YOUR GAME THIS TIME, HATTER? WHO IS THIS BANE?
WHAT'S HE AFTER -- AND WHY ARE YOU HELPING HIM?
IT'S LOCKED, HATTER...
I MAY HAVE TO JUST WATCH THE FRONT ENTRANCE.
TRANS-MITTER AND RECEIVER IN YOUR HAT -- BUT WHO'S USING IT?
OH, JUST FILM FREAK -- REPORTING ON GOTHAM'S NIGHT LIFE.
ALSO PART OF BANE'S PLAN?
THAT'S THE SECOND TIME YOU'VE MENTIONED THAT NAME... BUT, IN REPLY, I CAN ONLY SAY...
15

...WHO'S BANE?

I'M...

BANE...

SWUKK

...AND YOUR KILLER--

--IS DEAD. HIS VOICE... THE SAME... THEN IT IS HIM...

HATS-- STIMULATE ADRENAL CORTEX!

PING

UHRRRR...

PING

PING

RUAHRR...

RAHRRR...

PING

BRAM

SPTANG

16

17

43

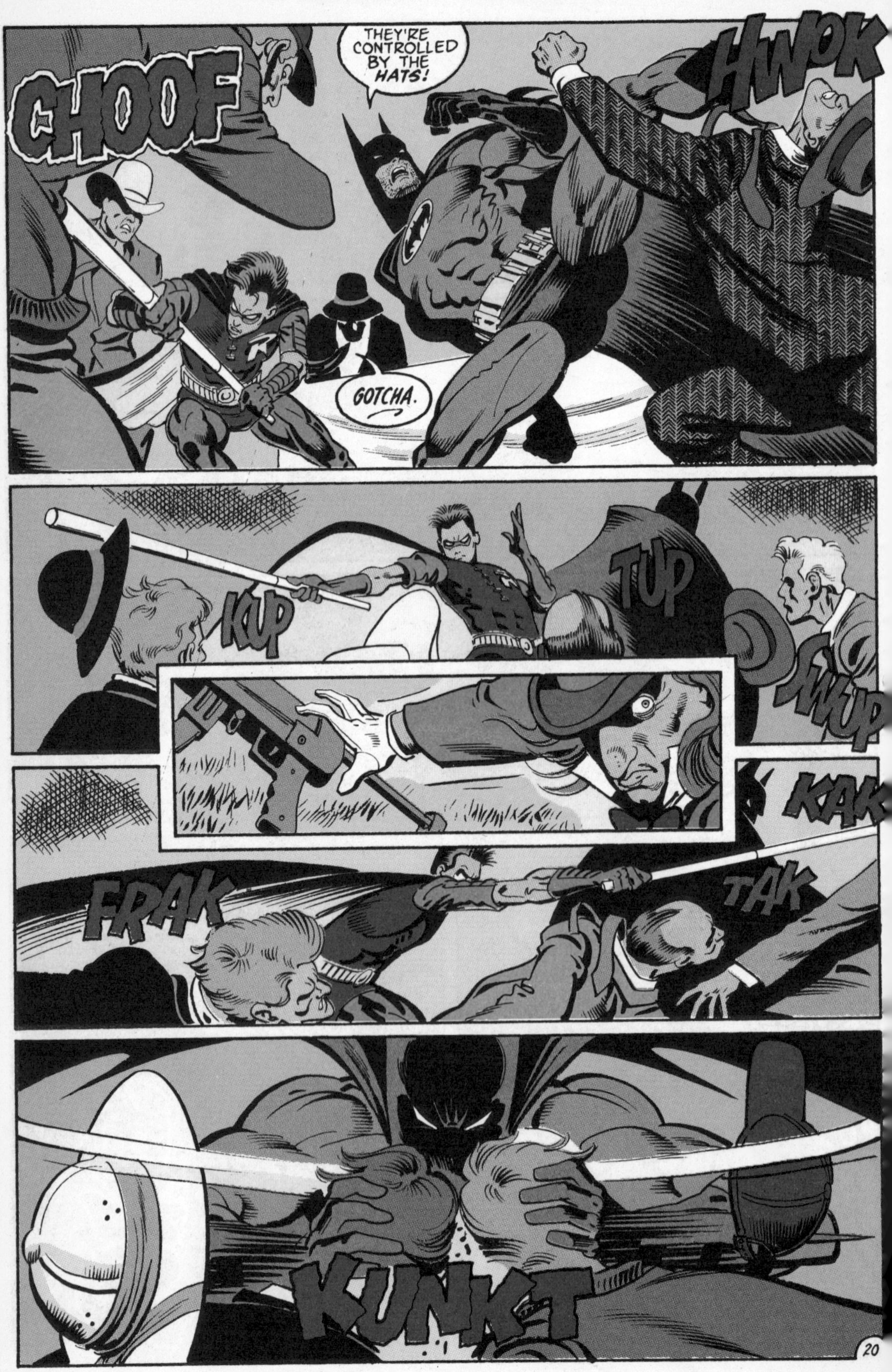
CHOOF
THEY'RE CONTROLLED BY THE HATS!
HWOK
GOTCHA.
KLIP
TUP
SWUP
KAK
FRAK
TAK
KUNKT
20

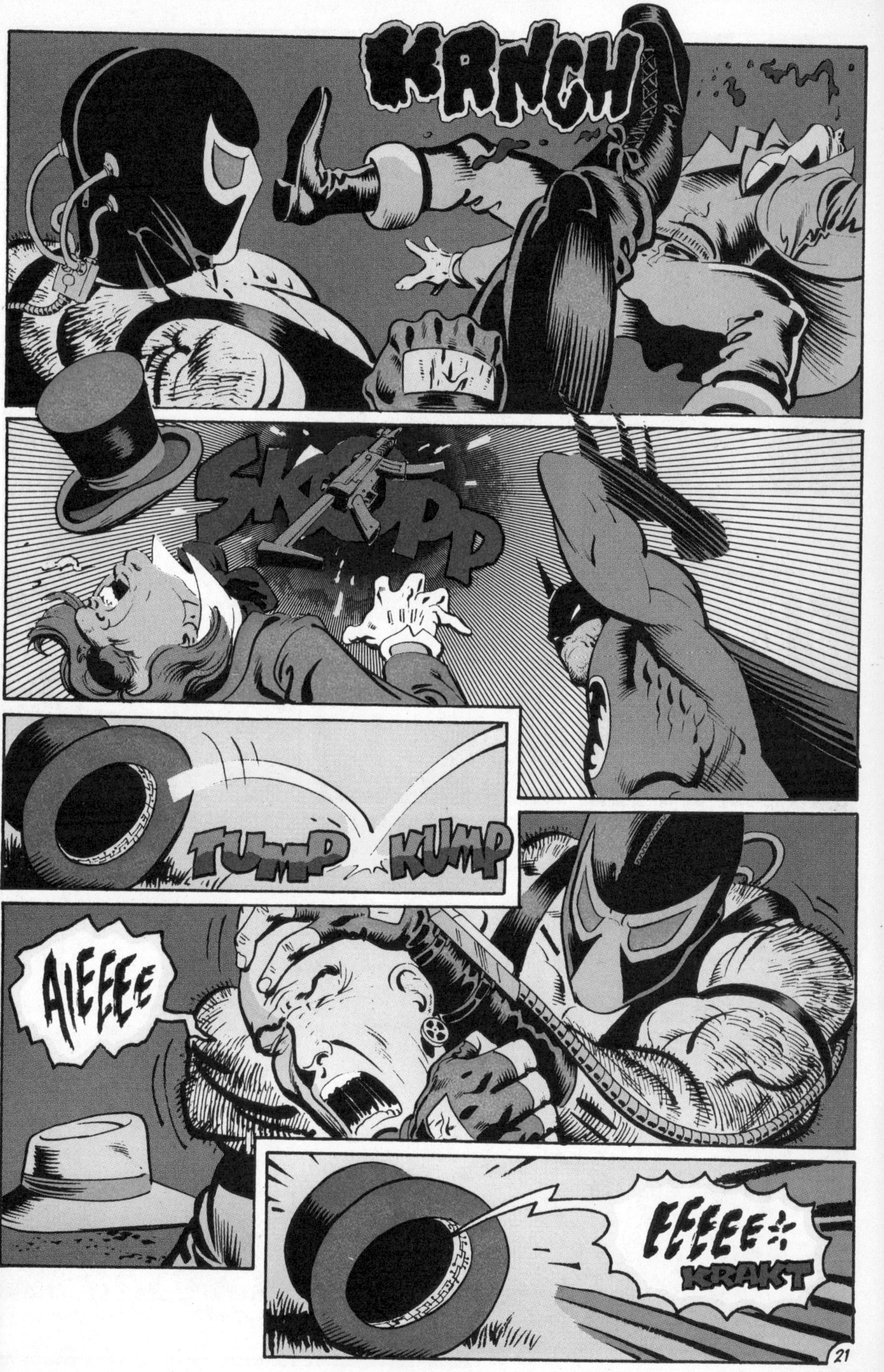
KRNCH
SKRUDD
TUMP
KUMP
AIEEEE
EEEEE
KRAKT
21

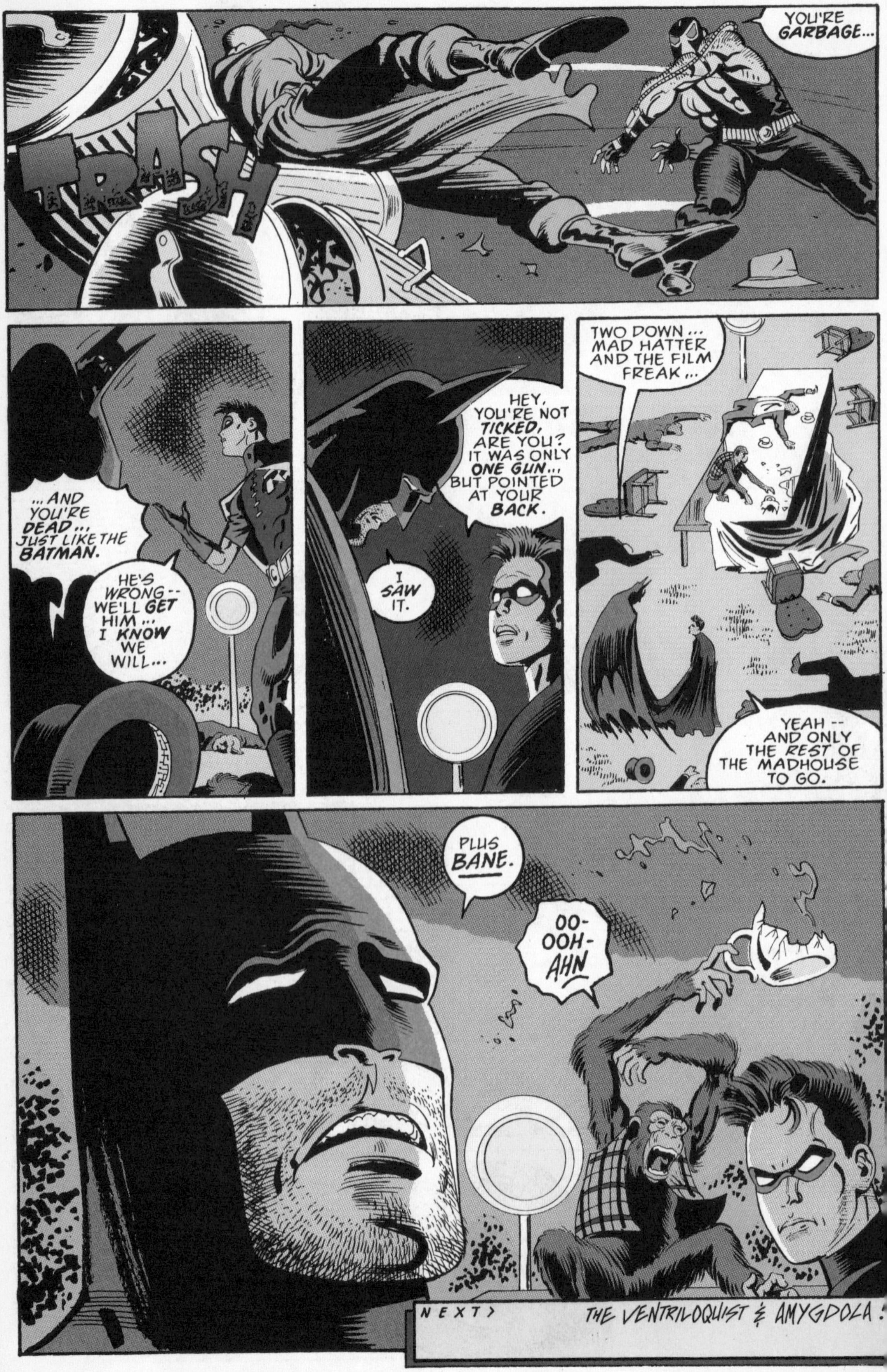
YOU'RE GARBAGE...
TRASH
...AND YOU'RE DEAD... JUST LIKE THE BATMAN.
HE'S WRONG -- WE'LL GET HIM... I KNOW WE WILL...
HEY, YOU'RE NOT TICKED, ARE YOU? IT WAS ONLY ONE GUN... BUT POINTED AT YOUR BACK.
I SAW IT.
TWO DOWN... MAD HATTER AND THE FILM FREAK...
YEAH -- AND ONLY THE REST OF THE MADHOUSE TO GO.
PLUS BANE.
OO-OOOH-AHN
NEXT > THE VENTRILOQUIST & AMYGDALA!

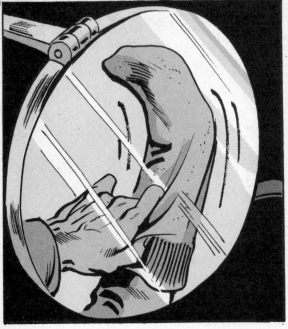

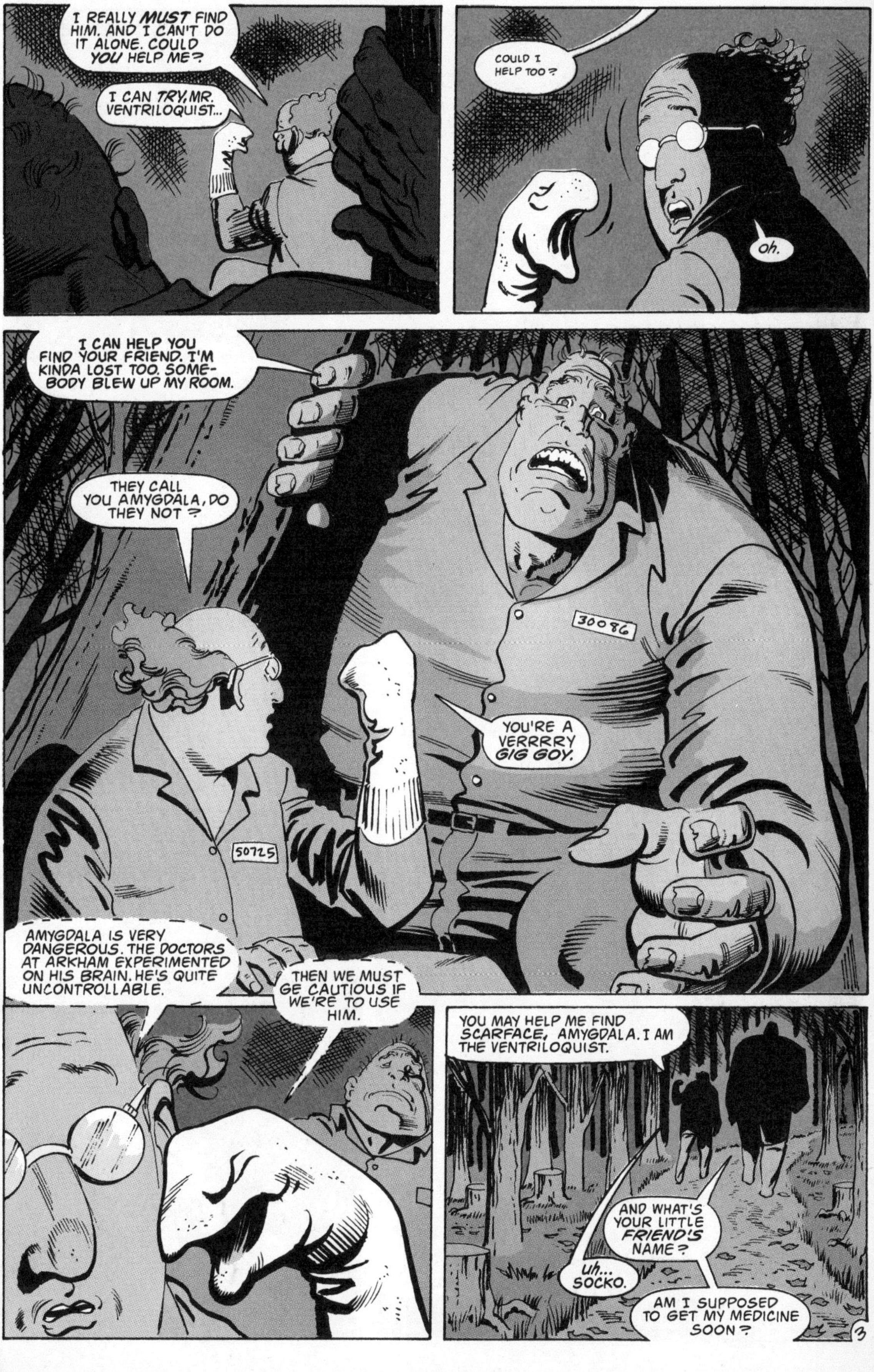
I REALLY MUST FIND HIM. AND I CAN'T DO IT ALONE. COULD YOU HELP ME?
I CAN TRY, MR. VENTRILOQUIST...
COULD I HELP TOO?
oh.
I CAN HELP YOU FIND YOUR FRIEND. I'M KINDA LOST TOO. SOMEBODY BLEW UP MY ROOM.
THEY CALL YOU AMYGDALA, DO THEY NOT?
30086
YOU'RE A VERRRRY GIG GOY.
50725
AMYGDALA IS VERY DANGEROUS. THE DOCTORS AT ARKHAM EXPERIMENTED ON HIS BRAIN. HE'S QUITE UNCONTROLLABLE.
THEN WE MUST GE CAUTIOUS IF WE'RE TO USE HIM.
YOU MAY HELP ME FIND SCARFACE, AMYGDALA. I AM THE VENTRILOQUIST.
AND WHAT'S YOUR LITTLE FRIEND'S NAME?
uh... SOCKO.
AM I SUPPOSED TO GET MY MEDICINE SOON?
3

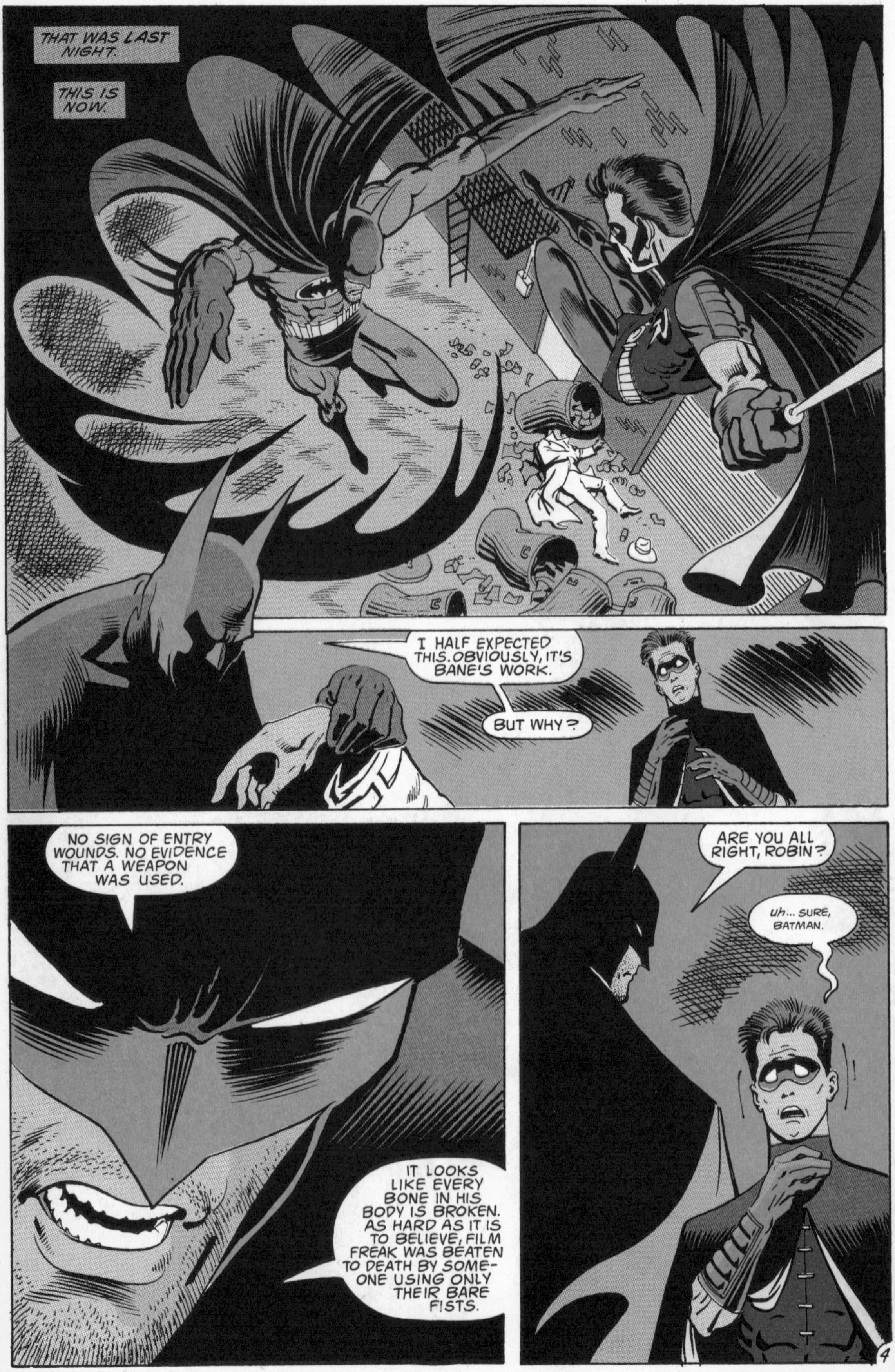
THAT WAS LAST NIGHT.
THIS IS NOW.
I HALF EXPECTED THIS. OBVIOUSLY, IT'S BANE'S WORK.
BUT WHY?
NO SIGN OF ENTRY WOUNDS. NO EVIDENCE THAT A WEAPON WAS USED.
IT LOOKS LIKE EVERY BONE IN HIS BODY IS BROKEN. AS HARD AS IT IS TO BELIEVE, FILM FREAK WAS BEATEN TO DEATH BY SOME-ONE USING ONLY THEIR BARE FISTS.
ARE YOU ALL RIGHT, ROBIN?
uh... SURE, BATMAN.
4

WE'D BETTER KEEP ROLLING. I WANT TO STAY AHEAD OF THE POLICE ON THIS.

HE'S DEAD?

THEY DON'T *GET* ANY DEADER THAN THIS.

YOU GUYS WANT TO STEP LIGHTER? THIS *IS* A CRIME SCENE.

LIEUTENANT KITCH, I DIDN'T KNOW YOU WERE CATCHING.

I'M NOT. I WAS TWO BLOCKS AWAY WHEN THE CALL CAME IN. I'LL STICK UNTIL HOMICIDE GETS HERE.

WANT I SHOULD RADIO FOR A MEAT WAGON?

ONE OF THE ARKHAM INMATES. WENT BY THE NAME *FILM FREAK*. A LONG NIGHT JUST GOT LONGER.

BETTER PUT A CALL IN TO THE COMMISSIONER.

TELL HIM WE DON'T HAVE TO LOOK FOR THIS ONE ANYMORE.

IT'S CALLED A MEDICAL EXAMINER'S VAN, PATROLMAN. EVEN A SKEL LIKE THIS DESERVES *SOME* RESPECT.

YOU *KNOW* THIS ONE, EL TEE?

5

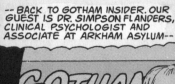

-- BACK TO GOTHAM INSIDER. OUR GUEST IS DR. SIMPSON FLANDERS, CLINICAL PSYCHOLOGIST AND ASSOCIATE AT ARKHAM ASYLUM--

-- WHICH IS MUCH IN THE NEWS TONIGHT. WHAT CAN WE EXPECT FROM THE MASS ESCAPE FROM ARKHAM, DOCTOR?

EXCUSE ME FOR SAYING SO, LINDA, BUT I THINK THE MEDIA ARE ACTING A BIT... HYSTERICAL.

AS I'VE DETAILED IN MY CURRENT BOOK, "I'M SANE AND SO ARE YOU," THESE PATIENTS ARE MERELY MISUNDERSTOOD.

THEY ARE CRYING OUT FOR HELP, LINDA.

I'm Sane and so YOU!

DR. ...

THERE HAVE BEEN A DOZEN HOMICIDES SINCE THE BREAKOUT.

WE'RE TALKING ABOUT THE MOST DANGEROUS COLLECTION OF PSYCHOPATHS EVER ASSEMBLED. THEY ARE HARDLY "MISUNDERSTOOD."

THAT'S YOUR INNATE PREJUDICE TOWARD THE MENTALLY DIVERGENT--

"MENTALLY DIVERGENT"? THAT'S A NEW ONE.

IT'S IN MY BOOK.

AND LET ME MAKE ANOTHER POINT. THESE PATIENTS ARE CONFUSED, LOST. THEY CANNOT OPERATE IN THE OUTSIDE WORLD.

YOU THINK THEY ARE A DANGER TO SOCIETY?

6

"WELL, THEY'RE IN GREATER DANGER FROM US THAN WE ARE FROM THEM."

F.O.I.A. THE OXYMORON

MAYBE SOME OF THEM ALREADY *ARE*.

NO JUSTICE, NO PEACE

DREAM BIG!

HEAVY HEAVY CLUB SOLID BLOOD

POST NO BILLS

DEMONZ

BEEP

WSHSHSH

BEEP

I'M SURE WE WON'T HAVE TO LOOK FOR *ALL* OF THEM.

LOVE

SKIDS

JUST DO IT

SOME OF THEM WILL BE LOOKING FOR *US*.

I'D PREFER TO BE ACTING MORE AND *RE*-ACTING LESS. BUT THERE'S NO RHYME OR REASON TO ANY OF THIS.

YET.

WE'LL STAY MOBILE FOR NOW. CHANCES ARE WE CAN NAIL MORE OF THE ESCAPEES BEFORE THEY CAN GET TO DEEP COVER.

NOT THAT I'M *COMFORTABLE* WITH THAT STRATEGY.

THAT'S WHY WE HAVE TO MOVE FAST. THE *REALLY* DANGEROUS ONES WILL BE THOSE WHO GET A CHANCE TO PLAN.

7

"THEN THE RANDOM VIOLENCE TURNS TO MORE *DELIBERATE* MAYHEM."

THE TAP ROOM

ah-hem.

GENTLEMEN...

YO. LOOK WHO IT IS.

WE'RE LOOKING FOR SCARFACE. HAVE ANY OF YOU GENTLEMEN SEEN HIM?

PERHAPS I MIGHT EVEN ENLIST YOUR AID IN SEARCHING FOR HIM.

HA HA HEE HEE HOO HOO HA HA

LAUGH AT SOCKO, WILL YOU?

WELL, CHUCKLE ALL YOU WANT AT *ME*...

8

56

57

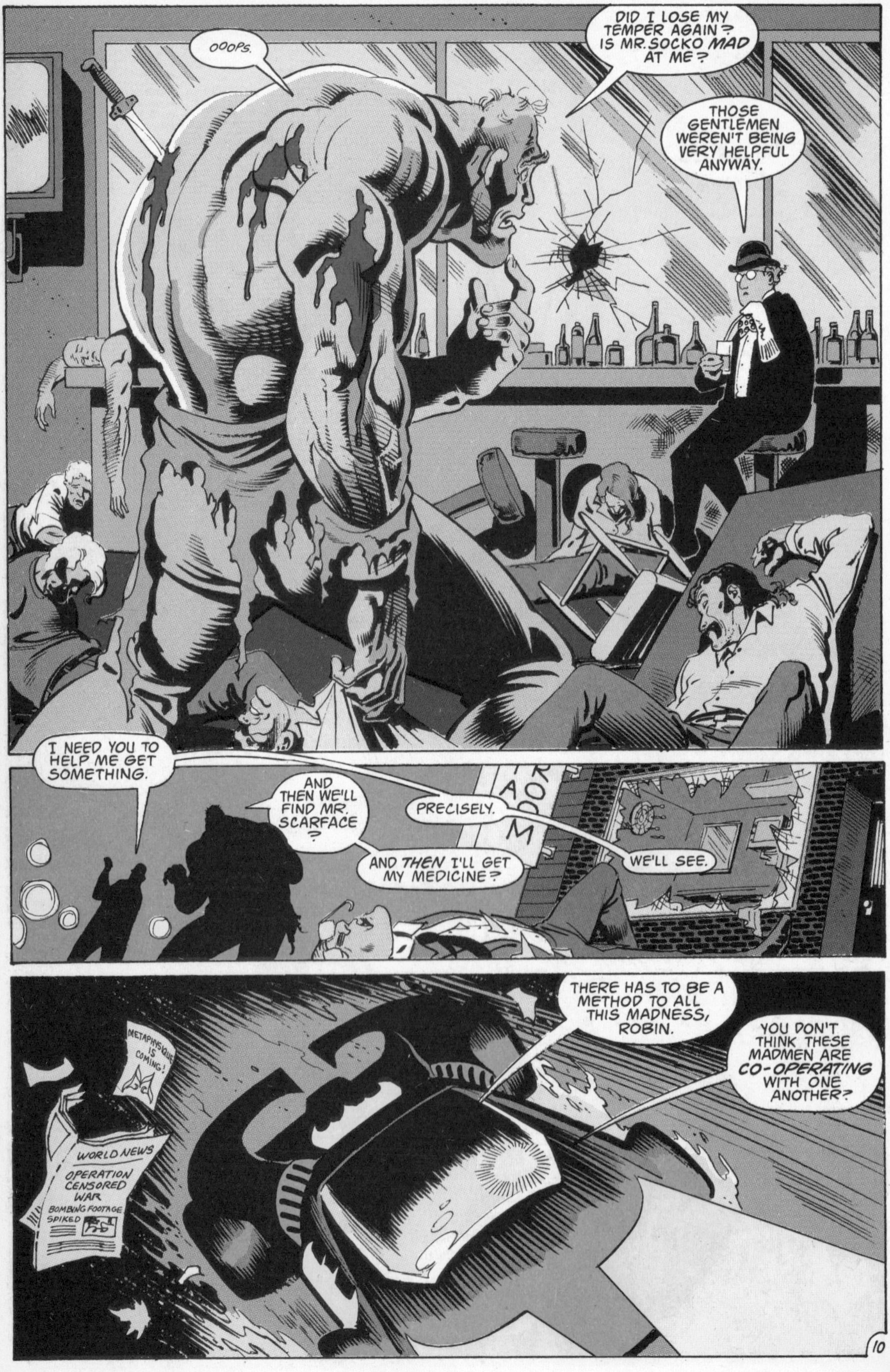
OOOPS.
DID I LOSE MY TEMPER AGAIN? IS MR. SOCKO MAD AT ME?
THOSE GENTLEMEN WEREN'T BEING VERY HELPFUL ANYWAY.
I NEED YOU TO HELP ME GET SOMETHING.
AND THEN WE'LL FIND MR. SCARFACE?
PRECISELY.
AND THEN I'LL GET MY MEDICINE?
WE'LL SEE.
ROOM
THERE HAS TO BE A METHOD TO ALL THIS MADNESS, ROBIN.
YOU DON'T THINK THESE MADMEN ARE CO-OPERATING WITH ONE ANOTHER?
METAPHYSIQUE IS COMING!
WORLD NEWS
OPERATION CENSORED WAR
BOMBING FOOTAGE SPIKED
10

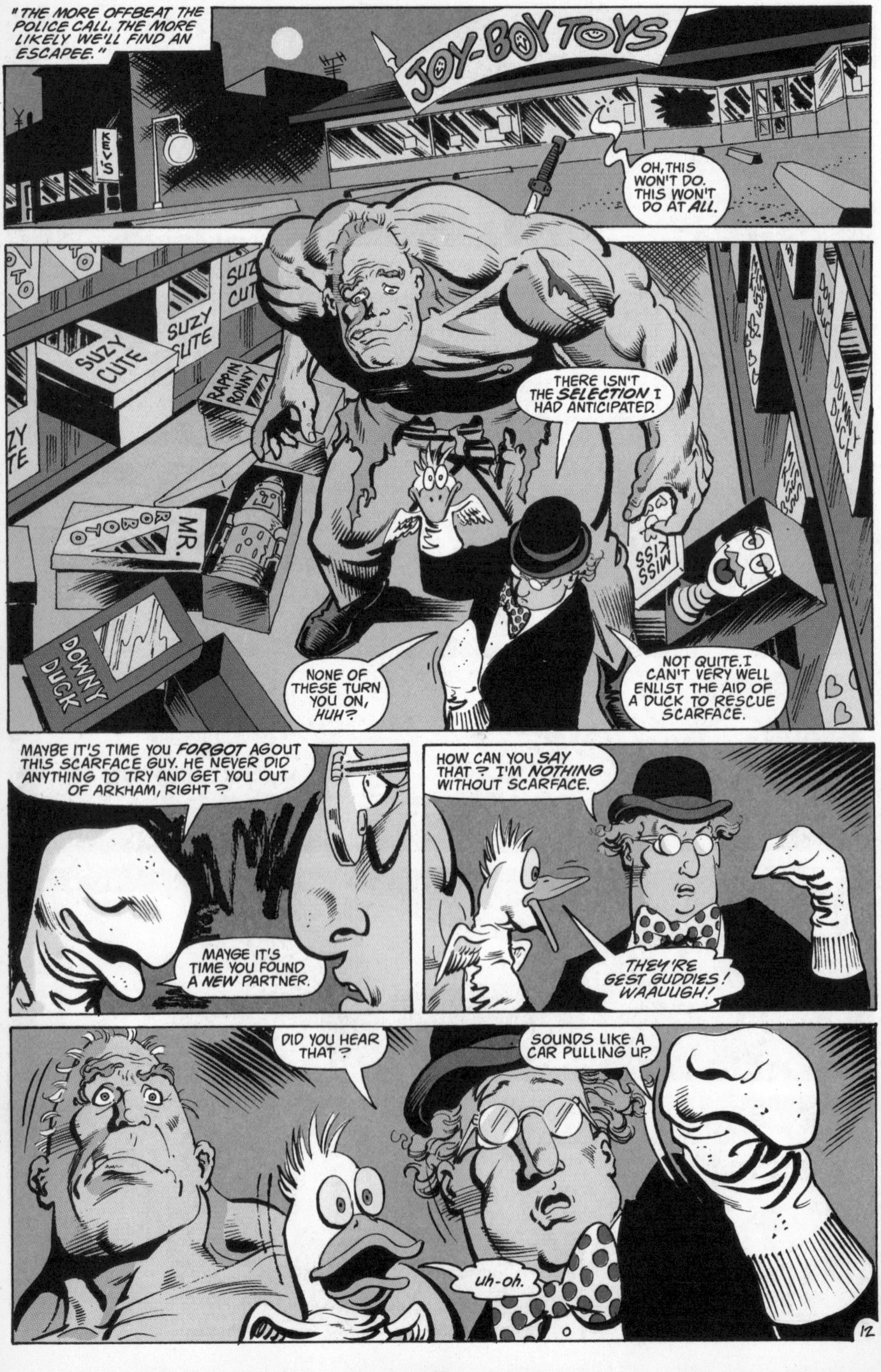
"THE MORE OFFBEAT THE POLICE CALL, THE MORE LIKELY WE'LL FIND AN ESCAPEE."
JOY-BOY TOYS
KEV'S
OH, THIS WON'T DO. THIS WON'T DO AT ALL.
SUZY CUTE
RAPPIN' RONNY
MR. ROBOTO
DOWNY DUCK
MISS KISS
THERE ISN'T THE SELECTION I HAD ANTICIPATED.
NONE OF THESE TURN YOU ON, HUH?
NOT QUITE. I CAN'T VERY WELL ENLIST THE AID OF A DUCK TO RESCUE SCARFACE.
MAYBE IT'S TIME YOU FORGOT AGOUT THIS SCARFACE GUY. HE NEVER DID ANYTHING TO TRY AND GET YOU OUT OF ARKHAM, RIGHT?
MAYGE IT'S TIME YOU FOUND A NEW PARTNER.
HOW CAN YOU SAY THAT? I'M NOTHING WITHOUT SCARFACE.
THEY'RE GEST GUDDIES! WAAUUGH!
DID YOU HEAR THAT?
SOUNDS LIKE A CAR PULLING UP.
uh-oh.
12

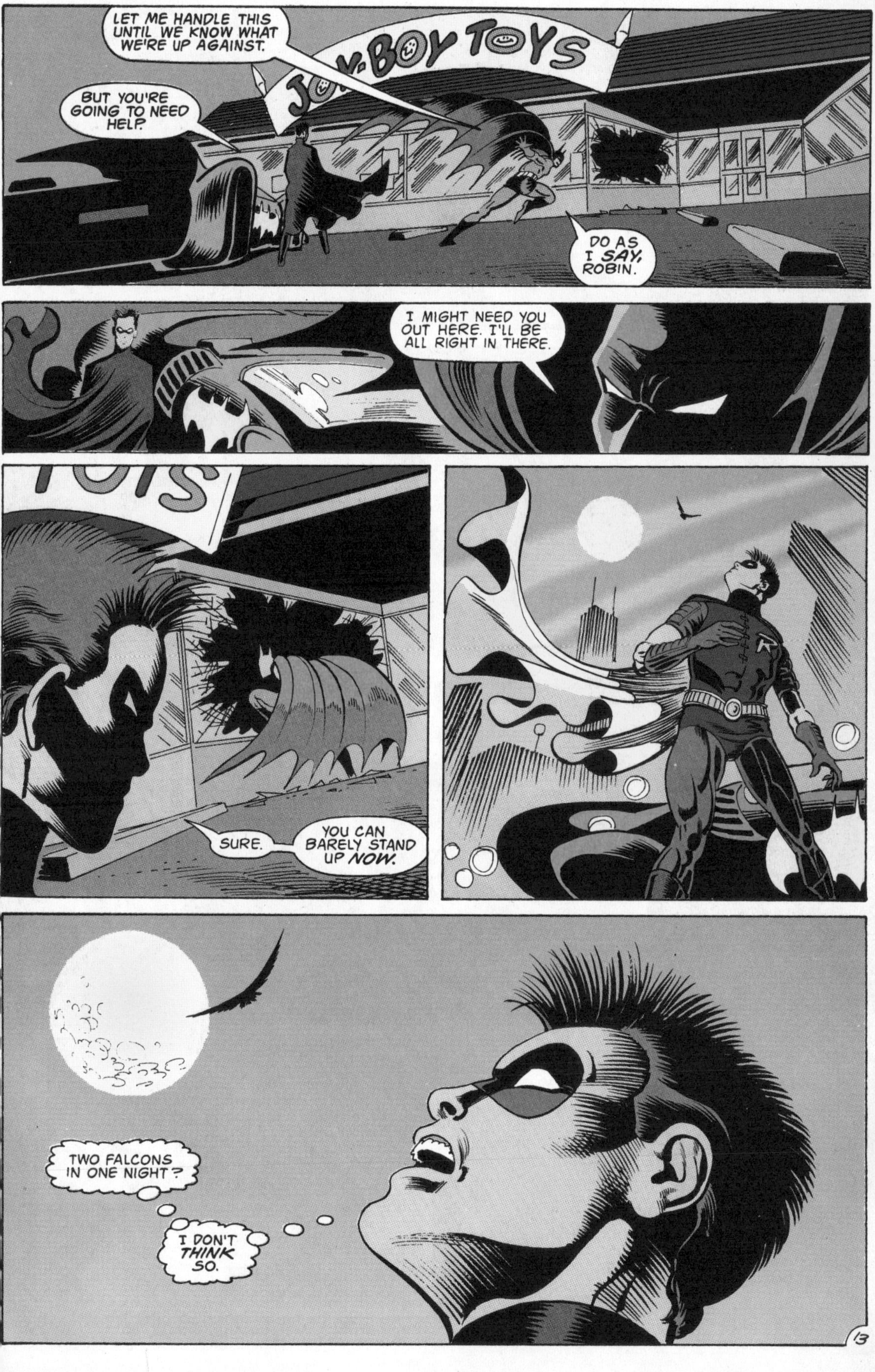
LET ME HANDLE THIS UNTIL WE KNOW WHAT WE'RE UP AGAINST.
JOY-BOY TOYS
BUT YOU'RE GOING TO NEED HELP.
DO AS I SAY, ROBIN.
I MIGHT NEED YOU OUT HERE. I'LL BE ALL RIGHT IN THERE.
TOYS
SURE.
YOU CAN BARELY STAND UP NOW.
TWO FALCONS IN ONE NIGHT?
I DON'T THINK SO.
13

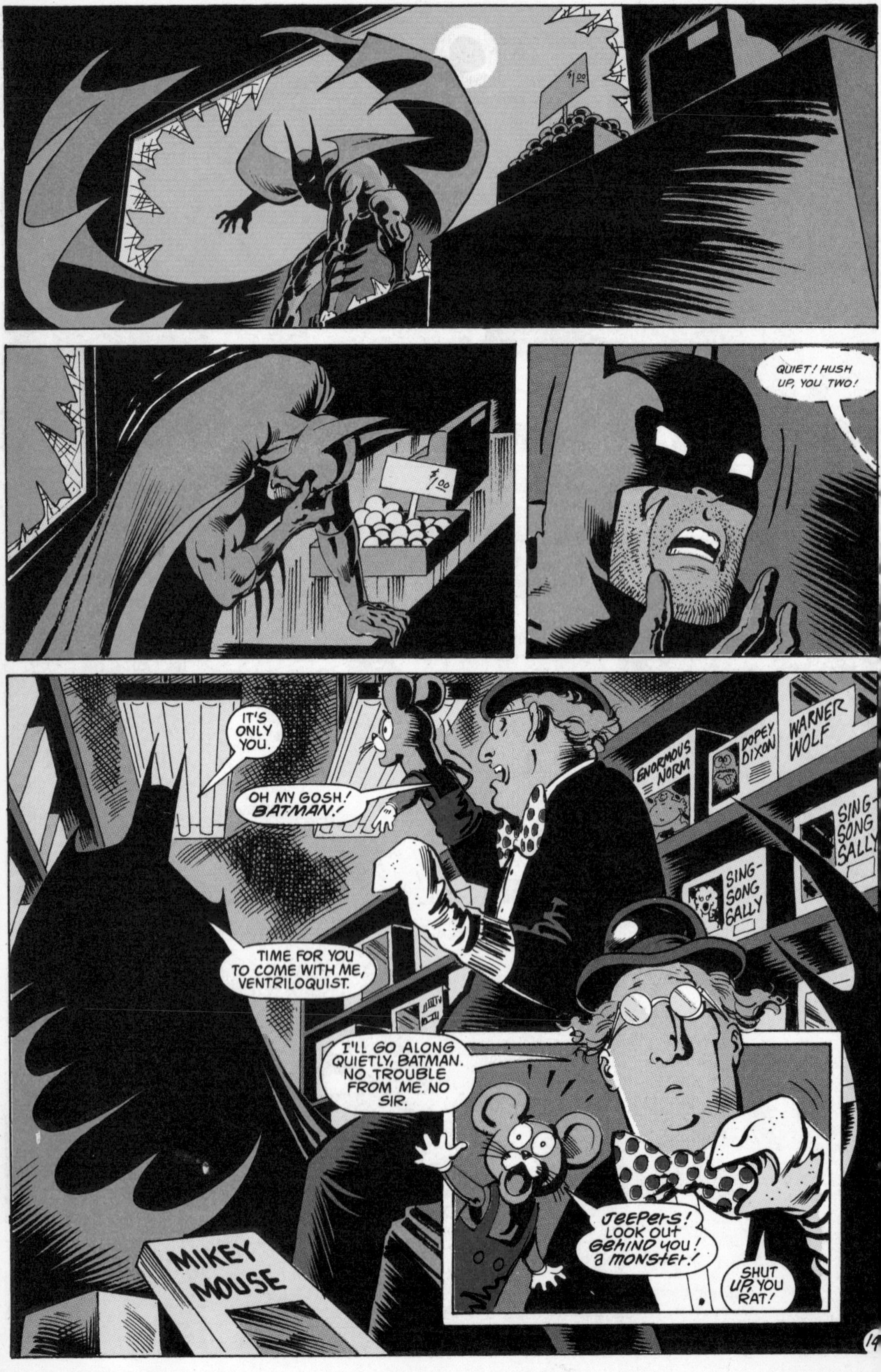
$1.00
$1.00
QUIET! HUSH UP, YOU TWO!
IT'S ONLY YOU.
OH MY GOSH! BATMAN!
ENORMOUS NORM
DOPEY DIXON
WARNER WOLF
SING-SONG SALLY
SING-SONG GALLY
TIME FOR YOU TO COME WITH ME, VENTRILOQUIST.
I'LL GO ALONG QUIETLY, BATMAN. NO TROUBLE FROM ME. NO SIR.
JEEPERS! LOOK OUT BEHIND YOU! A MONSTER!
SHUT UP, YOU RAT!
MIKEY MOUSE

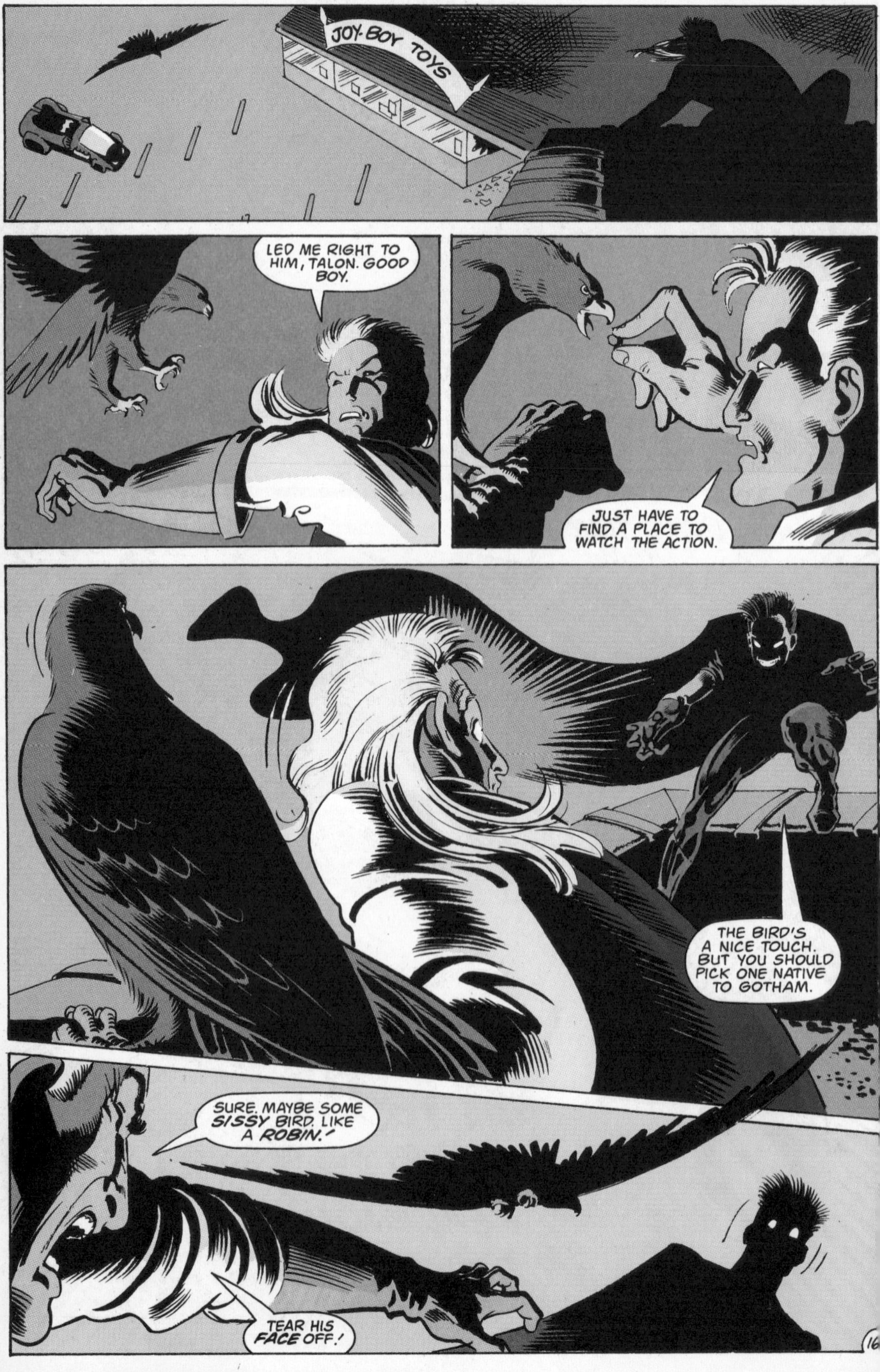
JOY-BOY TOYS
LED ME RIGHT TO HIM, TALON. GOOD BOY.
JUST HAVE TO FIND A PLACE TO WATCH THE ACTION.
THE BIRD'S A NICE TOUCH. BUT YOU SHOULD PICK ONE NATIVE TO GOTHAM.
SURE. MAYBE SOME *SISSY* BIRD. LIKE A *ROBIN*.'
TEAR HIS *FACE* OFF.'
16

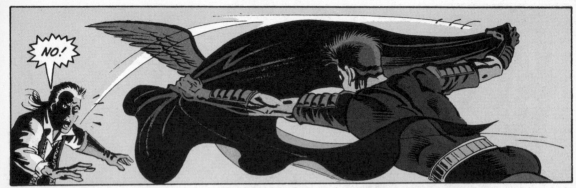

YOU PUT UP A GOOD FRONT, KID...

KIKKK

SNK

BUT YOU'LL NEVER GET A CHANCE TO WALK THE WALK.

BIRD. ANSWER ME, BIRD.

WHAT IS IT? I'M KINDA BUSY. I GOT THIS ROBIN BRAT DOWN FOR THE COUNT.

LEAVE HIM. I DO NOT WANT TO SHOW OUR HAND THIS SOON.

aw...

YOUR LUCKY NIGHT. YOU GET A STAY OF EXECUTION, KID.

OBEY ME, BIRD. COME TO ME. TROGG CAN TAKE OVER THE SURVEILLANCE.

SEE YOU LATER, PUNK.

NOT IF I SEE YOU FIRST.

2₁

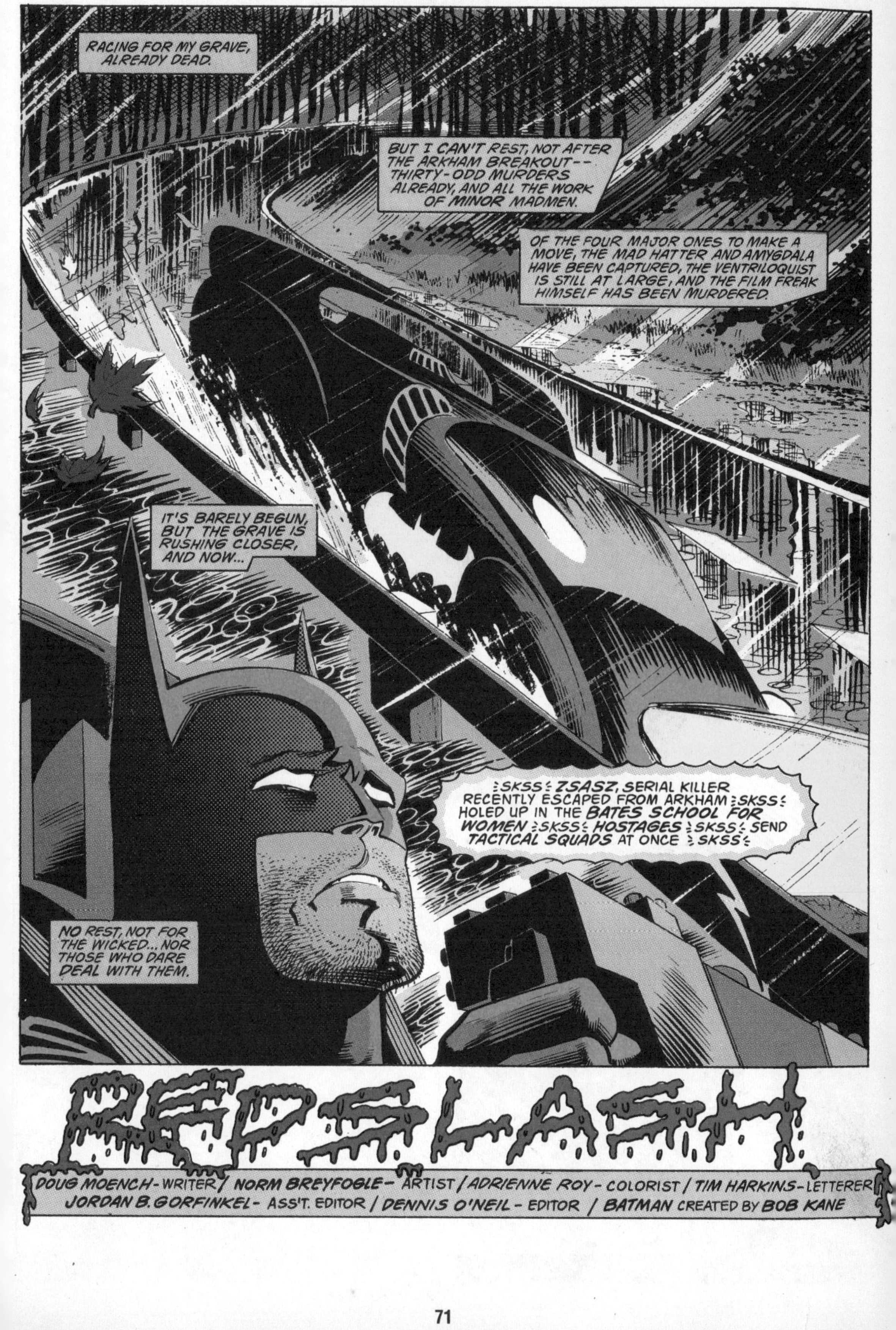
RACING FOR MY GRAVE, ALREADY DEAD.
BUT I CAN'T REST, NOT AFTER THE ARKHAM BREAKOUT-- THIRTY-ODD MURDERS ALREADY, AND ALL THE WORK OF MINOR MADMEN.
OF THE FOUR MAJOR ONES TO MAKE A MOVE, THE MAD HATTER AND AMYGDALA HAVE BEEN CAPTURED, THE VENTRILOQUIST IS STILL AT LARGE, AND THE FILM FREAK HIMSELF HAS BEEN MURDERED.
IT'S BARELY BEGUN, BUT THE GRAVE IS RUSHING CLOSER, AND NOW...
SKSS ZSASZ, SERIAL KILLER RECENTLY ESCAPED FROM ARKHAM SKSS HOLED UP IN THE BATES SCHOOL FOR WOMEN SKSS HOSTAGES SKSS SEND TACTICAL SQUADS AT ONCE SKSS
NO REST, NOT FOR THE WICKED... NOR THOSE WHO DARE DEAL WITH THEM.

RED SLASH

DOUG MOENCH-WRITER / NORM BREYFOGLE-ARTIST / ADRIENNE ROY-COLORIST / TIM HARKINS-LETTERER
JORDAN B. GORFINKEL-ASS'T. EDITOR / DENNIS O'NEIL-EDITOR / BATMAN CREATED BY BOB KANE

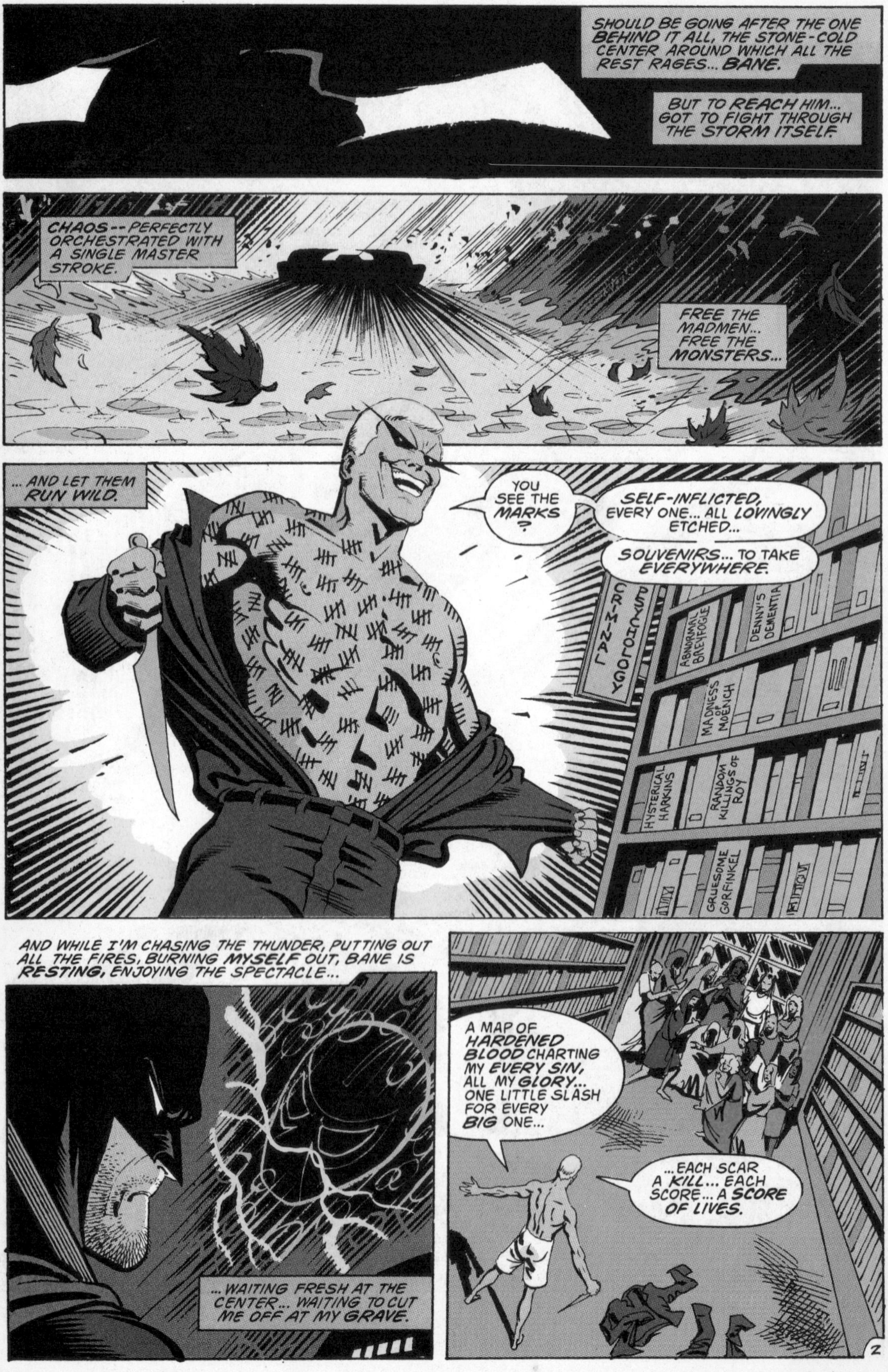
SHOULD BE GOING AFTER THE ONE BEHIND IT ALL, THE STONE-COLD CENTER AROUND WHICH ALL THE REST RAGES... BANE.
BUT TO REACH HIM... GOT TO FIGHT THROUGH THE STORM ITSELF.
CHAOS--PERFECTLY ORCHESTRATED WITH A SINGLE MASTER STROKE.
FREE THE MADMEN... FREE THE MONSTERS...
...AND LET THEM RUN WILD.
YOU SEE THE MARKS?
SELF-INFLICTED, EVERY ONE... ALL LOVINGLY ETCHED...
SOUVENIRS... TO TAKE EVERYWHERE.
CRIMINAL PSYCHOLOGY
ABNORMAL BREYFOGLE
DENNY'S DEMENTIA
MADNESS OF MOENCH
HYSTERICAL HARKINS
RANDOM KILLINGS OF ROY
GRUESOME GORFINKEL
AND WHILE I'M CHASING THE THUNDER, PUTTING OUT ALL THE FIRES, BURNING MYSELF OUT, BANE IS RESTING, ENJOYING THE SPECTACLE...
...WAITING FRESH AT THE CENTER... WAITING TO CUT ME OFF AT MY GRAVE.
A MAP OF HARDENED BLOOD CHARTING MY EVERY SIN, ALL MY GLORY... ONE LITTLE SLASH FOR EVERY BIG ONE...
...EACH SCAR A KILL... EACH SCORE... A SCORE OF LIVES.
2

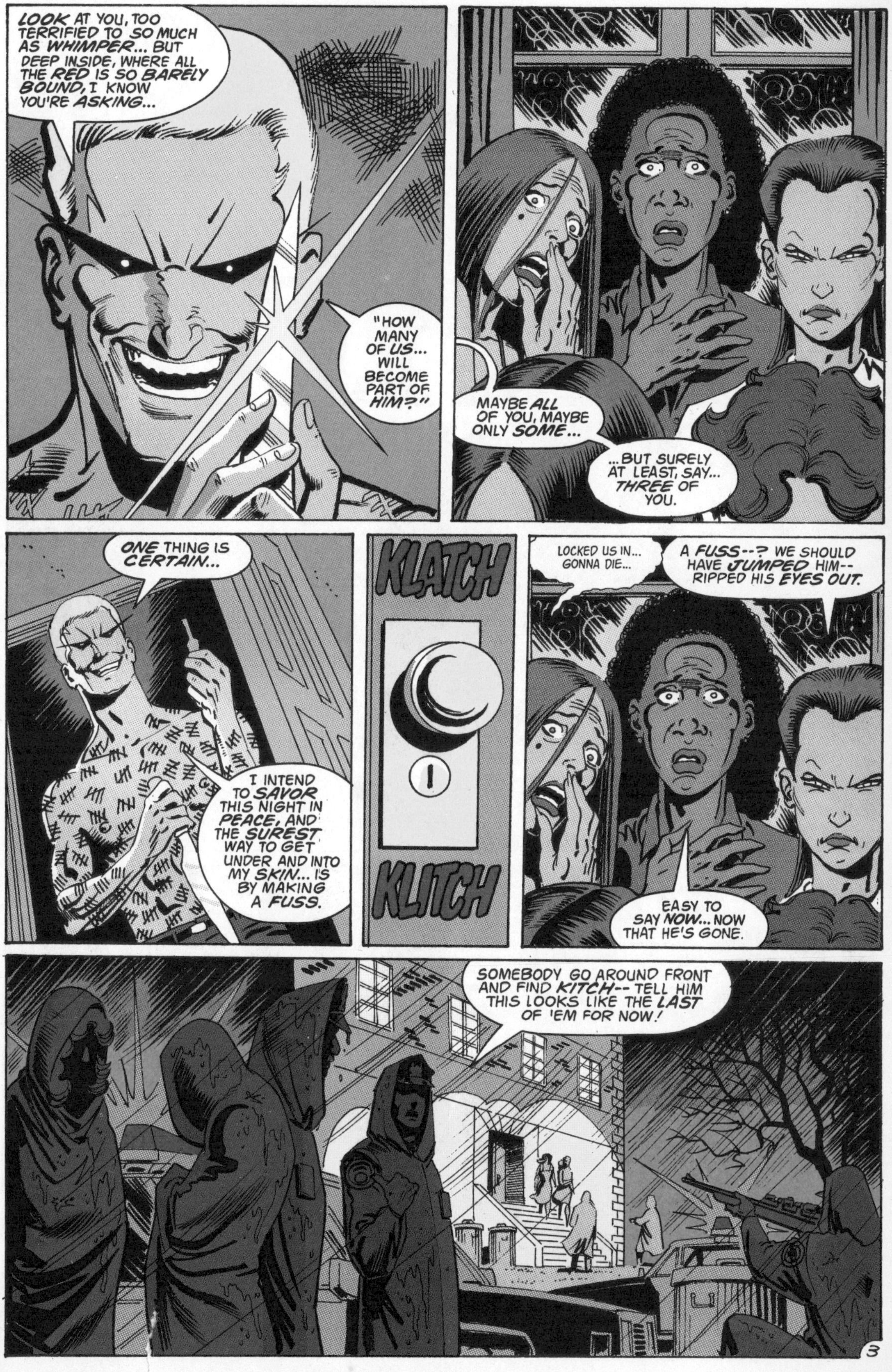
LOOK AT YOU, TOO TERRIFIED TO SO MUCH AS WHIMPER... BUT DEEP INSIDE, WHERE ALL THE RED IS SO BARELY BOUND, I KNOW YOU'RE ASKING...
"HOW MANY OF US... WILL BECOME PART OF HIM?"
MAYBE ALL OF YOU, MAYBE ONLY SOME...
...BUT SURELY AT LEAST, SAY... THREE OF YOU.
ONE THING IS CERTAIN...
I INTEND TO SAVOR THIS NIGHT IN PEACE, AND THE SUREST WAY TO GET UNDER AND INTO MY SKIN... IS BY MAKING A FUSS.
KLATCH
KLITCH
LOCKED US IN... GONNA DIE...
A FUSS--? WE SHOULD HAVE JUMPED HIM-- RIPPED HIS EYES OUT.
EASY TO SAY NOW... NOW THAT HE'S GONE.
SOMEBODY GO AROUND FRONT AND FIND KITCH-- TELL HIM THIS LOOKS LIKE THE LAST OF 'EM FOR NOW!
3

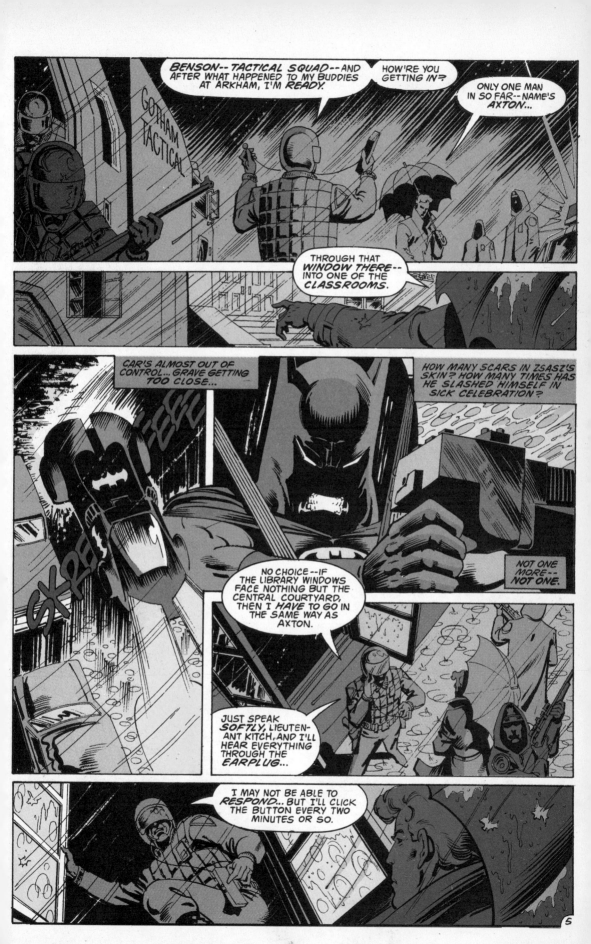

HE'LL BE *BACK*... BACK TO KILL US *ALL*...

Oh, STOP YOUR *SNIVELING*, ANN!

IF HE *DOES* COME BACK, I SAY WE *JUMP* HIM--ALL AT *ONCE!* NO *WAY* HE CAN KILL US *ALL.*

BUT HE *COULD* KILL *SOME* OF US -- AND *JUMPING* HIM MIGHT BE THE THING THAT *FORCES* HIM TO *DO* IT.

DIE... WE'RE GONNA DIE...

AXTON--? YOU *FIND* SOMETHING--?

ALL RIGHT, SO WE *HOLD BACK* AS LONG AS WE'RE ALL *OKAY*... BUT THE MOMENT HE TOUCHES *ONE* OF US -- ANY ONE OF US -- WE ALL *POUNCE* ON HIM, KICKING AND CLAWING WHERE IT *HURTS* MOST.

RIGHT--?

AW, NO... YOU FOUND *BLOOD...*

DIE... ALL GONNA DIE...

6

--TENSE STANDOFF *CONTINUES* AT GOTHAM'S *BATES SCHOOL FOR WOMEN,* WHERE POLICE ARE UNABLE TO MOVE WITHOUT RISK TO *HOSTAGES' LIVES...*

LOTTA *COPS,* BANE-- BUT NO *BATMAN* YET.

IN OTHER NEWS...

HE'LL *BE* THERE, BIRD.

I THINK MAYBE THE BATMAN'S RIPE FOR HIS FALL *RIGHT NOW.*

NO. HE'S *PHYSICALLY* WEAKENED -- AND DEPLETED MORE WITH EACH NEW EXPLOSION OF MADNESS -- BUT HIS *MIND* IS STILL *STRONG...*

HE IS *NOT* READY TO BE BROKEN... NOT QUITE *YET.*

PROBABLY-- BUT I'M BEGINNIN' TO *WONDER* ABOUT HIM, BANE-- ESPECIALLY AFTER RUNNIN' INTO HIS *LITTLE* PARTNER.

THE KID'S *GOOD,* BUT ANY MAN WHO *RELIES* ON A KID MAY BE *OVERRATED...*

KRIK

WHEN HE *IS,* I WILL *KNOW* IT... AND THEN, THE PIECES WILL *STAY BROKEN.*

8

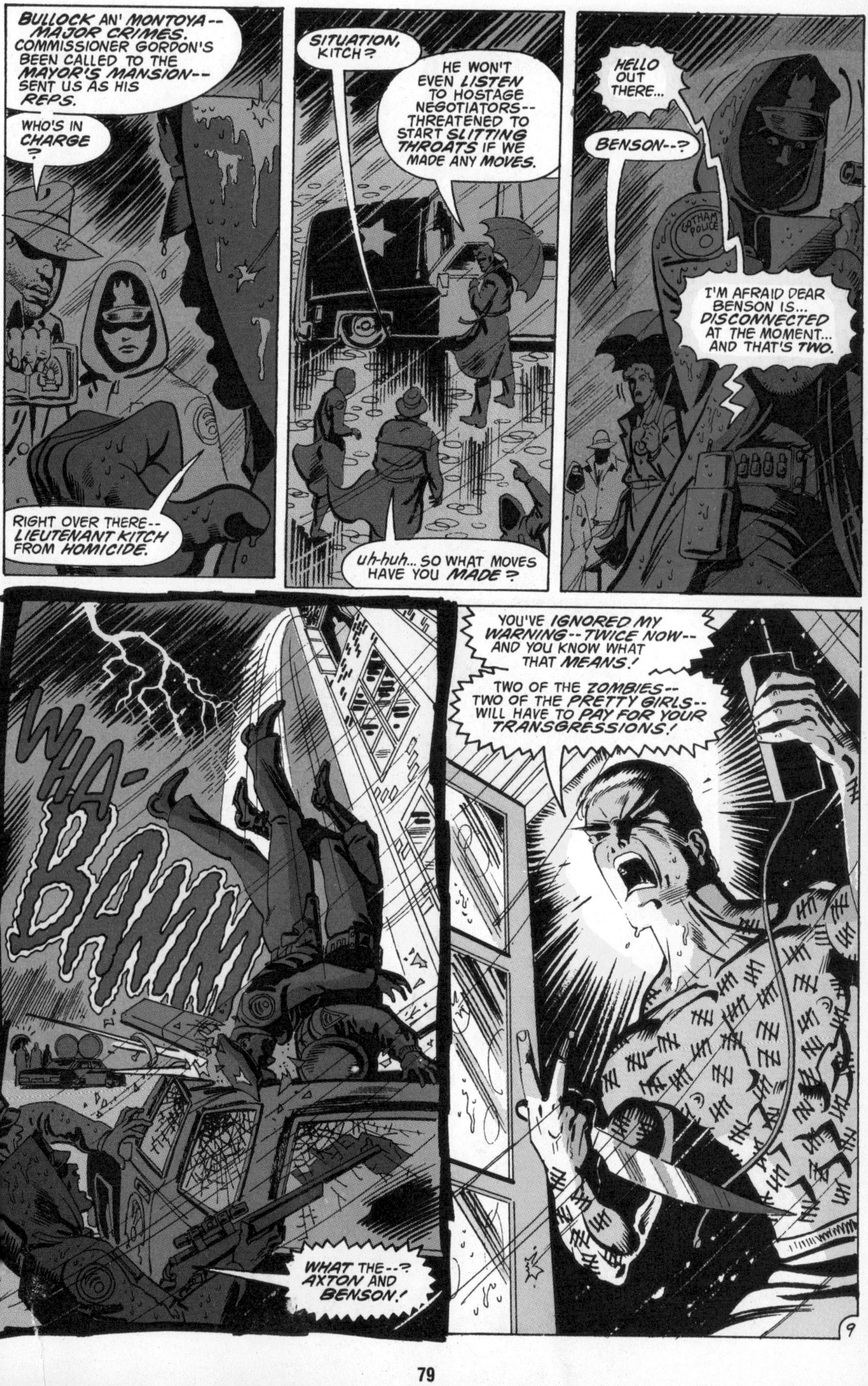
BULLOCK AN' MONTOYA-- MAJOR CRIMES. COMMISSIONER GORDON'S BEEN CALLED TO THE MAYOR'S MANSION-- SENT US AS HIS REPS.
WHO'S IN CHARGE?
RIGHT OVER THERE-- LIEUTENANT KITCH FROM HOMICIDE.
SITUATION, KITCH?
HE WON'T EVEN LISTEN TO HOSTAGE NEGOTIATORS-- THREATENED TO START SLITTING THROATS IF WE MADE ANY MOVES.
uh-huh... SO WHAT MOVES HAVE YOU MADE?
HELLO OUT THERE...
BENSON--?
GOTHAM POLICE
I'M AFRAID DEAR BENSON IS... DISCONNECTED AT THE MOMENT... AND THAT'S TWO.
WHA-BAM
WHAT THE--? AXTON AND BENSON!
YOU'VE IGNORED MY WARNING--TWICE NOW-- AND YOU KNOW WHAT THAT MEANS!
TWO OF THE ZOMBIES-- TWO OF THE PRETTY GIRLS-- WILL HAVE TO PAY FOR YOUR TRANSGRESSIONS!
9

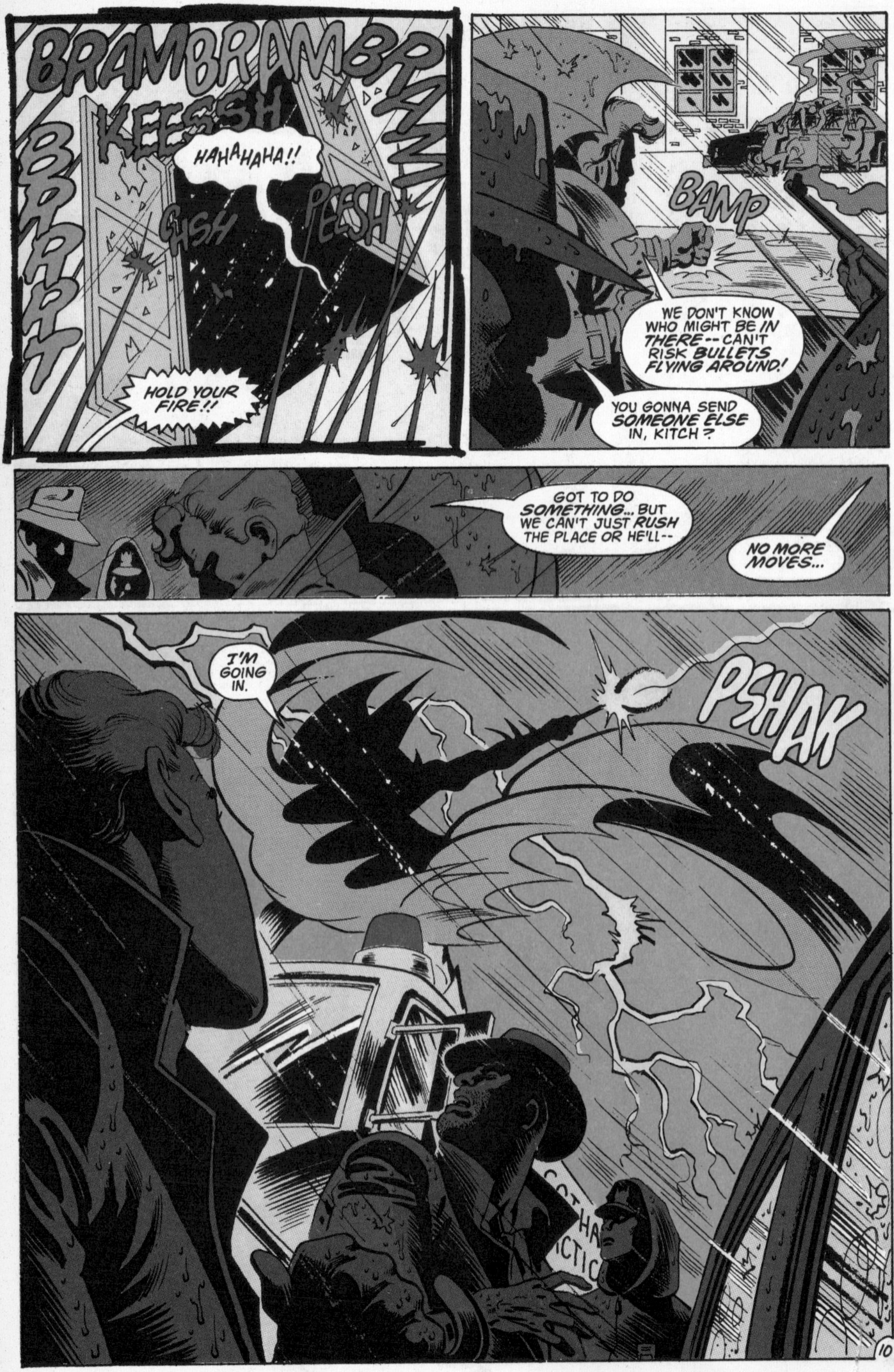
BRAMBRAMBRAM
BRRRRT
KEESSH
HAHAHAHA!!
CHSH
PEESH
HOLD YOUR FIRE!!
BAMP
WE DON'T KNOW WHO MIGHT BE IN THERE-- CAN'T RISK BULLETS FLYING AROUND!
YOU GONNA SEND SOMEONE ELSE IN, KITCH?
GOT TO DO SOMETHING... BUT WE CAN'T JUST RUSH THE PLACE OR HE'LL--
NO MORE MOVES...
I'M GOING IN.
PSHAK
10

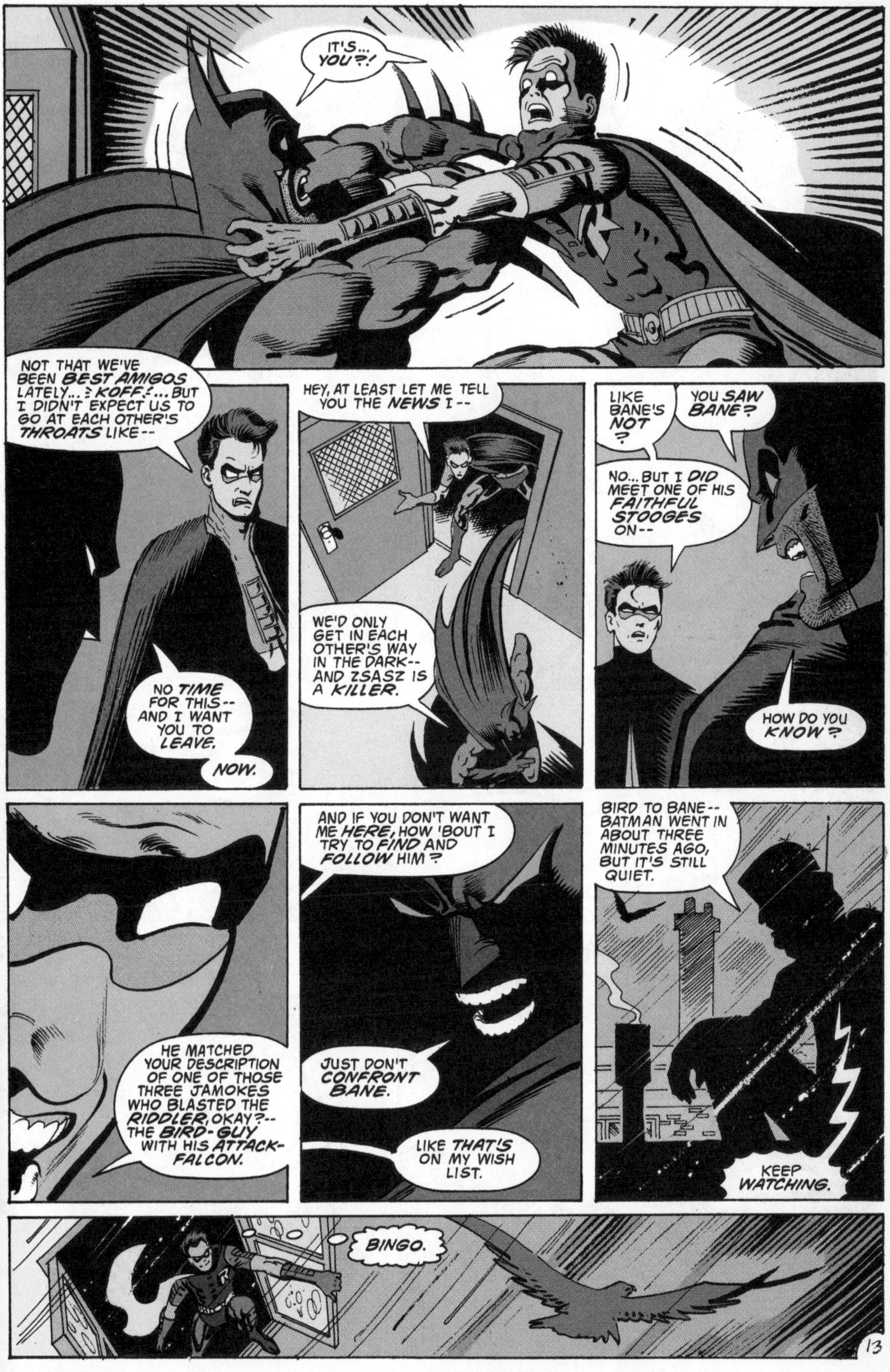
IT'S... YOU?!
NOT THAT WE'VE BEEN BEST AMIGOS LATELY... KOFF!... BUT I DIDN'T EXPECT US TO GO AT EACH OTHER'S THROATS LIKE--
NO TIME FOR THIS-- AND I WANT YOU TO LEAVE.
NOW.
HEY, AT LEAST LET ME TELL YOU THE NEWS I--
WE'D ONLY GET IN EACH OTHER'S WAY IN THE DARK-- AND ZSASZ IS A KILLER.
LIKE BANE'S NOT?
YOU SAW BANE?
NO... BUT I DID MEET ONE OF HIS FAITHFUL STOOGES ON--
HOW DO YOU KNOW?
HE MATCHED YOUR DESCRIPTION OF ONE OF THOSE THREE JAMOKES WHO BLASTED THE RIDDLER, OKAY?-- THE BIRD-GUY WITH HIS ATTACK-FALCON.
AND IF YOU DON'T WANT ME HERE, HOW 'BOUT I TRY TO FIND AND FOLLOW HIM?
JUST DON'T CONFRONT BANE.
LIKE THAT'S ON MY WISH LIST.
BIRD TO BANE-- BATMAN WENT IN ABOUT THREE MINUTES AGO, BUT IT'S STILL QUIET.
KEEP WATCHING.
BINGO.
13

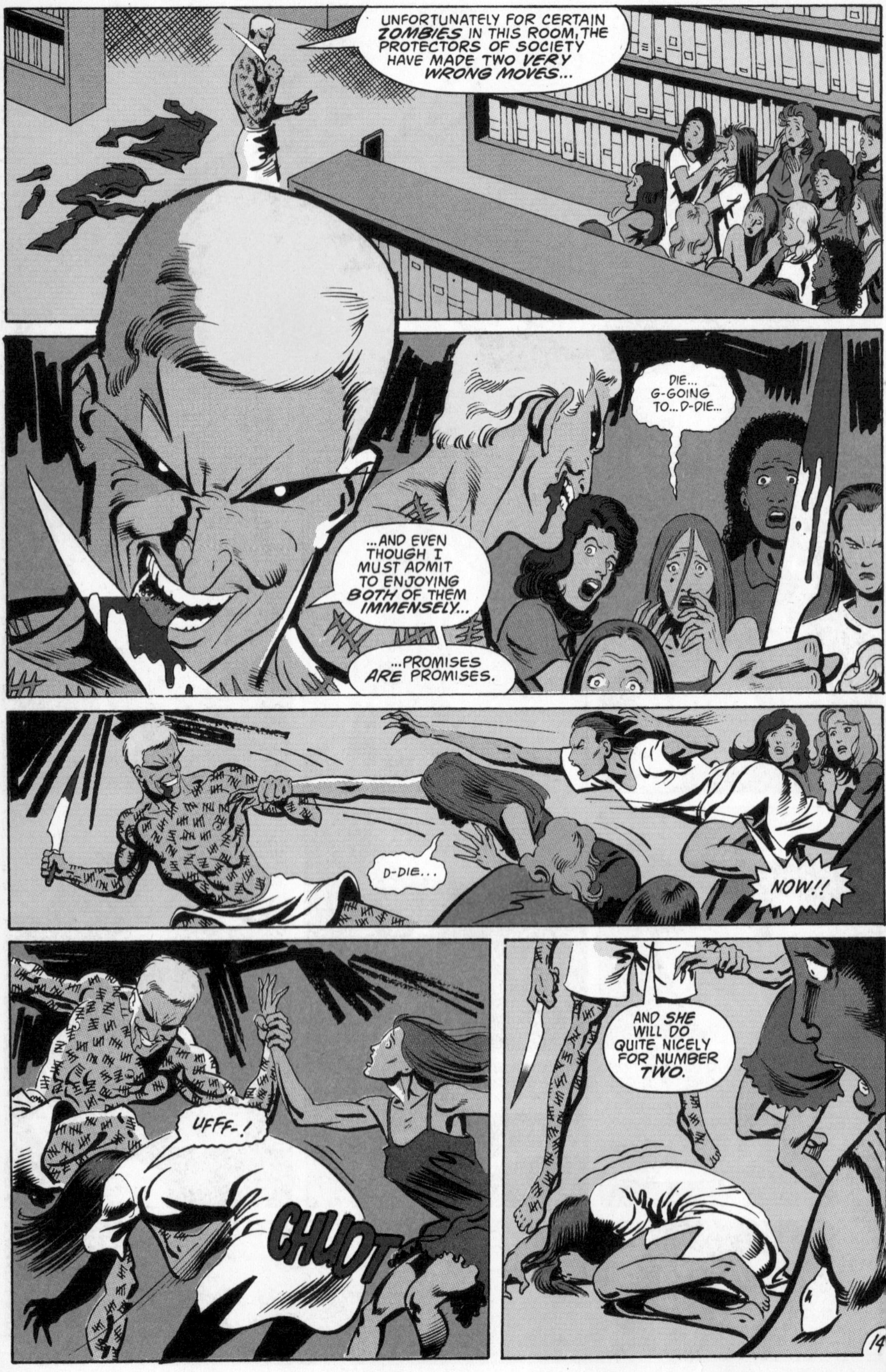
UNFORTUNATELY FOR CERTAIN ZOMBIES IN THIS ROOM, THE PROTECTORS OF SOCIETY HAVE MADE TWO VERY WRONG MOVES...
DIE... G-GOING TO... D-DIE...
...AND EVEN THOUGH I MUST ADMIT TO ENJOYING BOTH OF THEM IMMENSELY...
...PROMISES ARE PROMISES.
D-DIE...
NOW!!
UFFF-!
CHUDT
AND SHE WILL DO QUITE NICELY FOR NUMBER TWO.
14

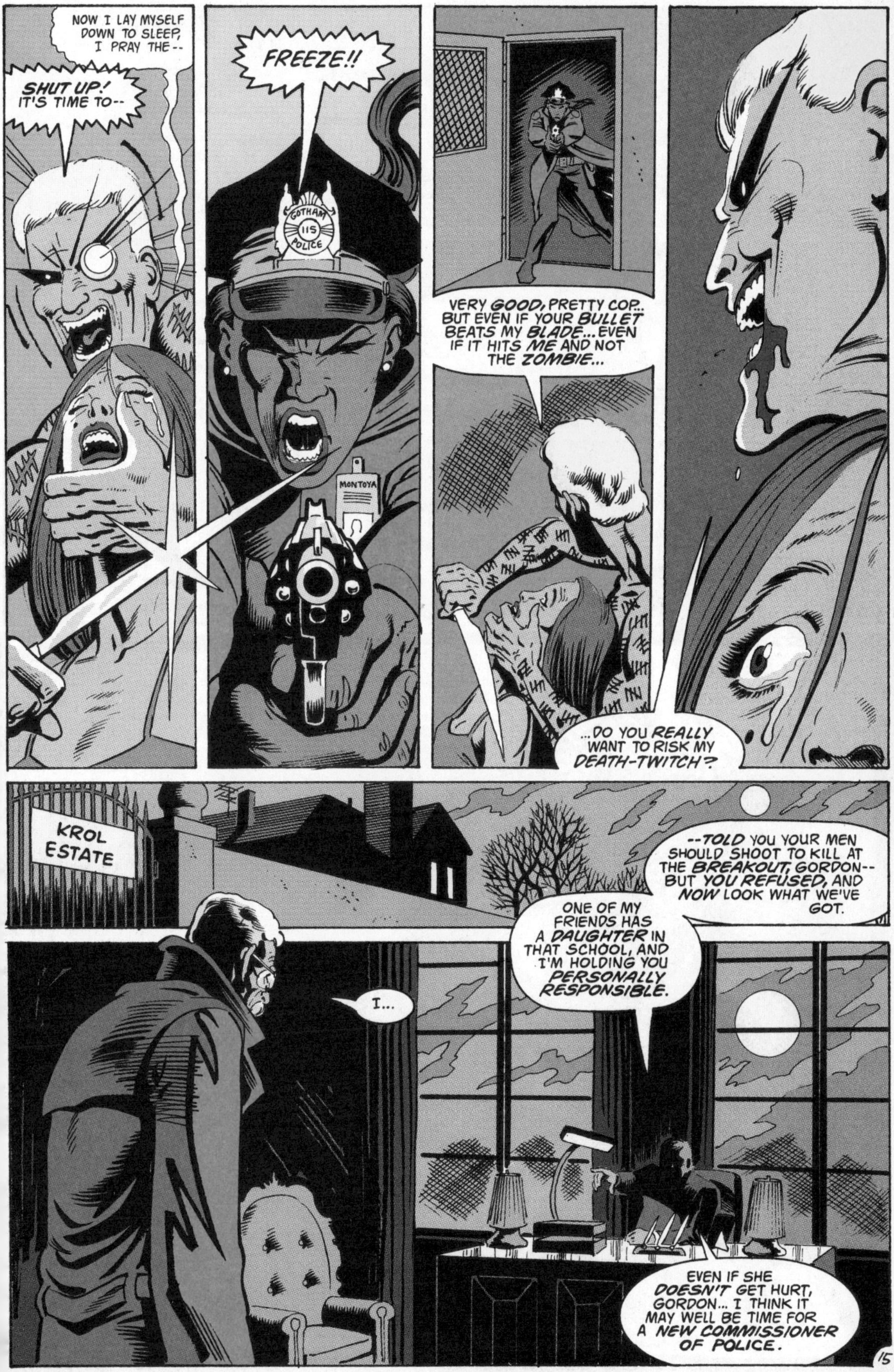
NOW I LAY MYSELF DOWN TO SLEEP, I PRAY THE--
SHUT UP! IT'S TIME TO--
FREEZE!!
GOTHAM 115 POLICE
MONTOYA
VERY GOOD, PRETTY COP... BUT EVEN IF YOUR BULLET BEATS MY BLADE... EVEN IF IT HITS ME AND NOT THE ZOMBIE...
...DO YOU REALLY WANT TO RISK MY DEATH-TWITCH?
KROL ESTATE
--TOLD YOU YOUR MEN SHOULD SHOOT TO KILL AT THE BREAKOUT, GORDON-- BUT YOU REFUSED, AND NOW LOOK WHAT WE'VE GOT.
ONE OF MY FRIENDS HAS A DAUGHTER IN THAT SCHOOL, AND I'M HOLDING YOU PERSONALLY RESPONSIBLE.
I...
EVEN IF SHE DOESN'T GET HURT, GORDON... I THINK IT MAY WELL BE TIME FOR A NEW COMMISSIONER OF POLICE.
15

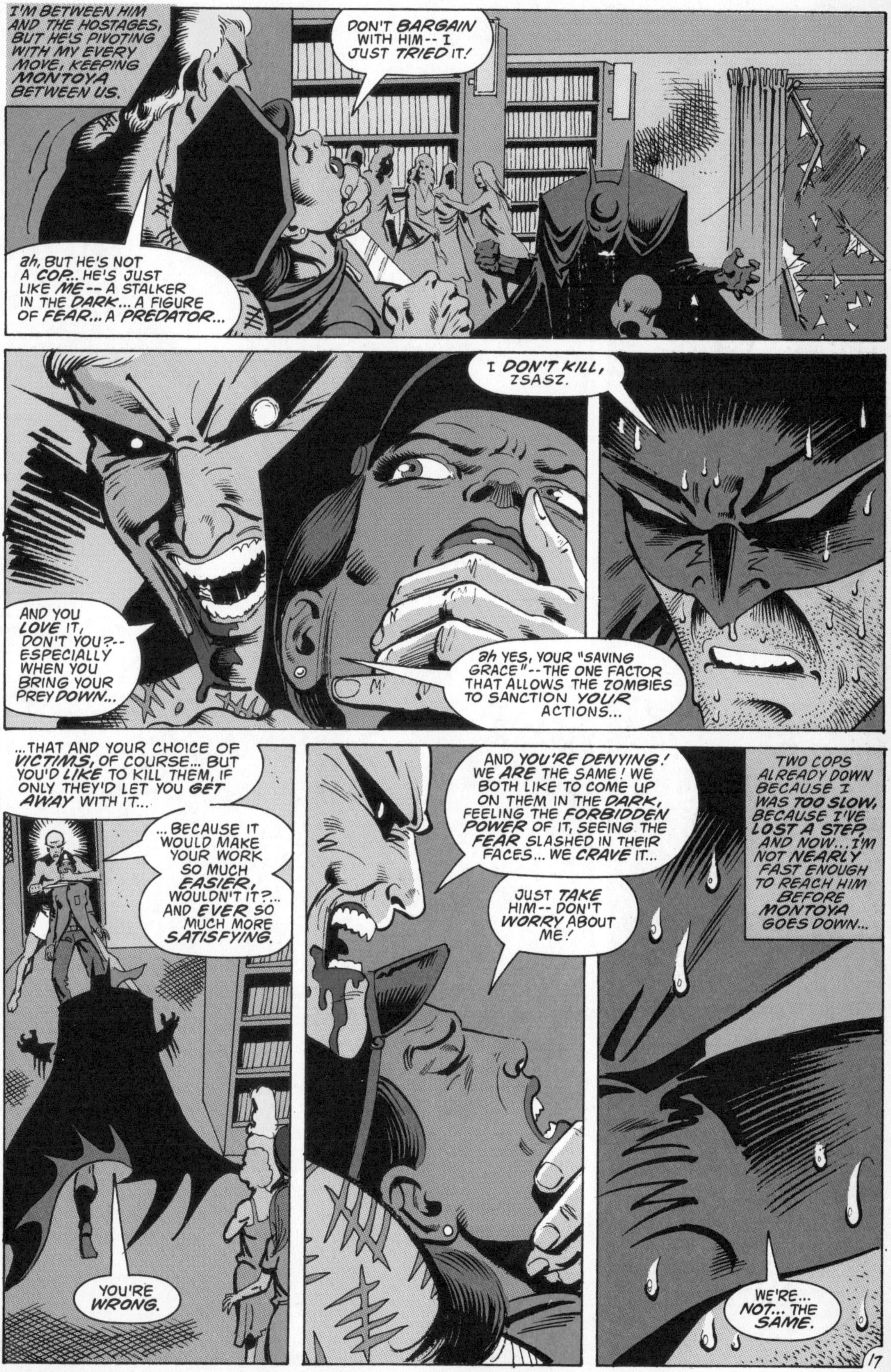
I'M BETWEEN HIM AND THE HOSTAGES, BUT HE'S PIVOTING WITH MY EVERY MOVE, KEEPING MONTOYA BETWEEN US.
DON'T BARGAIN WITH HIM-- I JUST TRIED IT!
ah, BUT HE'S NOT A COP.. HE'S JUST LIKE ME-- A STALKER IN THE DARK... A FIGURE OF FEAR... A PREDATOR...
I DON'T KILL, ZSASZ.
AND YOU LOVE IT, DON'T YOU?-- ESPECIALLY WHEN YOU BRING YOUR PREY DOWN...
ah YES, YOUR "SAVING GRACE"-- THE ONE FACTOR THAT ALLOWS THE ZOMBIES TO SANCTION YOUR ACTIONS...
...THAT AND YOUR CHOICE OF VICTIMS, OF COURSE... BUT YOU'D LIKE TO KILL THEM, IF ONLY THEY'D LET YOU GET AWAY WITH IT...
...BECAUSE IT WOULD MAKE YOUR WORK SO MUCH EASIER, WOULDN'T IT?... AND EVER SO MUCH MORE SATISFYING.
YOU'RE WRONG.
AND YOU'RE DENYING! WE ARE THE SAME! WE BOTH LIKE TO COME UP ON THEM IN THE DARK, FEELING THE FORBIDDEN POWER OF IT, SEEING THE FEAR SLASHED IN THEIR FACES... WE CRAVE IT...
JUST TAKE HIM-- DON'T WORRY ABOUT ME!
TWO COPS ALREADY DOWN BECAUSE I WAS TOO SLOW, BECAUSE I'VE LOST A STEP, AND NOW... I'M NOT NEARLY FAST ENOUGH TO REACH HIM BEFORE MONTOYA GOES DOWN...
WE'RE... NOT... THE SAME.
17

BUT I SUSPECT THAT'S ALREADY BEGUN TO CHANGE, HASN'T IT?

WHAT DO YOU MEAN?

SOMEONE LOOSED THE HORDES OF ARKHAM-- ALL YOUR MOST DANGEROUS PREY-- WHICH MEANS SOMEONE HAS IT IN FOR YOU...

...SOMEONE WHO MAY BE STALKING YOU RIGHT NOW, WAITING AND WATCHING FOR JUST THE RIGHT MOMENT OF FEAR AND WEAKNESS...THE PERFECT MOMENT TO POUNCE.

OH, THERE IS ONE DIFFERENCE! I STALK THE FRESH ONES, THE CLEAN ONES, WHILE YOU STALK THE ONES FOULED WITH BLOOD... ME AND MINE...

...SO I KNOW THE THRILL FROM BOTH SIDES...UNLIKE YOU!

I SEE I'M RIGHT... AND MAYBE YOU EVEN KNOW WHO IT IS.

AS IF YOU DON'T KNOW BANE'S NAME. WHAT'S HIS PLAN, ZSASZ? WHAT DOES HE WANT?

YOU ARE JUST LIKE ME... PARANOID...BUT IT'S THRILLING, ISN'T IT? --TO BE BOTH HUNTER AND HUNTED, KNOWING DEEP INSIDE YOU DESERVE TO BE BROUGHT DOWN...

...DOOMED TO BRING DOOM... AND DOOMED TO PAY FOR IT.

KUNK

TUD

TAKE HIM!

CHUP

18

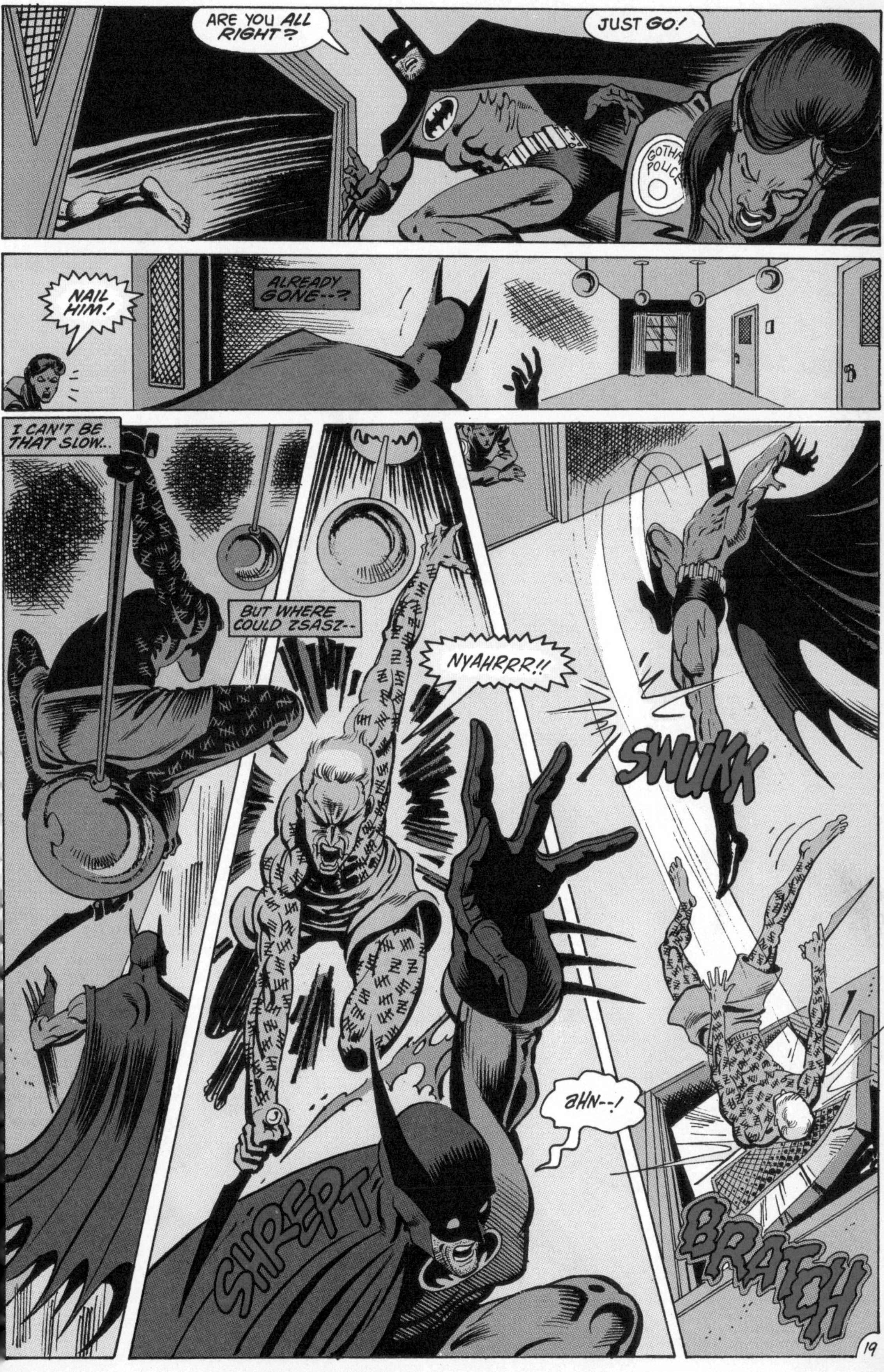
ARE YOU ALL RIGHT?
JUST GO!
NAIL HIM!
ALREADY GONE--?
I CAN'T BE THAT SLOW..
BUT WHERE COULD ZSASZ--
NYAHRRR!!
SWUKK
AHN--!
SHREPT
BRATCH
19

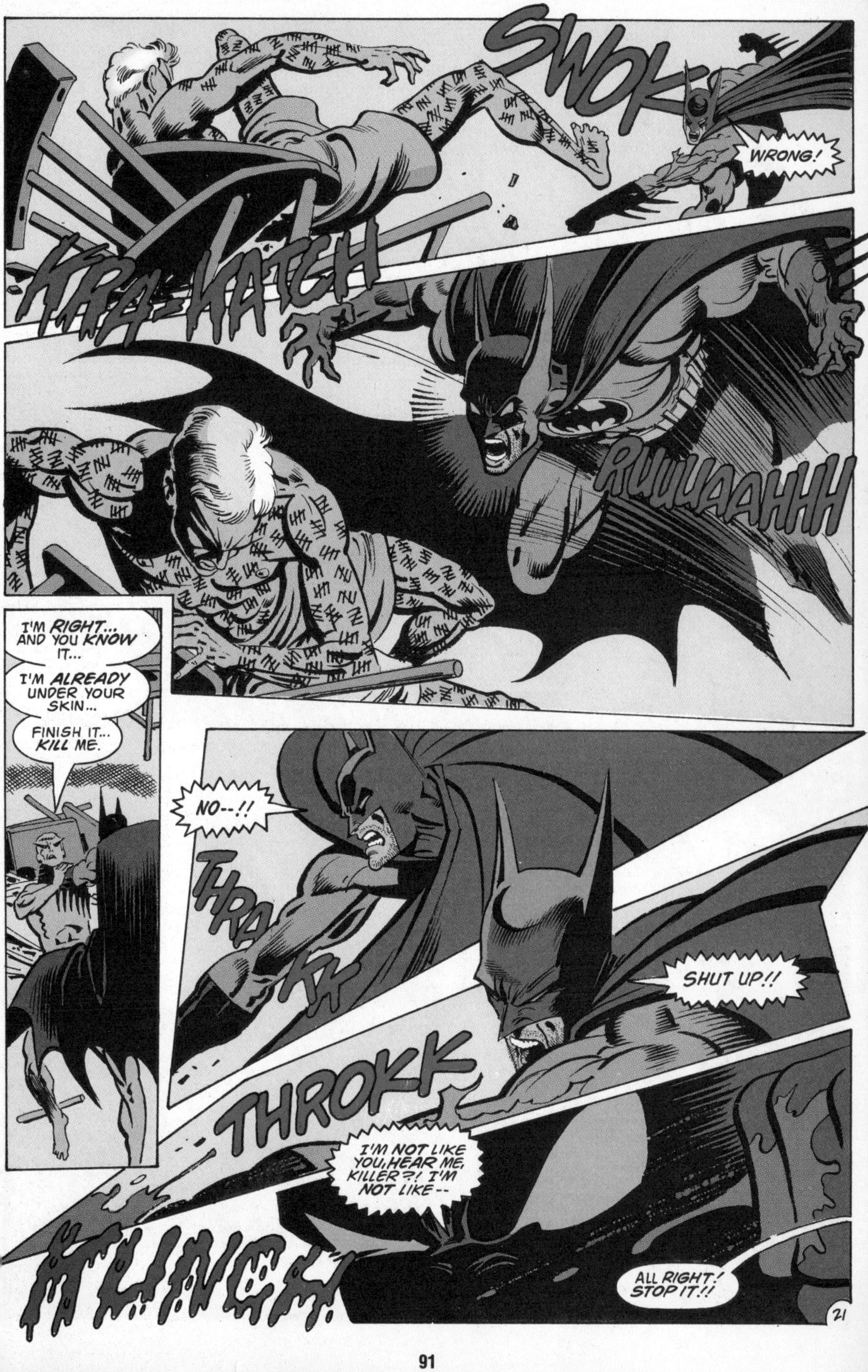
SWOK
WRONG!
KRA-KATCH
RUUUAAHHH
I'M RIGHT... AND YOU KNOW IT...
I'M ALREADY UNDER YOUR SKIN...
FINISH IT... KILL ME.
NO--!!
THRAKK
SHUT UP!!
THROKK
I'M NOT LIKE YOU, HEAR ME, KILLER?! I'M NOT LIKE--
TUNCH!
ALL RIGHT! STOP IT!!
21

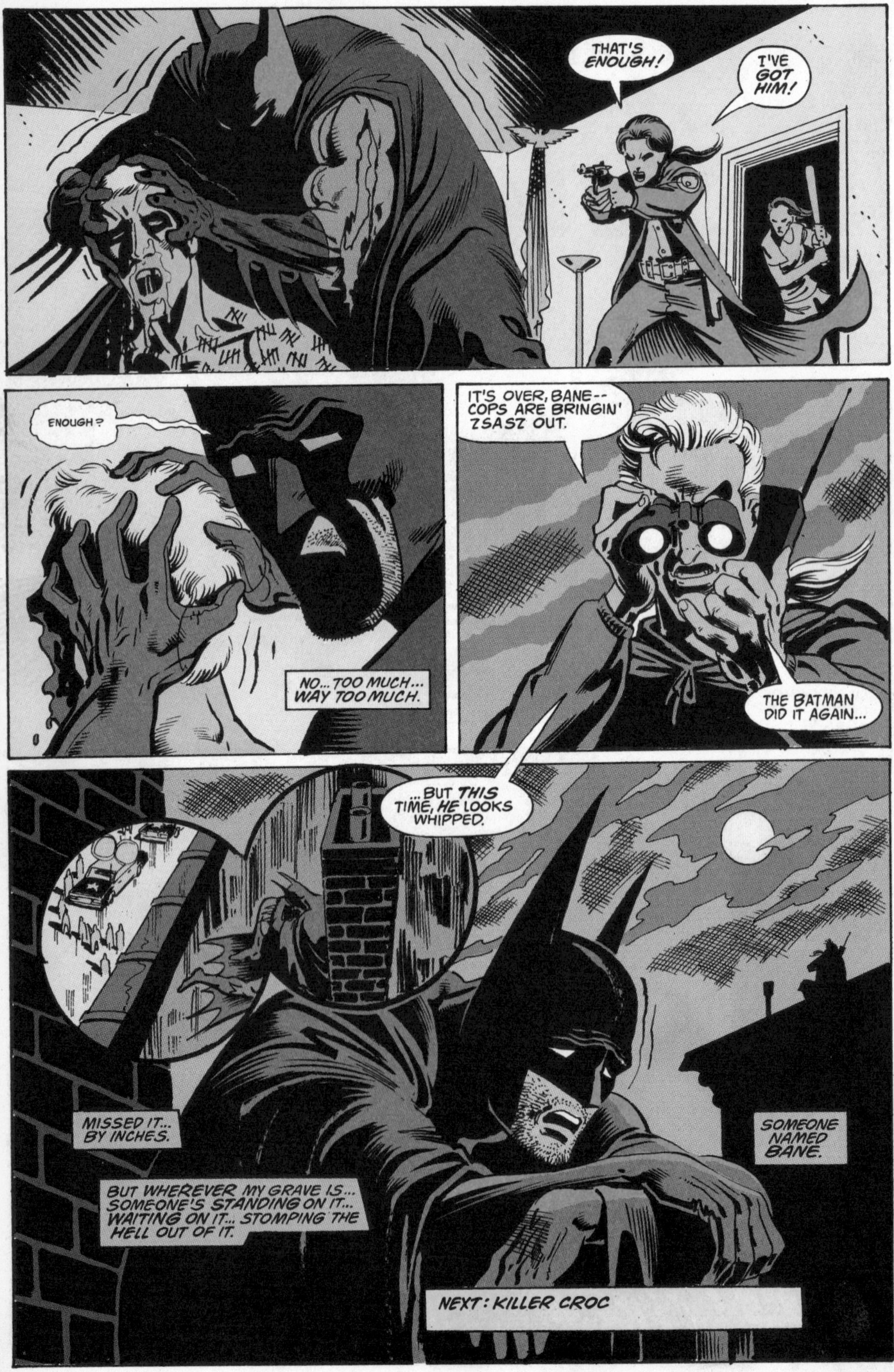
THAT'S ENOUGH!
I'VE GOT HIM!
ENOUGH?
NO... TOO MUCH... WAY TOO MUCH.
IT'S OVER, BANE-- COPS ARE BRINGIN' ZSASZ OUT.
THE BATMAN DID IT AGAIN...
...BUT THIS TIME, HE LOOKS WHIPPED.
MISSED IT... BY INCHES.
BUT WHEREVER MY GRAVE IS... SOMEONE'S STANDING ON IT... WAITING ON IT... STOMPING THE HELL OUT OF IT.
SOMEONE NAMED BANE.
NEXT: KILLER CROC

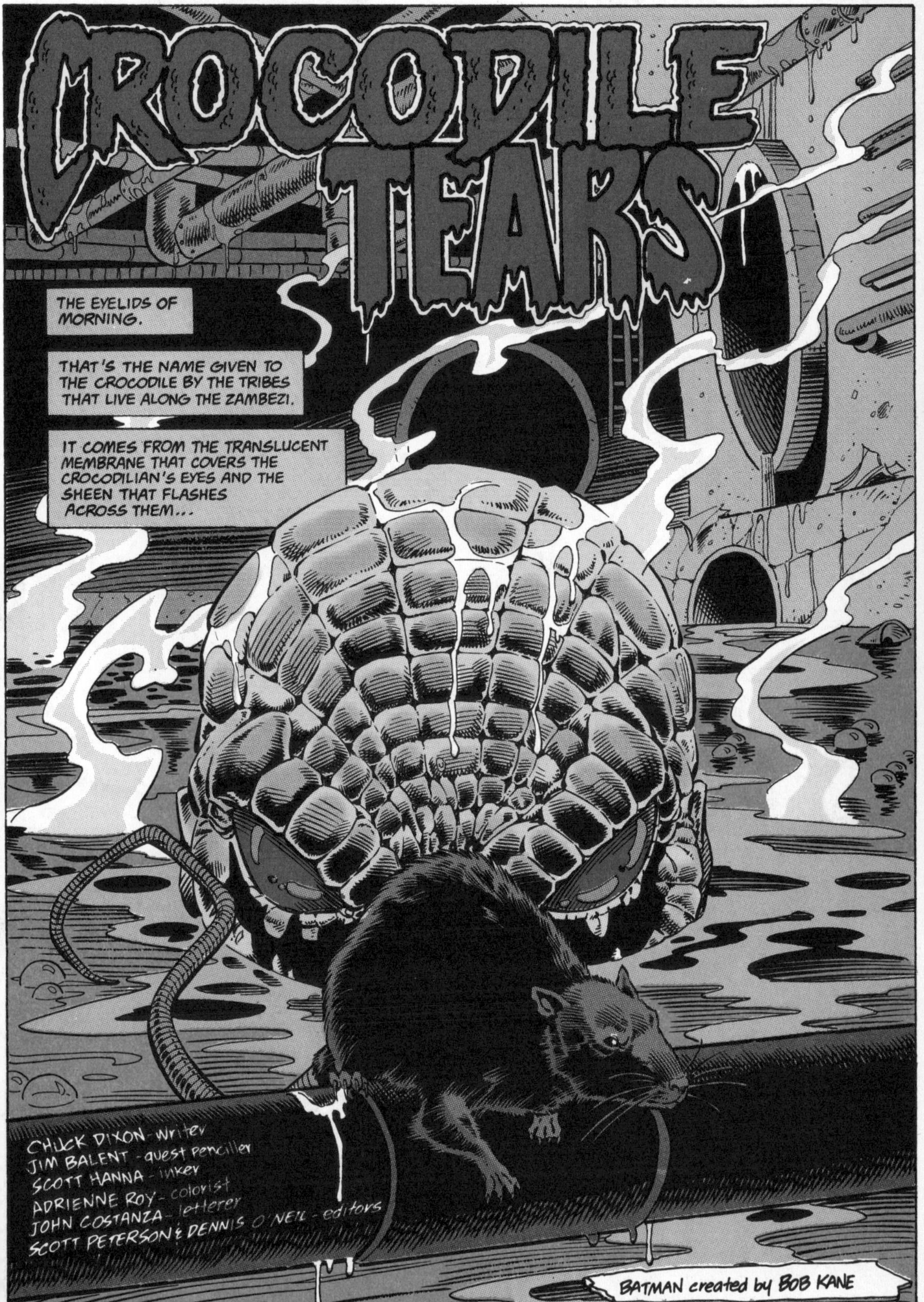
CROCODILE TEARS
THE EYELIDS OF MORNING.
THAT'S THE NAME GIVEN TO THE CROCODILE BY THE TRIBES THAT LIVE ALONG THE ZAMBEZI.
IT COMES FROM THE TRANSLUCENT MEMBRANE THAT COVERS THE CROCODILIAN'S EYES AND THE SHEEN THAT FLASHES ACROSS THEM...
CHUCK DIXON - writer
JIM BALENT - guest penciller
SCOTT HANNA - inker
ADRIENNE ROY - colorist
JOHN COSTANZA - letterer
SCOTT PETERSON & DENNIS O'NEIL - editors
BATMAN created by BOB KANE

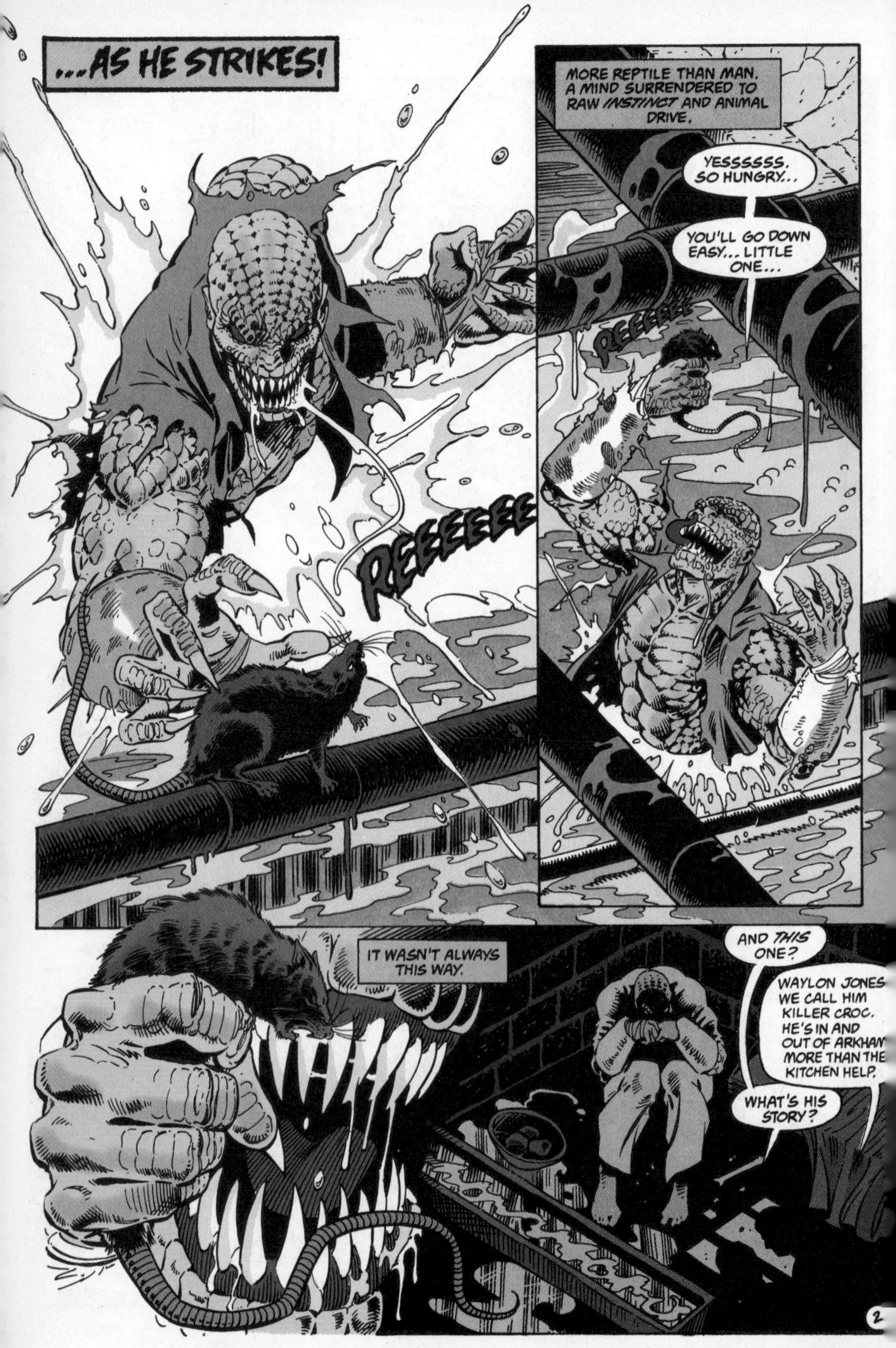

...AS HE STRIKES!
REEEEEE
MORE REPTILE THAN MAN. A MIND SURRENDERED TO RAW INSTINCT AND ANIMAL DRIVE.
YESSSSSS. SO HUNGRY...
YOU'LL GO DOWN EASY... LITTLE ONE...
REEEEEE
IT WASN'T ALWAYS THIS WAY.
AND THIS ONE?
WAYLON JONES. WE CALL HIM KILLER CROC. HE'S IN AND OUT OF ARKHAM MORE THAN THE KITCHEN HELP.
WHAT'S HIS STORY?
2

YOU'D NEVER KNOW IT TO *LOOK* AT HIM BUT HE RAN GOTHAM'S TOP MOB FOR A WHILE. NOW HE'S JUST ANOTHER HOPELESS NUTJOB.

HE BREAK HIS ARMS IN HERE?

NAW, THAT'S THE WAY THE COPS FOUND HIM. SOMEBODY HANDED HIM A REAL BEATING.

JEEZ, I'D HATE TO MEET *THAT GUY*.

ANY IDEA WHO RACKED HIM UP?

CROC WAS IN NO SHAPE TO TELL US. I DOUBT HE EVEN *KNOWS*.

"THAT LUNATIC LOST WHAT-EVER MIND HE HAD A LONG TIME AGO."

BUT HE *KNOWS*. HE KNOWS THE NAME OF THE ONE WHO HURT HIM.

BAAAAARAANE!

THE NAME THAT RUNS THROUGH HIS MIND LIKE AN ENDLESS SHRIEK.

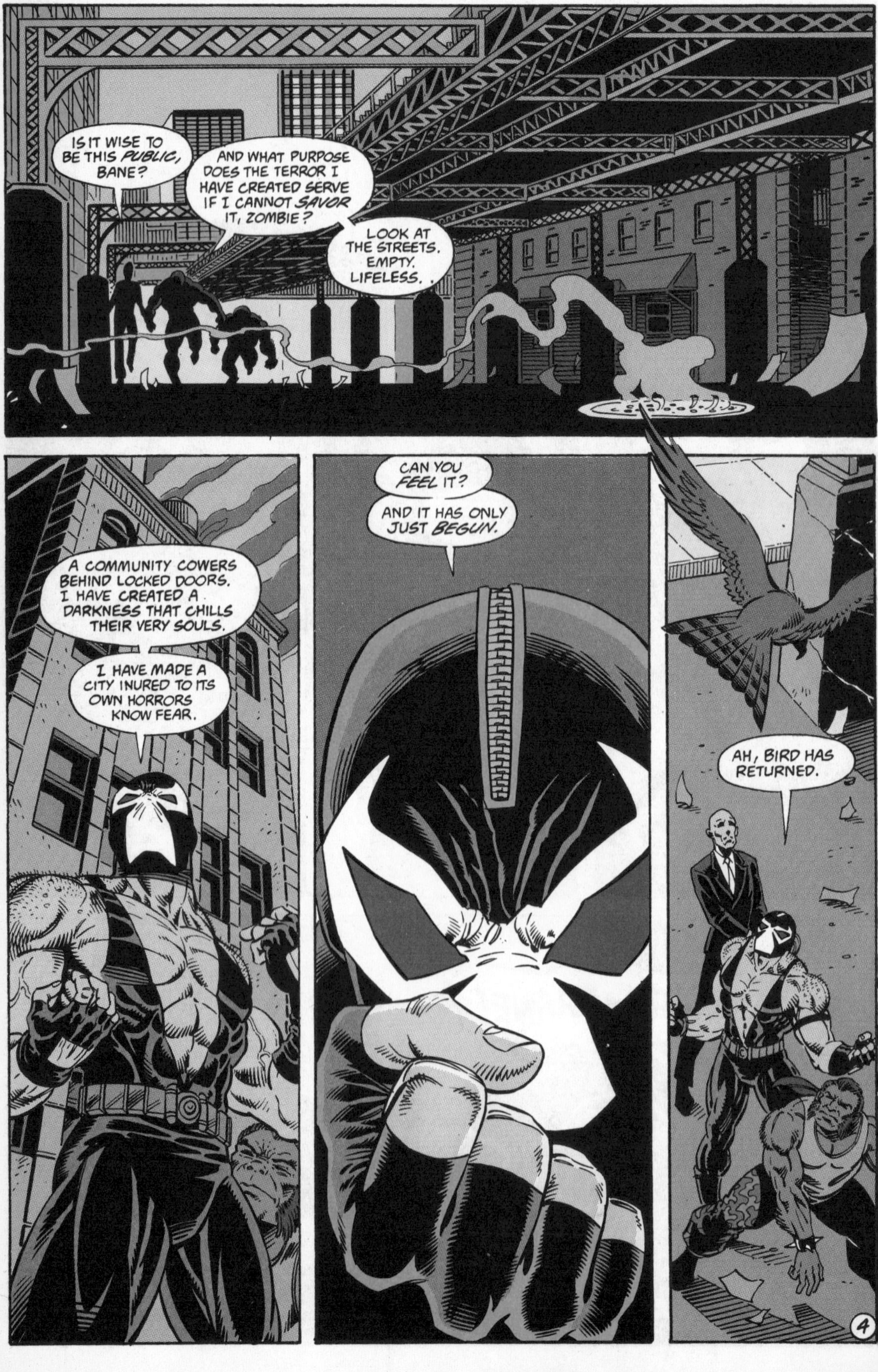
IS IT WISE TO BE THIS PUBLIC, BANE?
AND WHAT PURPOSE DOES THE TERROR I HAVE CREATED SERVE IF I CANNOT SAVOR IT, ZOMBIE?
LOOK AT THE STREETS. EMPTY. LIFELESS.
A COMMUNITY COWERS BEHIND LOCKED DOORS. I HAVE CREATED A DARKNESS THAT CHILLS THEIR VERY SOULS.
I HAVE MADE A CITY INURED TO ITS OWN HORRORS KNOW FEAR.
CAN YOU FEEL IT?
AND IT HAS ONLY JUST BEGUN.
AH, BIRD HAS RETURNED.
4

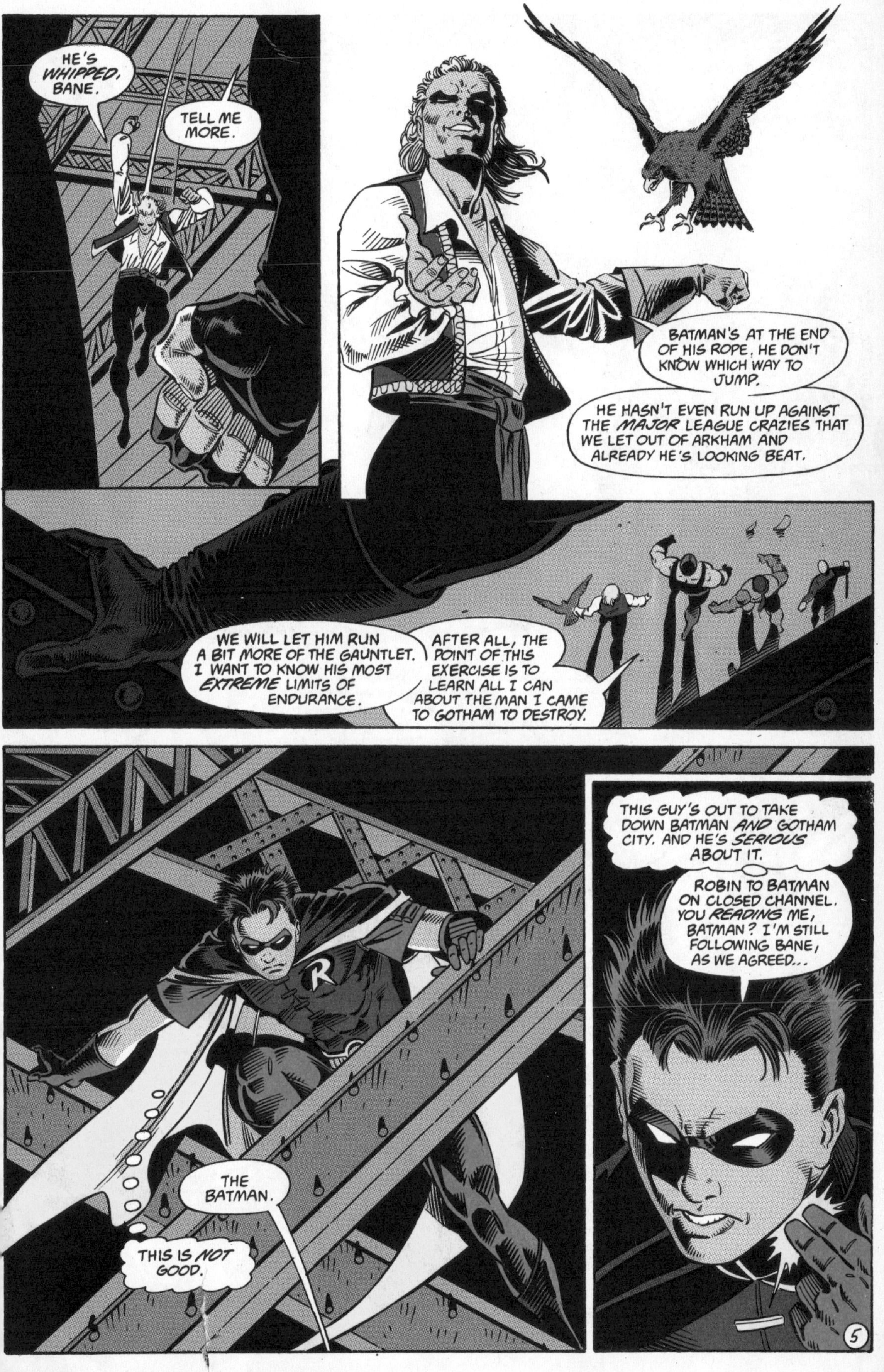
HE'S WHIPPED, BANE.
TELL ME MORE.
BATMAN'S AT THE END OF HIS ROPE. HE DON'T KNOW WHICH WAY TO JUMP.
HE HASN'T EVEN RUN UP AGAINST THE MAJOR LEAGUE CRAZIES THAT WE LET OUT OF ARKHAM AND ALREADY HE'S LOOKING BEAT.
WE WILL LET HIM RUN A BIT MORE OF THE GAUNTLET. I WANT TO KNOW HIS MOST EXTREME LIMITS OF ENDURANCE.
AFTER ALL, THE POINT OF THIS EXERCISE IS TO LEARN ALL I CAN ABOUT THE MAN I CAME TO GOTHAM TO DESTROY.
THE BATMAN.
THIS IS NOT GOOD.
THIS GUY'S OUT TO TAKE DOWN BATMAN AND GOTHAM CITY. AND HE'S SERIOUS ABOUT IT.
ROBIN TO BATMAN ON CLOSED CHANNEL. YOU READING ME, BATMAN? I'M STILL FOLLOWING BANE, AS WE AGREED...
5

"BESIDES, I GOT A LOT OF OTHER LOONIES TO LOOK FOR."

MR. DETWEILER...?

MR. DETWEILER, ATTORNEY AT LAW...?

WHUZZ?

WHAH?

WHAT IS THIS? WHO ARE YOU?

YOU CAN CALL ME *SOCKO*, COUNSELOR. AND YOU ALREADY KNOW YOUR VALUED CLIENT, THE VENTRILOQUIST.

WHAT DO YOU WANT?

YOU WERE THE LAST TO DEFEND MY PAL AND HIS GUDDY SCARFACE. WE WANT TO KNOW WHERE SCARFACE GOT TO.

THIS IS ALL ABOUT THAT STUPID *PUPPET*? YOU'RE *NUTS*. WHY SHOULD I HELP YOU FIND *ANY*THING?

'CAUSE GULLETS MAKE NASTY HOLES.

"DARNED IF YOU DO, DARNED IF YOU DON'T." THAT'S *SOCK* HUMOR, COUNSELOR.

7

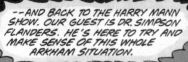

--AND BACK TO THE HARRY MANN SHOW. OUR GUEST IS DR. SIMPSON FLANDERS. HE'S HERE TO TRY AND MAKE SENSE OF THIS WHOLE ARKHAM SITUATION.

HARRY **MANN** SHOW

WE'VE GOT A CITY PARALYZED WITH FEAR. THE STREETS ARE FULL OF WACKOS WITH ASSAULT WEAPONS, AND YOU THINK YOU'VE GOT THE SOLUTION?

I DO, HARRY.

YOU SEE, ALL OF THIS PANIC AND STRESS HAS CREATED A HOSTILE ENVIRONMENT FOR THE INMATES.

FEAR FEEDS ON FEAR AND ONLY SERVES TO MAKE MATTERS WORSE.

YOU'RE SAYING THAT BY BEING AFRAID OF AN ARMY OF HOMICIDAL MANIACS LOOSE ON OUR STREETS WE'RE ANTAGONIZING THEM?

EXACTLY. AS DETAILED IN MY BOOK, "I'M SANE AND SO ARE YOU," THE MENTALLY DIVERGENT SHOULD BE MADE TO FEEL AT EASE IN OUR ENVIRONMENT.

A CLIMATE OF MISTRUST AND SUSPICION ONLY TENDS TO MAKE THEM FEEL INSECURE IN THEIR CHOICE OF LIFESTYLES.

I'M **SANE** AND SO ARE **YOU**

DR. SIMPSON FLANDERS

WE'VE GOT A BODY COUNT HEADING TOWARD THE TRIPLE DIGITS.

THAT'S A "LIFE-STYLE"?

8

Pacific Grove Public Library
09/13/2022 15:40
Checked Out Today
Batman knightfall
Barcode: 37487002132211
Date Due: Tuesday, October 4, 2022

Batman knightfall
Barcode: 37487002132237
Date Due: Tuesday, October 4, 2022

Batman
Barcode: 37487003001183
Date Due: Tuesday, October 4, 2022

Batgirl
Barcode: 37487002927800
Date Due: Tuesday, October 4, 2022

Teen Titans : Beast Boy loves Raven
Barcode: 37487003256464
Date Due: Tuesday, October 4, 2022

Teen Titans
Barcode: 37487002980965
Date Due: Tuesday, October 4, 2022

Dracula
Barcode: 37487002549869
Date Due: Tuesday, October 4, 2022

8 mile
Barcode: 37487003041841
**Date Due: Tuesday, September 27,
2022**

**You saved a total of $154.48 by
using the library to borrow these
items!**

You can renew your items at
catalog.pacificgrovelibrary.org/
or by calling (831) 648-5760

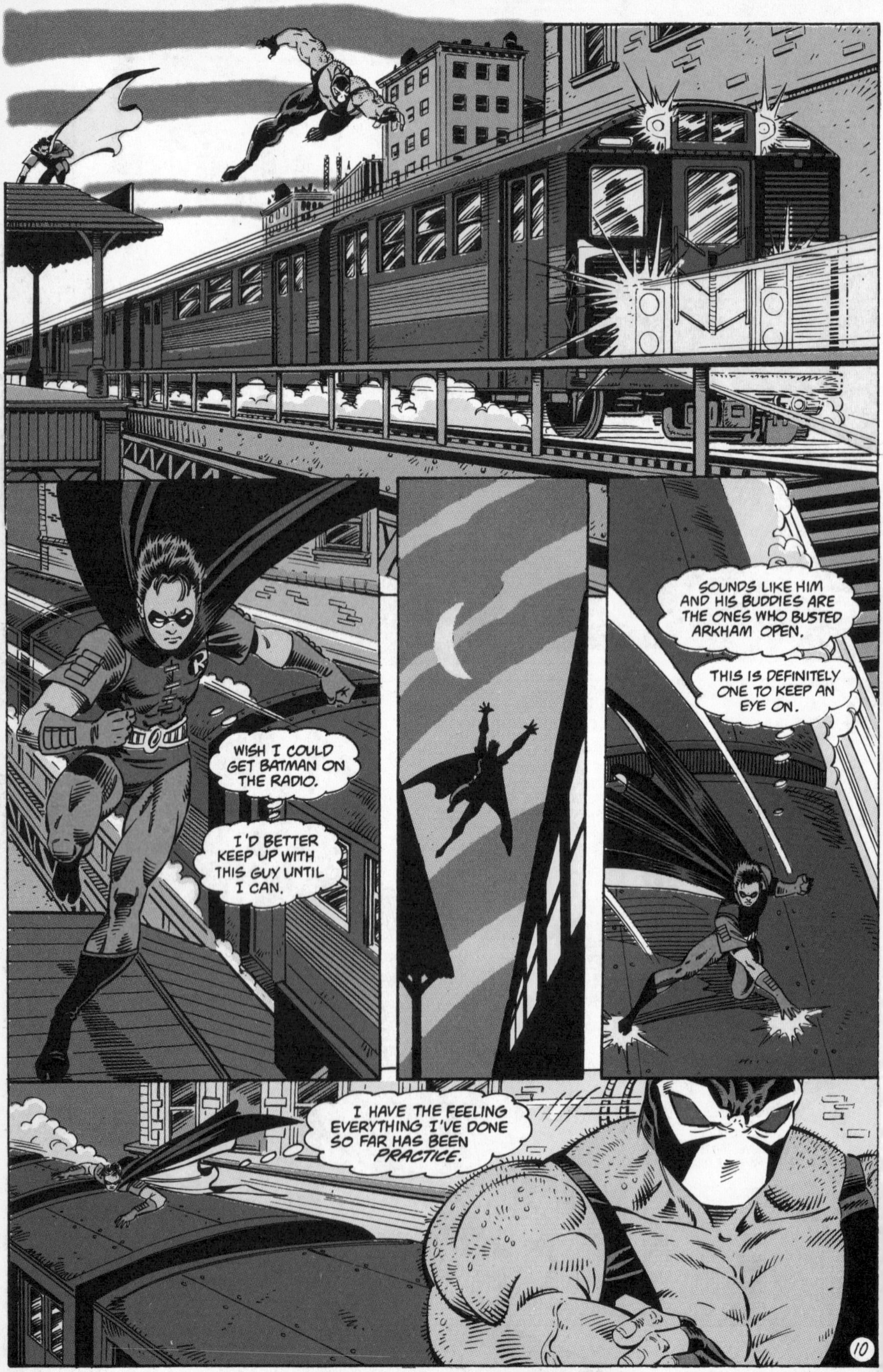
WISH I COULD GET BATMAN ON THE RADIO.
I'D BETTER KEEP UP WITH THIS GUY UNTIL I CAN.
SOUNDS LIKE HIM AND HIS BUDDIES ARE THE ONES WHO BUSTED ARKHAM OPEN.
THIS IS DEFINITELY ONE TO KEEP AN EYE ON.
I HAVE THE FEELING EVERYTHING I'VE DONE SO FAR HAS BEEN *PRACTICE*.
10

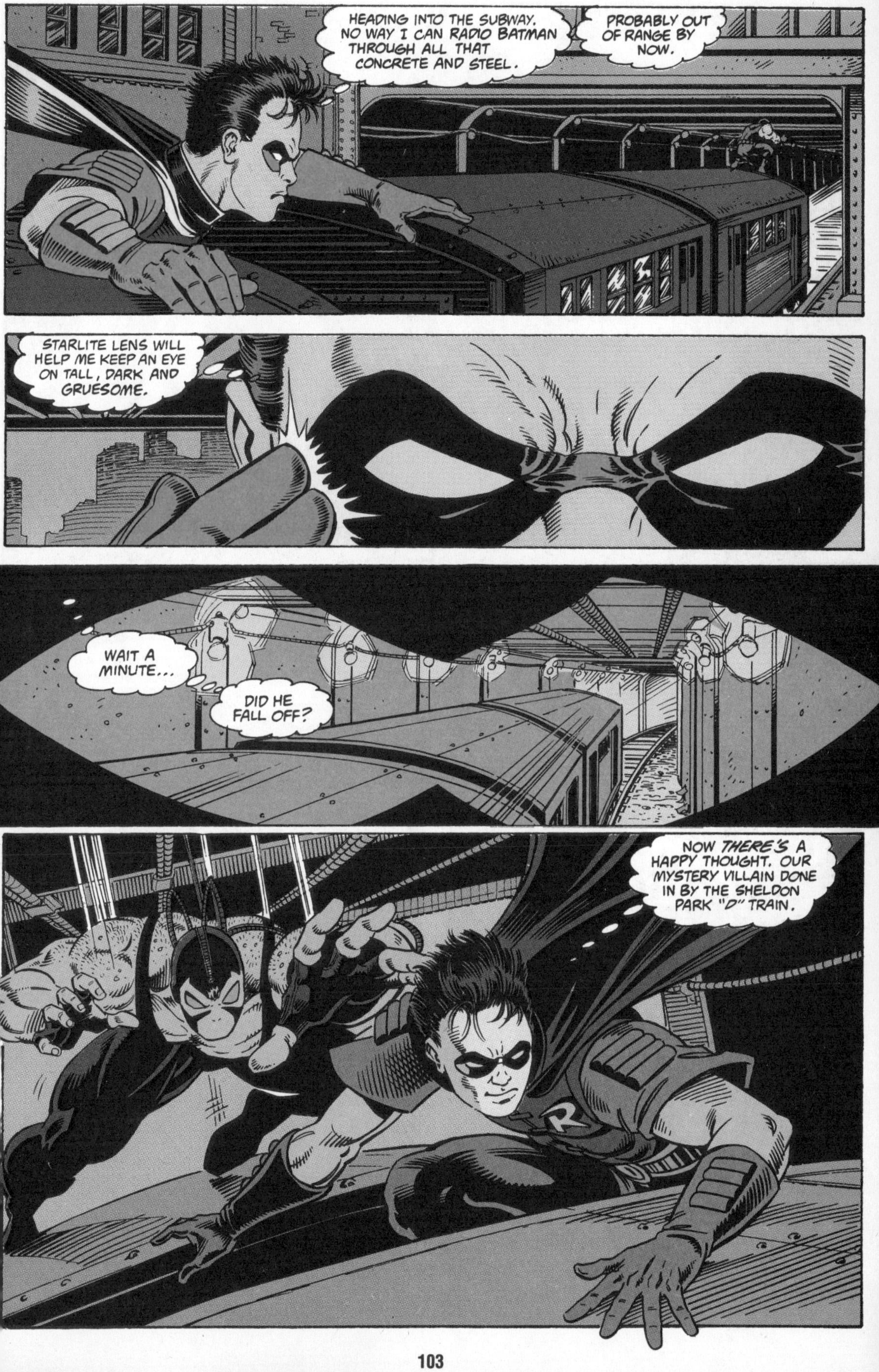
HEADING INTO THE SUBWAY. NO WAY I CAN RADIO BATMAN THROUGH ALL THAT CONCRETE AND STEEL.
PROBABLY OUT OF RANGE BY NOW.
STARLITE LENS WILL HELP ME KEEP AN EYE ON TALL, DARK AND GRUESOME.
WAIT A MINUTE...
DID HE FALL OFF?
NOW THERE'S A HAPPY THOUGHT. OUR MYSTERY VILLAIN DONE IN BY THE SHELDON PARK "D" TRAIN.

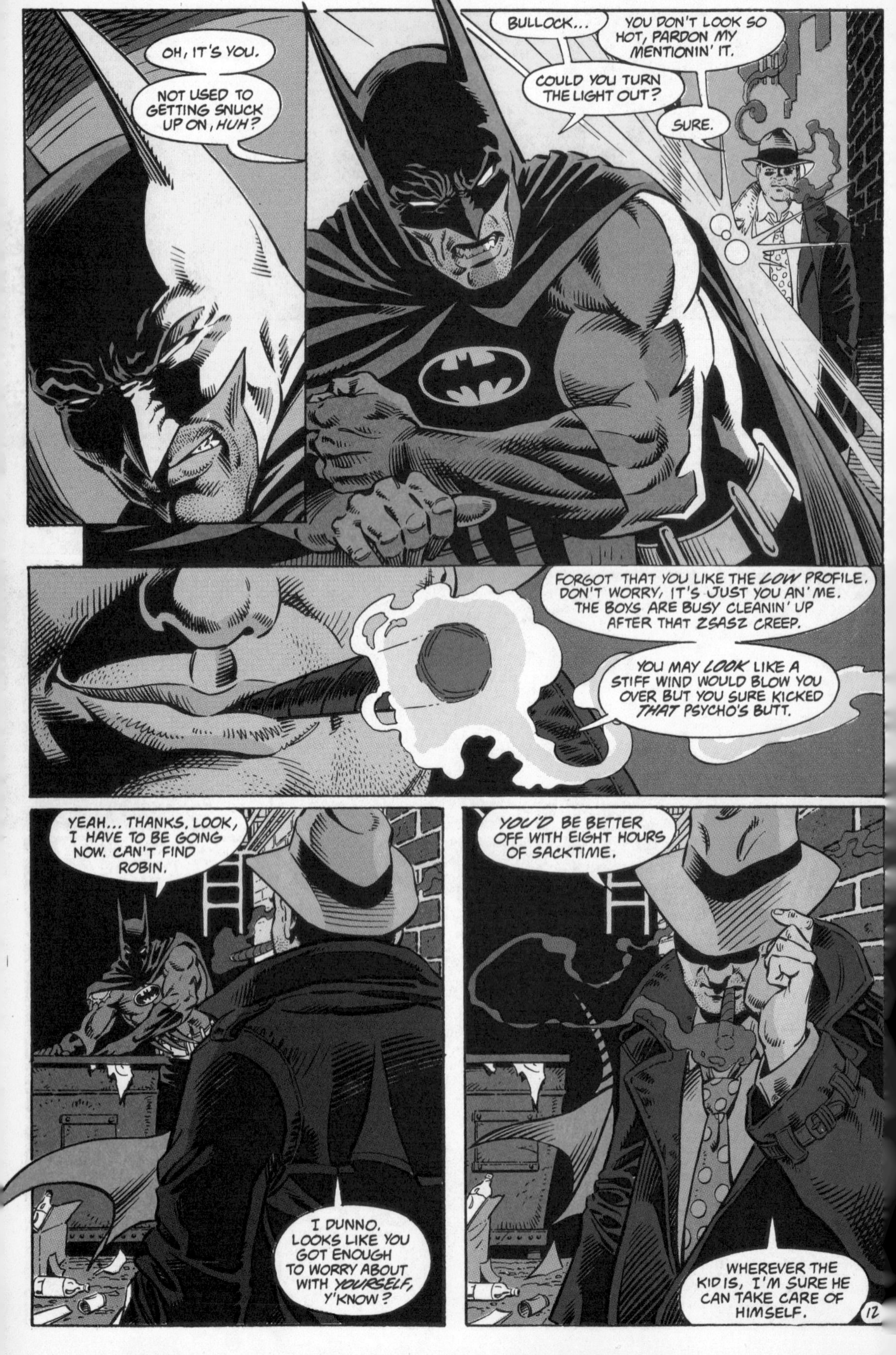
OH, IT'S YOU.
NOT USED TO GETTING SNUCK UP ON, HUH?
BULLOCK...
YOU DON'T LOOK SO HOT, PARDON MY MENTIONIN' IT.
COULD YOU TURN THE LIGHT OUT?
SURE.
FORGOT THAT YOU LIKE THE LOW PROFILE. DON'T WORRY, IT'S JUST YOU AN' ME. THE BOYS ARE BUSY CLEANIN' UP AFTER THAT ZSASZ CREEP.
YOU MAY LOOK LIKE A STIFF WIND WOULD BLOW YOU OVER BUT YOU SURE KICKED THAT PSYCHO'S BUTT.
YEAH... THANKS. LOOK, I HAVE TO BE GOING NOW. CAN'T FIND ROBIN.
I DUNNO. LOOKS LIKE YOU GOT ENOUGH TO WORRY ABOUT WITH YOURSELF, Y'KNOW?
YOU'D BE BETTER OFF WITH EIGHT HOURS OF SACKTIME.
WHEREVER THE KID IS, I'M SURE HE CAN TAKE CARE OF HIMSELF.
12

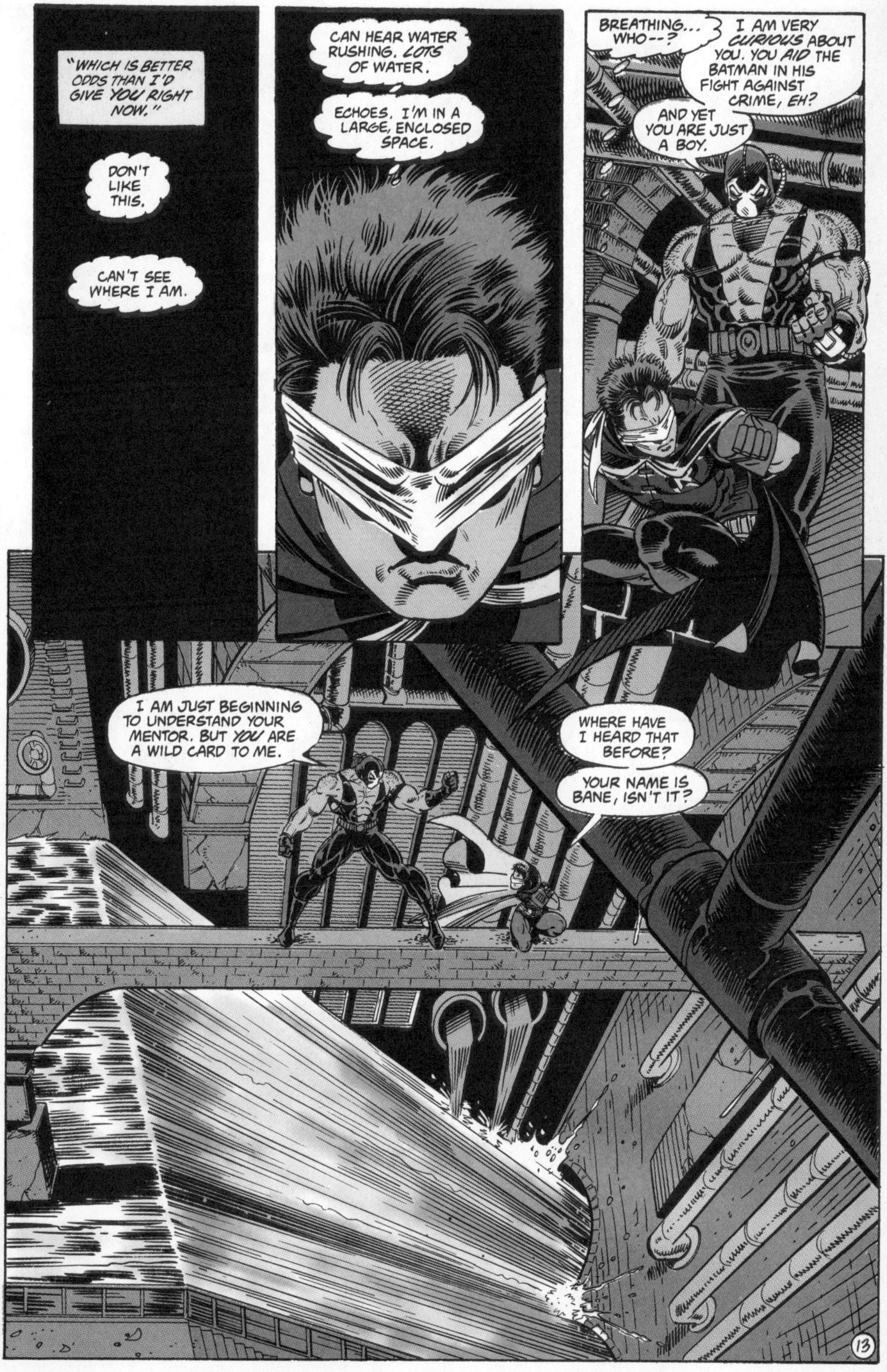
"WHICH IS BETTER ODDS THAN I'D GIVE YOU RIGHT NOW."
DON'T LIKE THIS.
CAN'T SEE WHERE I AM.
CAN HEAR WATER RUSHING. LOTS OF WATER.
ECHOES. I'M IN A LARGE, ENCLOSED SPACE.
BREATHING... WHO--?
I AM VERY CURIOUS ABOUT YOU. YOU AID THE BATMAN IN HIS FIGHT AGAINST CRIME, EH?
AND YET YOU ARE JUST A BOY.
I AM JUST BEGINNING TO UNDERSTAND YOUR MENTOR. BUT YOU ARE A WILD CARD TO ME.
WHERE HAVE I HEARD THAT BEFORE?
YOUR NAME IS BANE, ISN'T IT?
13

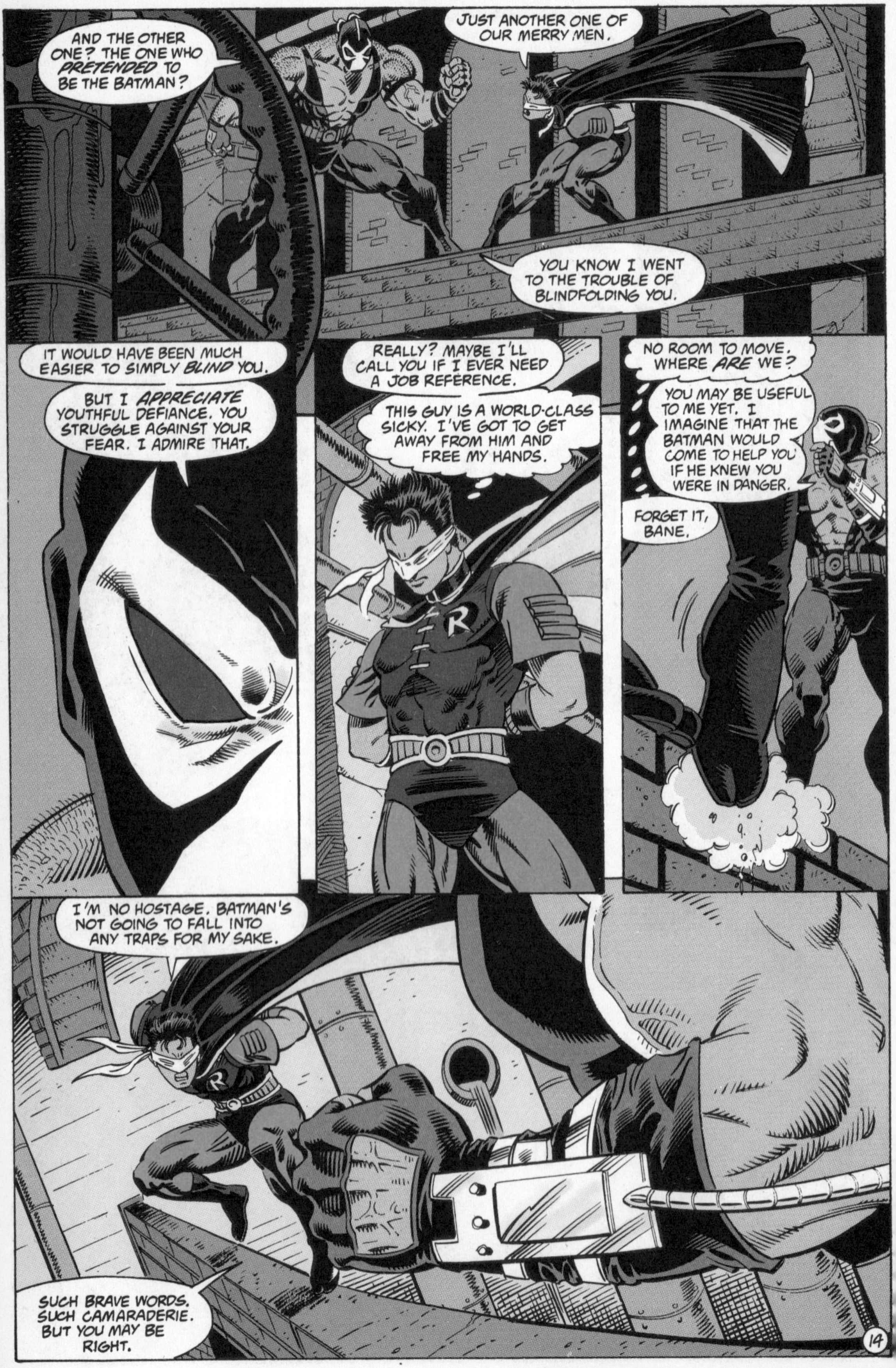
AND THE OTHER ONE? THE ONE WHO *PRETENDED* TO BE THE BATMAN?
JUST ANOTHER ONE OF OUR MERRY MEN.
YOU KNOW I WENT TO THE TROUBLE OF BLINDFOLDING YOU.
IT WOULD HAVE BEEN MUCH EASIER TO SIMPLY *BLIND* YOU.
BUT I *APPRECIATE* YOUTHFUL DEFIANCE. YOU STRUGGLE AGAINST YOUR FEAR. I ADMIRE THAT.
REALLY? MAYBE I'LL CALL YOU IF I EVER NEED A JOB REFERENCE.
THIS GUY IS A WORLD-CLASS SICKY. I'VE GOT TO GET AWAY FROM HIM AND FREE MY HANDS.
NO ROOM TO MOVE. WHERE *ARE* WE?
YOU MAY BE USEFUL TO ME YET. I IMAGINE THAT THE BATMAN WOULD COME TO HELP YOU IF HE KNEW YOU WERE IN DANGER.
FORGET IT, BANE.
I'M NO HOSTAGE. BATMAN'S NOT GOING TO FALL INTO ANY TRAPS FOR MY SAKE.
SUCH BRAVE WORDS. SUCH CAMARADERIE. BUT YOU MAY BE RIGHT.
14

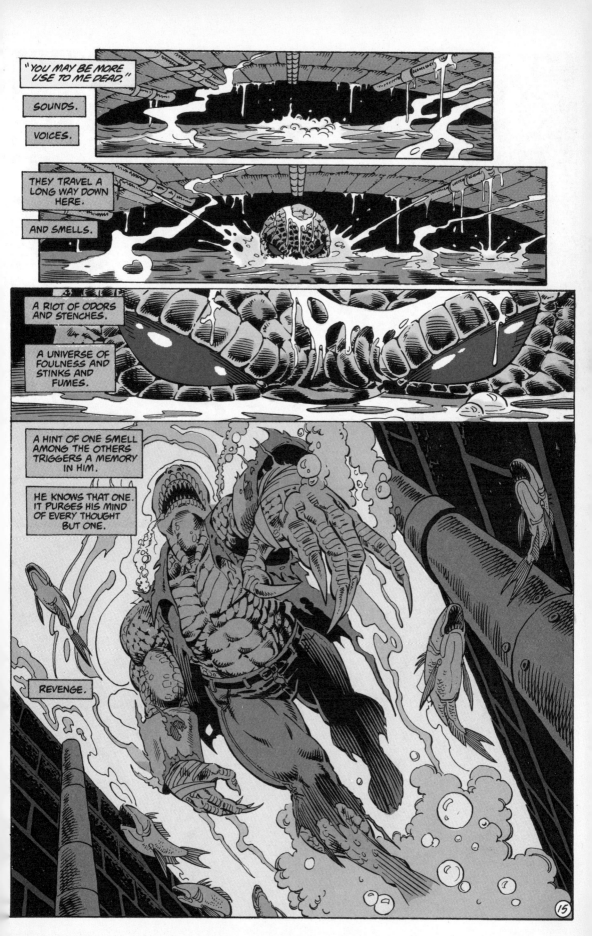

"YOU MAY BE MORE USE TO ME DEAD."

SOUNDS.

VOICES.

THEY TRAVEL A LONG WAY DOWN HERE.

AND SMELLS.

A RIOT OF ODORS AND STENCHES.

A UNIVERSE OF FOULNESS AND STINKS AND FUMES.

A HINT OF ONE SMELL AMONG THE OTHERS TRIGGERS A MEMORY IN HIM.

HE KNOWS THAT ONE. IT PURGES HIS MIND OF EVERY THOUGHT BUT ONE.

REVENGE.

15

111

112

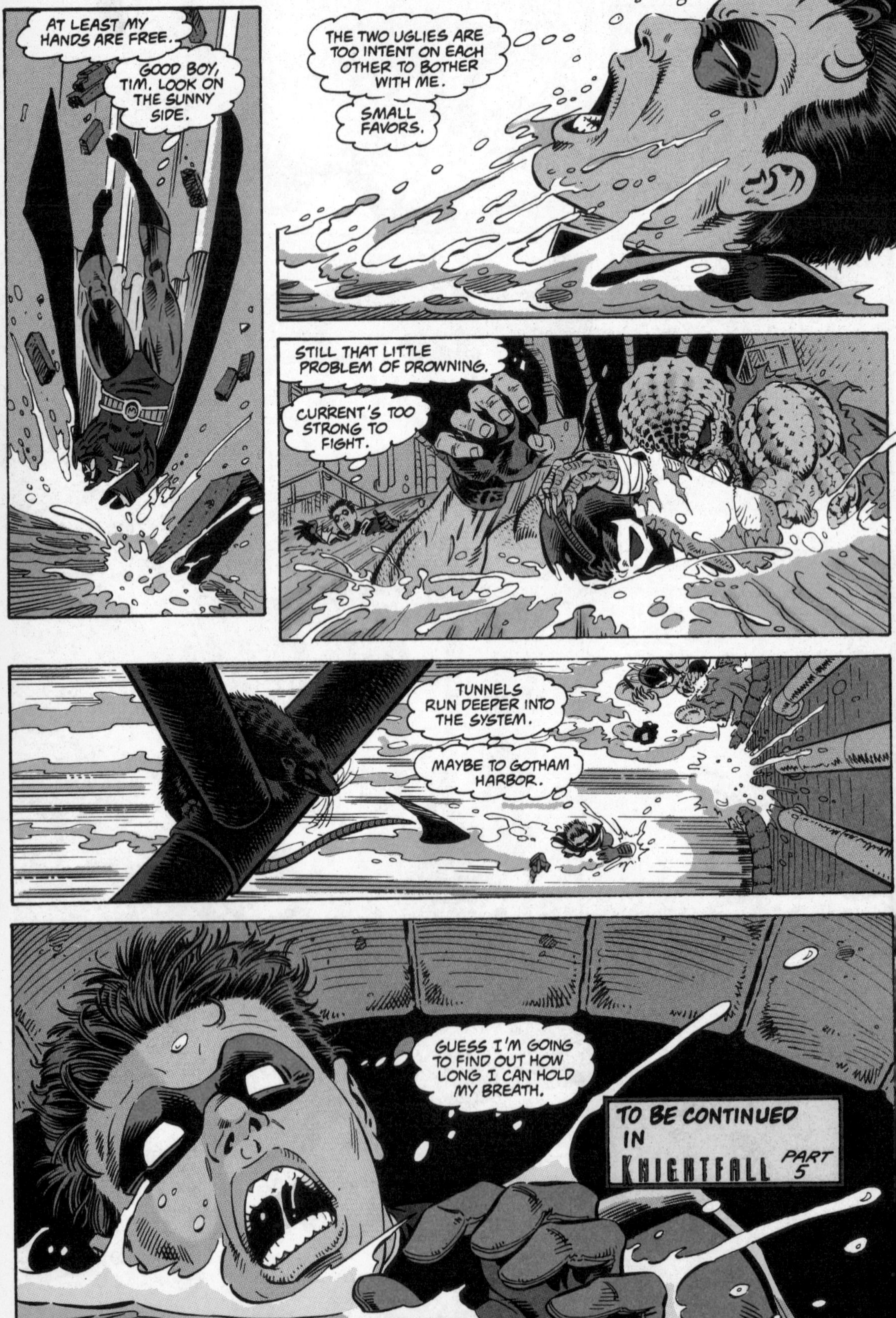
AT LEAST MY HANDS ARE FREE.
GOOD BOY, TIM. LOOK ON THE SUNNY SIDE.
THE TWO UGLIES ARE TOO INTENT ON EACH OTHER TO BOTHER WITH ME.
SMALL FAVORS.
STILL THAT LITTLE PROBLEM OF DROWNING.
CURRENT'S TOO STRONG TO FIGHT.
TUNNELS RUN DEEPER INTO THE SYSTEM.
MAYBE TO GOTHAM HARBOR.
GUESS I'M GOING TO FIND OUT HOW LONG I CAN HOLD MY BREATH.
TO BE CONTINUED IN KNIGHTFALL PART 5

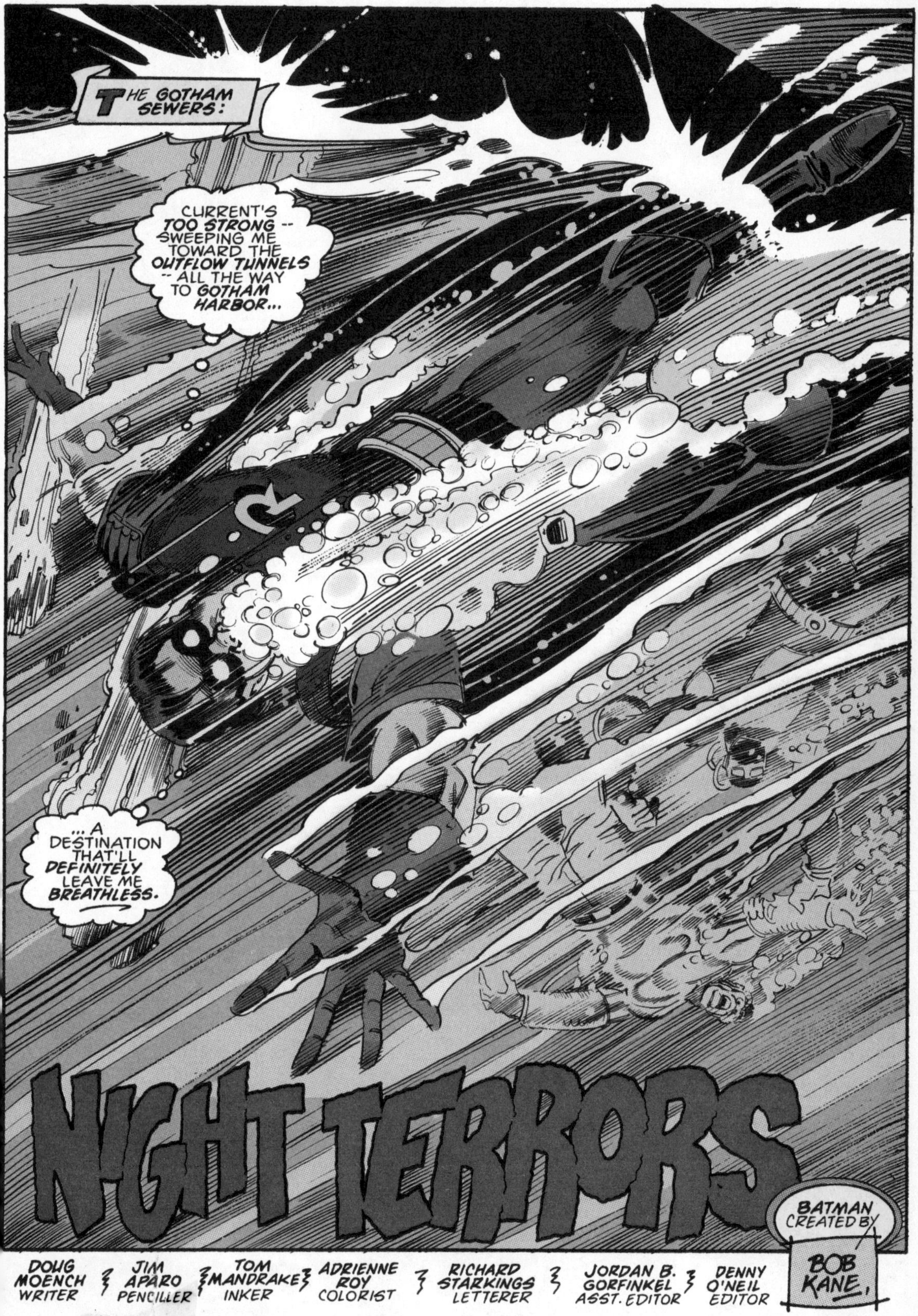
THE GOTHAM SEWERS:
CURRENT'S TOO STRONG -- SWEEPING ME TOWARD THE OUTFLOW TUNNELS -- ALL THE WAY TO GOTHAM HARBOR...
...A DESTINATION THAT'LL DEFINITELY LEAVE ME BREATHLESS.
NIGHT TERRORS
BATMAN CREATED BY BOB KANE,
DOUG MOENCH WRITER
JIM APARO PENCILLER
TOM MANDRAKE INKER
ADRIENNE ROY COLORIST
RICHARD STARKINGS LETTERER
JORDAN B. GORFINKEL ASST. EDITOR
DENNY O'NEIL EDITOR

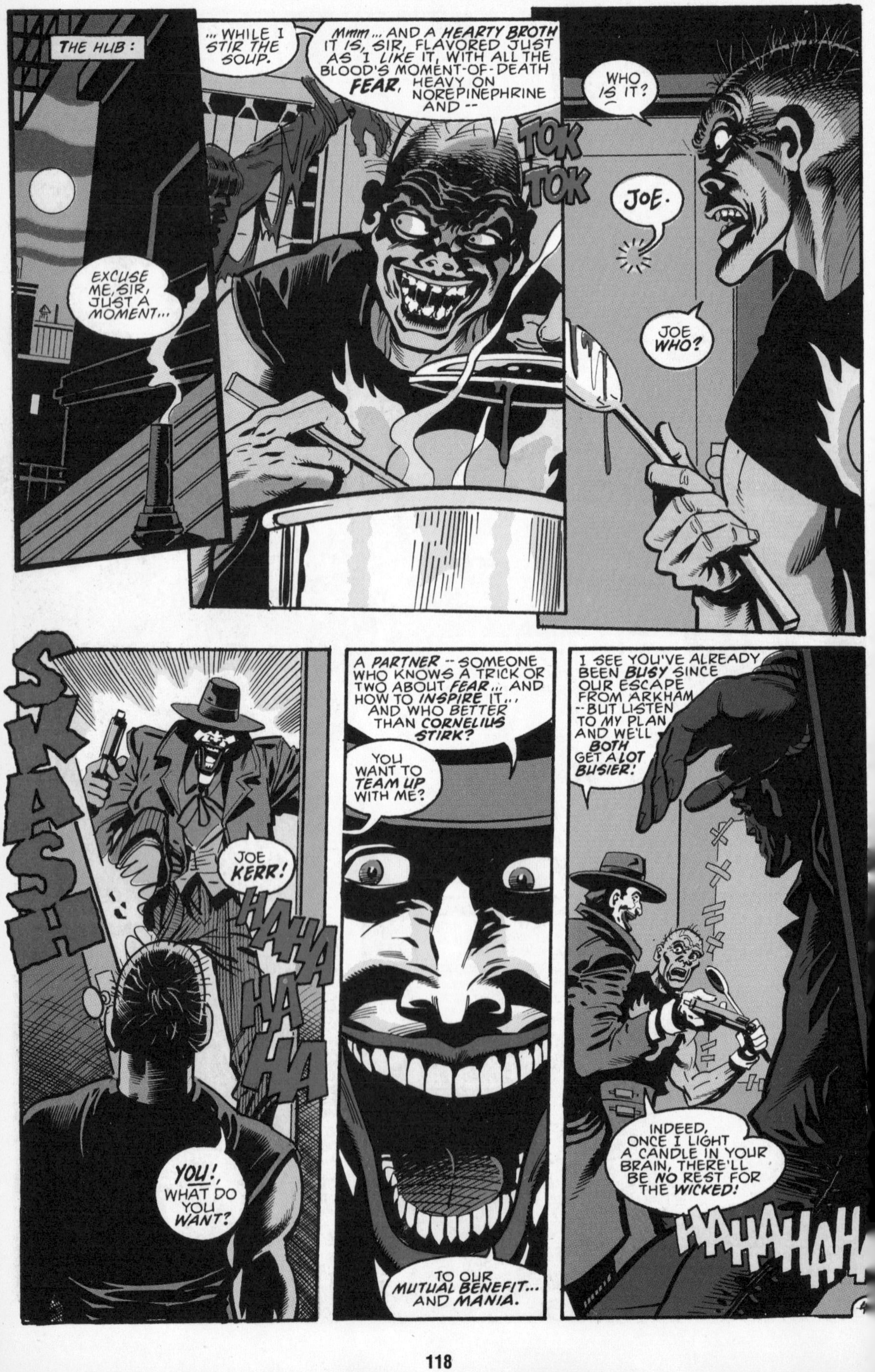
THE HUB:
... WHILE I STIR THE SOUP.
Mmm... AND A HEARTY BROTH IT IS, SIR, FLAVORED JUST AS I LIKE IT, WITH ALL THE BLOOD'S MOMENT-OF-DEATH FEAR, HEAVY ON NOREPINEPHRINE AND --
TOK TOK
EXCUSE ME, SIR, JUST A MOMENT...
WHO IS IT?
JOE.
JOE WHO?
SKASH
JOE KERR!
HAHAHA HA HA
YOU!, WHAT DO YOU WANT?
A PARTNER -- SOMEONE WHO KNOWS A TRICK OR TWO ABOUT FEAR... AND HOW TO INSPIRE IT... AND WHO BETTER THAN CORNELIUS STIRK?
YOU WANT TO TEAM UP WITH ME?
TO OUR MUTUAL BENEFIT... AND MANIA.
I SEE YOU'VE ALREADY BEEN BUSY SINCE OUR ESCAPE FROM ARKHAM --BUT LISTEN TO MY PLAN AND WE'LL BOTH GET A LOT BUSIER!
INDEED, ONCE I LIGHT A CANDLE IN YOUR BRAIN, THERE'LL BE NO REST FOR THE WICKED!
HAHAHAH

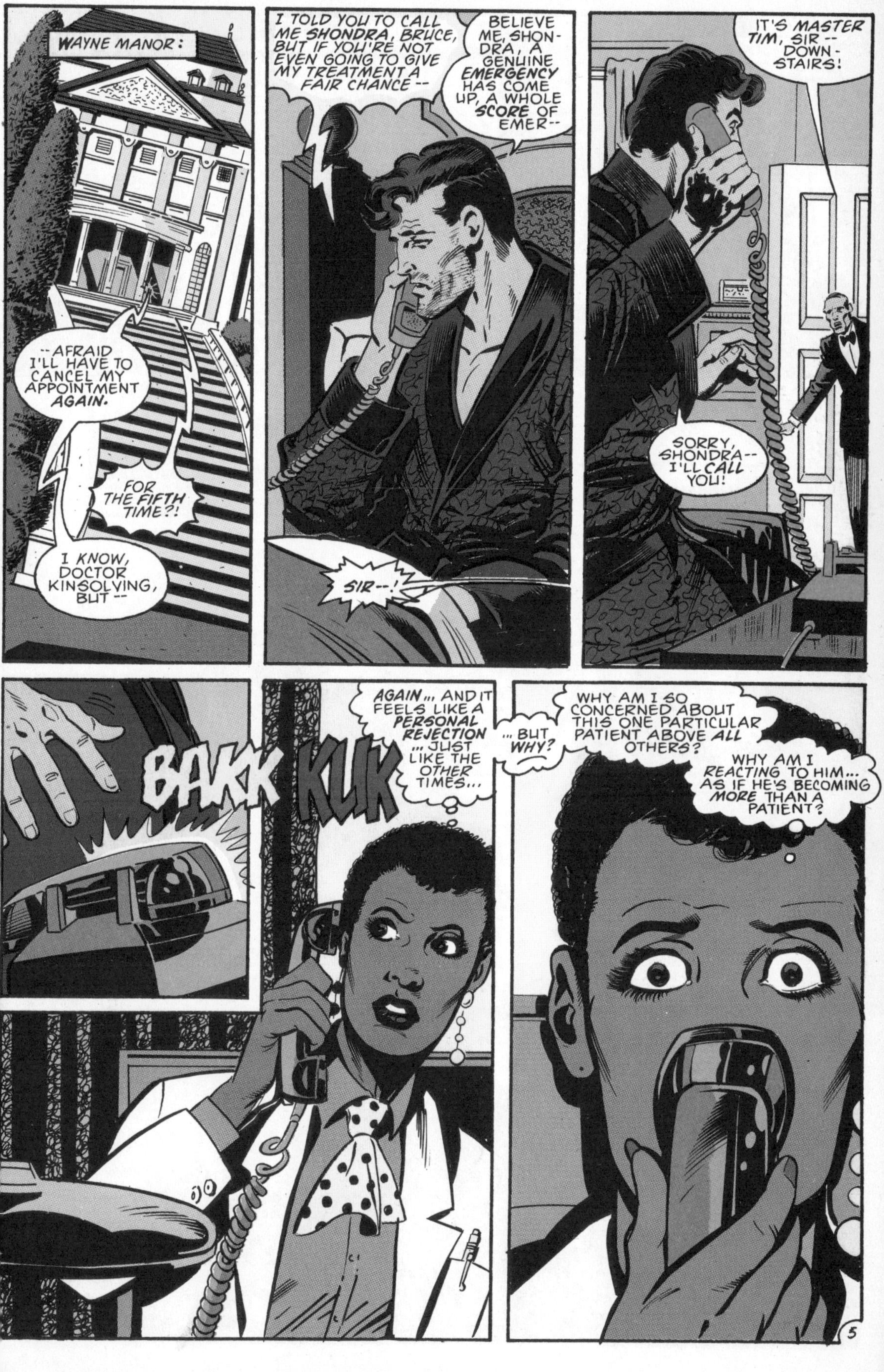
WAYNE MANOR:
--AFRAID I'LL HAVE TO CANCEL MY APPOINTMENT AGAIN.
FOR THE FIFTH TIME?!
I KNOW, DOCTOR KINSOLVING, BUT --
I TOLD YOU TO CALL ME SHONDRA, BRUCE, BUT IF YOU'RE NOT EVEN GOING TO GIVE MY TREATMENT A FAIR CHANCE --
BELIEVE ME, SHONDRA, A GENUINE EMERGENCY HAS COME UP, A WHOLE SCORE OF EMER--
SIR--!
IT'S MASTER TIM, SIR -- DOWNSTAIRS!
SORRY, SHONDRA-- I'LL CALL YOU!
BAKK KLIK
AGAIN... AND IT FEELS LIKE A PERSONAL REJECTION ... JUST LIKE THE OTHER TIMES...
... BUT WHY?
WHY AM I SO CONCERNED ABOUT THIS ONE PARTICULAR PATIENT ABOVE ALL OTHERS?
WHY AM I REACTING TO HIM... AS IF HE'S BECOMING MORE THAN A PATIENT?
5

I ONLY TOOK A BRIEF DIP IN THE *SEWERS*--

BREATHE THE VAPORS.

--BUT YOU'VE BEEN WALLOWING NONSTOP IN *HELL*.

DON'T *WORRY* ABOUT ME -- I *KNOW* WHERE I'VE BEEN, AND IT'S ONLY THE *BEGINNING*.

THERE ARE *MANIACS* TO STOP -- AND BANE'S INTENTIONS TO *LEARN*.

WHY WOULD HE AND KILLER CROC TRY TO *KILL* EACH OTHER -- AFTER HE BROKE CROC OUT OF *ARKHAM*? IS THE PLAN GOING *SOUR*?

MAYBE THERE *IS* NO MASTER PLAN.

GOT TO BE.

HEY, HE ALSO BUSTED THE *RIDDLER* OUT OF ARKHAM, DIDN'T HE --? AFTER HIS THREE STOOGES TRIED TO *WASTE* RIDDLER WITH *AUTOMATIC* WEAPONS...

TOO RANDOM FOR SOMEONE AS *CALCULATING* AS *BANE*...

SO MAYBE THE *PURPOSE* BEHIND THE ARKHAM BREAK-OUT WAS NOTHING BUT *CHAOS* -- OR AT MOST A PLAN TO CREATE *DIVERSIONS* ALL OVER THE PLACE, AND WITH YOU *LESS* THAN *ONE-HUNDRED PER CENT* --

BESIDES, THE RIDDLER WAS ALL *PUMPED UP* -- FROM THE SAME VENOM BANE IS APPARENTLY USING, WHICH MEANS BANE *ENHANCED* THE RIDDLER BEFORE HIS THREE ACCOMPLICES TRIED TO *KILL* HIM...

...IF THEY *ARE* HIS ACCOMPLICES.

THEY *ARE* -- OR AT LEAST THE *BIRD-GUY* IS -- I HEARD 'EM COMMUNICATING BY RADIO.

AND MAYBE THE *RANDOM-NESS* IS THE PLAN.

7

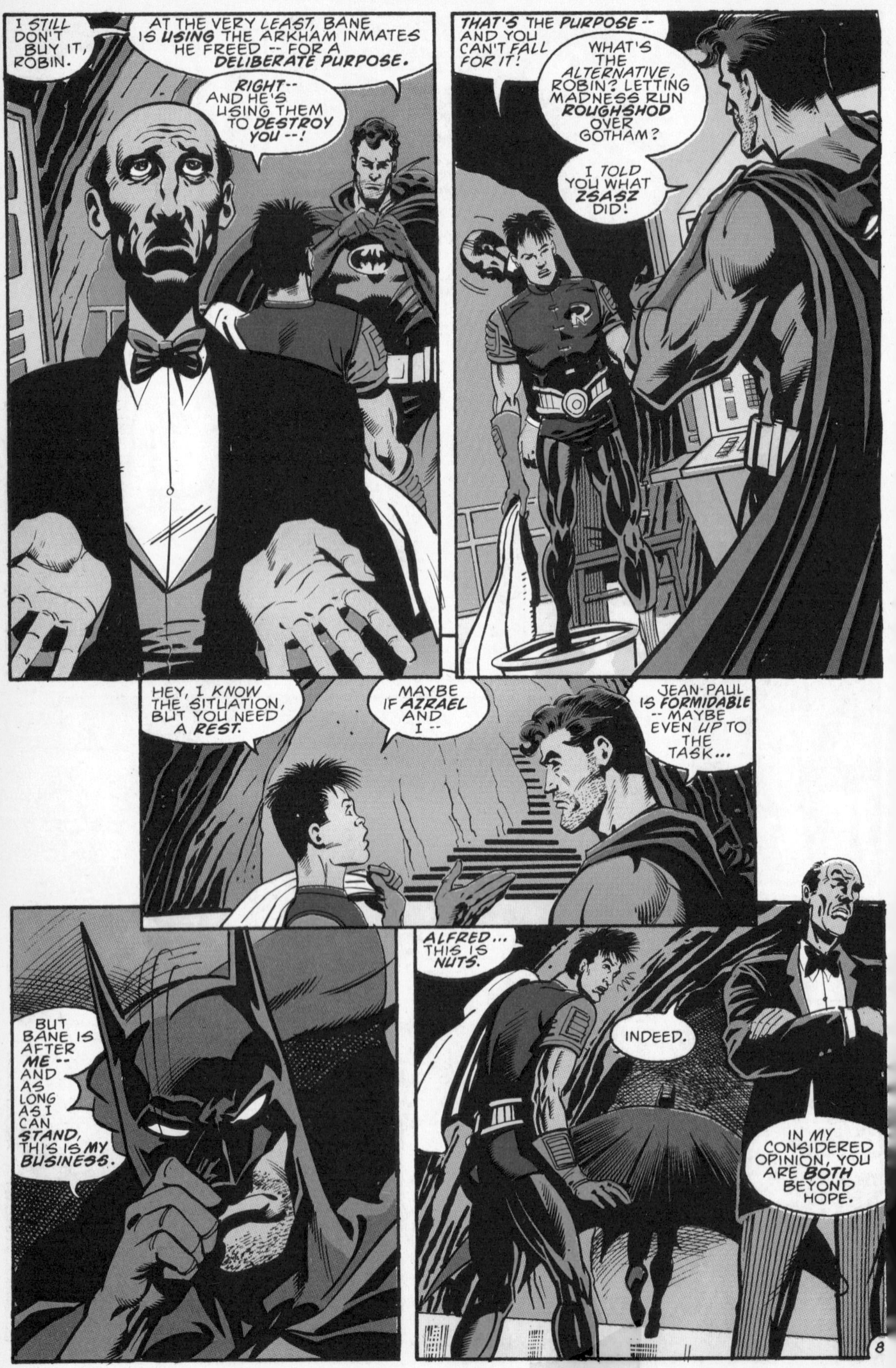
I STILL DON'T BUY IT, ROBIN.
AT THE VERY LEAST, BANE IS USING THE ARKHAM INMATES HE FREED -- FOR A DELIBERATE PURPOSE.
RIGHT-- AND HE'S USING THEM TO DESTROY YOU--!
THAT'S THE PURPOSE -- AND YOU CAN'T FALL FOR IT!
WHAT'S THE ALTERNATIVE, ROBIN? LETTING MADNESS RUN ROUGHSHOD OVER GOTHAM?
I TOLD YOU WHAT ZSASZ DID!
HEY, I KNOW THE SITUATION, BUT YOU NEED A REST.
MAYBE IF AZRAEL AND I --
JEAN-PAUL IS FORMIDABLE -- MAYBE EVEN UP TO THE TASK...
BUT BANE IS AFTER ME -- AND AS LONG AS I CAN STAND, THIS IS MY BUSINESS.
ALFRED... THIS IS NUTS.
INDEED.
IN MY CONSIDERED OPINION, YOU ARE BOTH BEYOND HOPE.
8

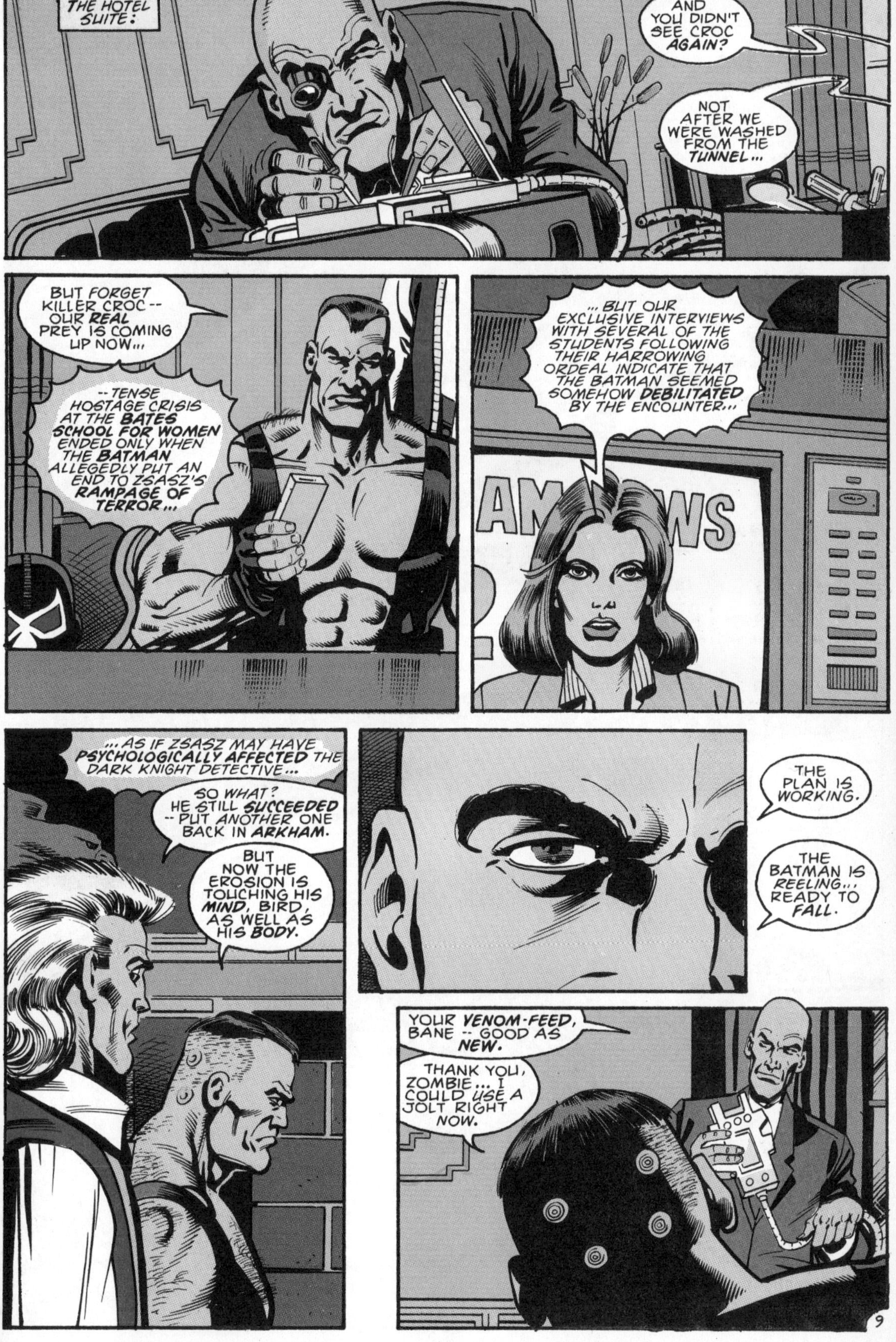

THE HOTEL SUITE:
AND YOU DIDN'T SEE CROC AGAIN?
NOT AFTER WE WERE WASHED FROM THE TUNNEL...
BUT FORGET KILLER CROC -- OUR REAL PREY IS COMING UP NOW...
--TENSE HOSTAGE CRISIS AT THE BATES SCHOOL FOR WOMEN ENDED ONLY WHEN THE BATMAN ALLEGEDLY PUT AN END TO ZSASZ'S RAMPAGE OF TERROR...
...BUT OUR EXCLUSIVE INTERVIEWS WITH SEVERAL OF THE STUDENTS FOLLOWING THEIR HARROWING ORDEAL INDICATE THAT THE BATMAN SEEMED SOMEHOW DEBILITATED BY THE ENCOUNTER...
...AS IF ZSASZ MAY HAVE PSYCHOLOGICALLY AFFECTED THE DARK KNIGHT DETECTIVE...
SO WHAT? HE STILL SUCCEEDED -- PUT ANOTHER ONE BACK IN ARKHAM.
BUT NOW THE EROSION IS TOUCHING HIS MIND, BIRD, AS WELL AS HIS BODY.
THE PLAN IS WORKING.
THE BATMAN IS REELING... READY TO FALL.
YOUR VENOM-FEED, BANE -- GOOD AS NEW.
THANK YOU, ZOMBIE... I COULD USE A JOLT RIGHT NOW.
9

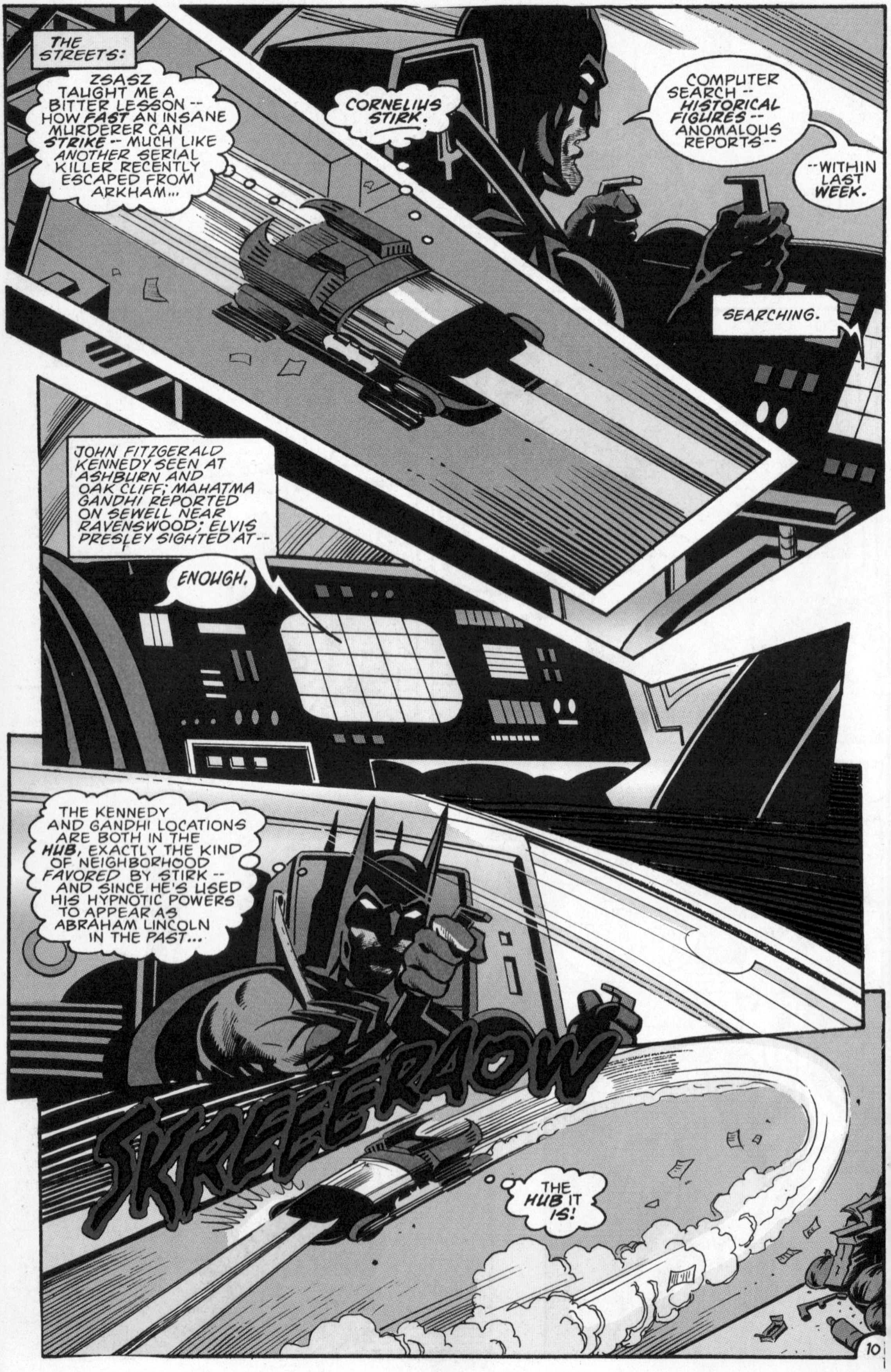
THE STREETS:
ZSASZ TAUGHT ME A BITTER LESSON -- HOW FAST AN INSANE MURDERER CAN STRIKE -- MUCH LIKE ANOTHER SERIAL KILLER RECENTLY ESCAPED FROM ARKHAM...
CORNELIUS STIRK.
COMPUTER SEARCH -- HISTORICAL FIGURES -- ANOMALOUS REPORTS--
--WITHIN LAST WEEK.
SEARCHING.
JOHN FITZGERALD KENNEDY SEEN AT ASHBURN AND OAK CLIFF; MAHATMA GANDHI REPORTED ON SEWELL NEAR RAVENSWOOD; ELVIS PRESLEY SIGHTED AT--
ENOUGH.
THE KENNEDY AND GANDHI LOCATIONS ARE BOTH IN THE HUB, EXACTLY THE KIND OF NEIGHBORHOOD FAVORED BY STIRK -- AND SINCE HE'S USED HIS HYPNOTIC POWERS TO APPEAR AS ABRAHAM LINCOLN IN THE PAST...
SKREEERAOW
THE HUB IT IS!
10

KRATCH

12

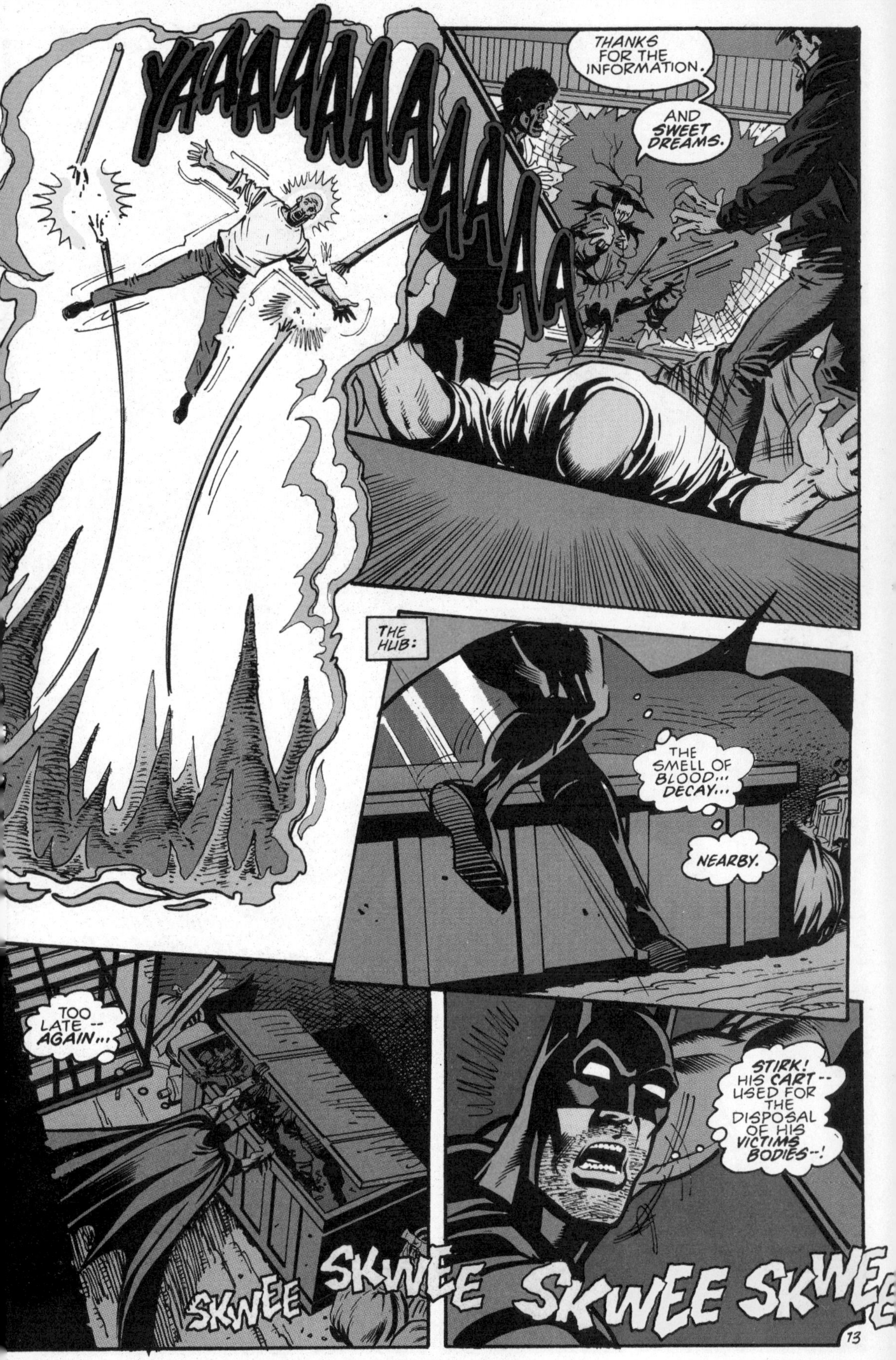
YAAAAAAAAAAAAAA
THANKS FOR THE INFORMATION.
AND SWEET DREAMS.
THE HUB:
THE SMELL OF BLOOD... DECAY...
NEARBY.
TOO LATE -- AGAIN...
STIRK! HIS CART -- USED FOR THE DISPOSAL OF HIS VICTIMS BODIES--!
SKWEE SKWEE
SKWEE SKWEE
13

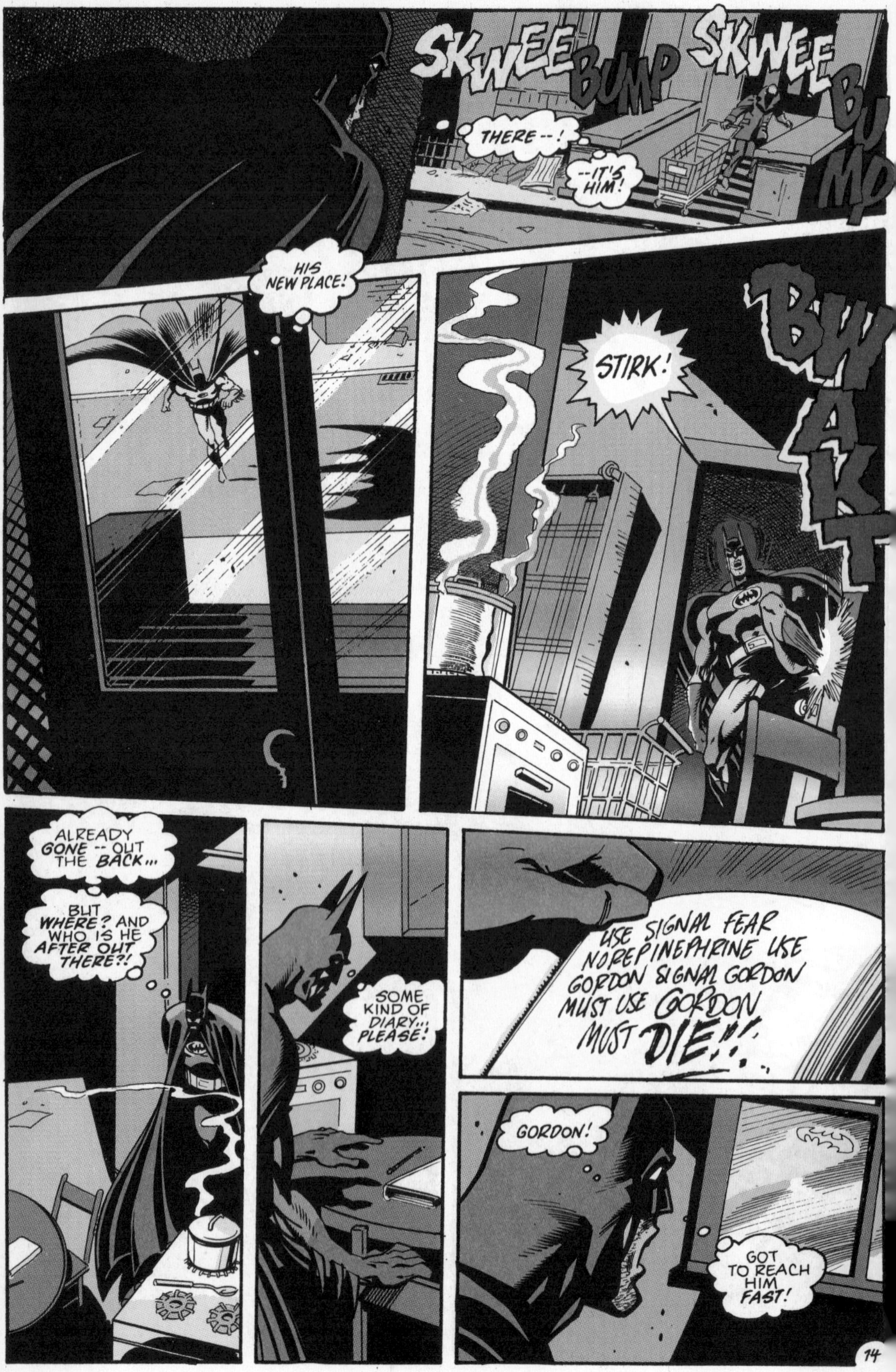

SKWEE
BUMP
SKWEE
BUMP
THERE--!
--IT'S HIM!
HIS NEW PLACE!
STIRK!
BWAKT
ALREADY GONE -- OUT THE BACK...
BUT WHERE? AND WHO IS HE AFTER OUT THERE?!
SOME KIND OF DIARY... PLEASE!
USE SIGNAL FEAR NOREPINEPHRINE USE GORDON SIGNAL GORDON MUST USE GORDON MUST DIE!!!
GORDON!
GOT TO REACH HIM FAST!
14

THE APARTMENT OF JEAN-PAUL VALLEY:

... AND EVEN IF HE DOESN'T *WANT* US, I'VE GOT A BAD FEELING HE'LL *NEED* US.

I'LL BE *READY*, ROBIN.

-- GETTING *WORRIED* ABOUT HIM, PAUL... *REAL* WORRIED...

I *SWEAR* IT.

POLICE HQ:

OVER *HERE*, GORDON.

ABOUT TIME --

-- THOUGHT YOU'D *NEVER* ANSWER THE SIGNAL.

MAYOR KROL'S THREAT-ENING TO CALL OUT THE *NATIONAL GUARD...*

IT'D MEAN LOSING MY *JOB*... RIGHT AFTER SARAH AND I JUST GOT *MARRIED...*

... AND IF I LEAVE AS *POLICE COMMISSIONER*... IT'D PROBABLY MEAN THE END OF *YOU* TOO.

15

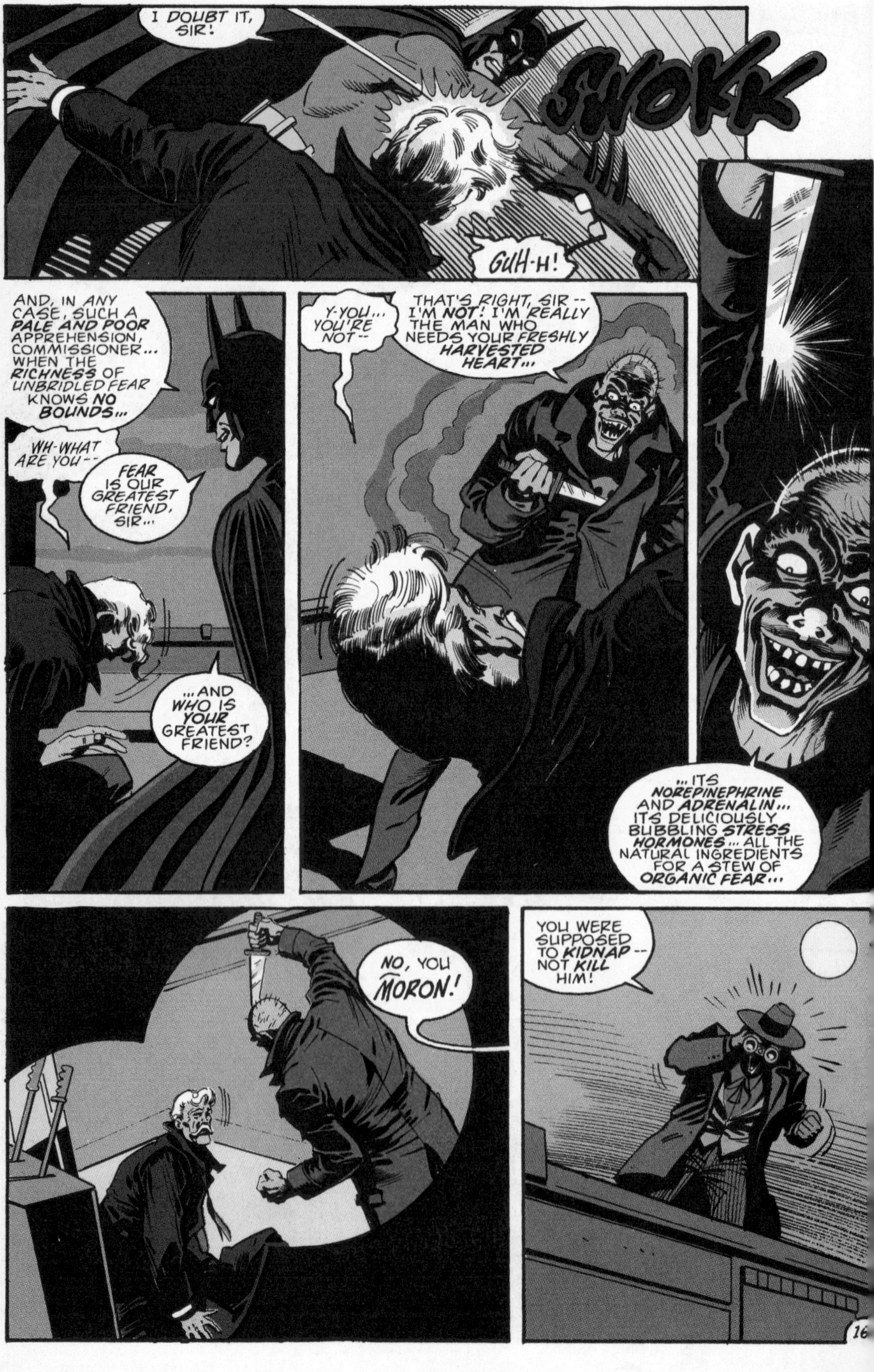
I DOUBT IT, SIR!
SNOKK
GUH-H!
AND, IN ANY CASE, SUCH A PALE AND POOR APPREHENSION, COMMISSIONER... WHEN THE RICHNESS OF UNBRIDLED FEAR KNOWS NO BOUNDS...
WH-WHAT ARE YOU--
FEAR IS OUR GREATEST FRIEND, SIR...
...AND WHO IS YOUR GREATEST FRIEND?
Y-YOU... YOU'RE NOT--
THAT'S RIGHT, SIR -- I'M NOT! I'M REALLY THE MAN WHO NEEDS YOUR FRESHLY HARVESTED HEART...
...ITS NOREPINEPHRINE AND ADRENALIN... ITS DELICIOUSLY BUBBLING STRESS HORMONES... ALL THE NATURAL INGREDIENTS FOR A STEW OF ORGANIC FEAR...
NO, YOU MORON!
YOU WERE SUPPOSED TO KIDNAP -- NOT KILL HIM!
16

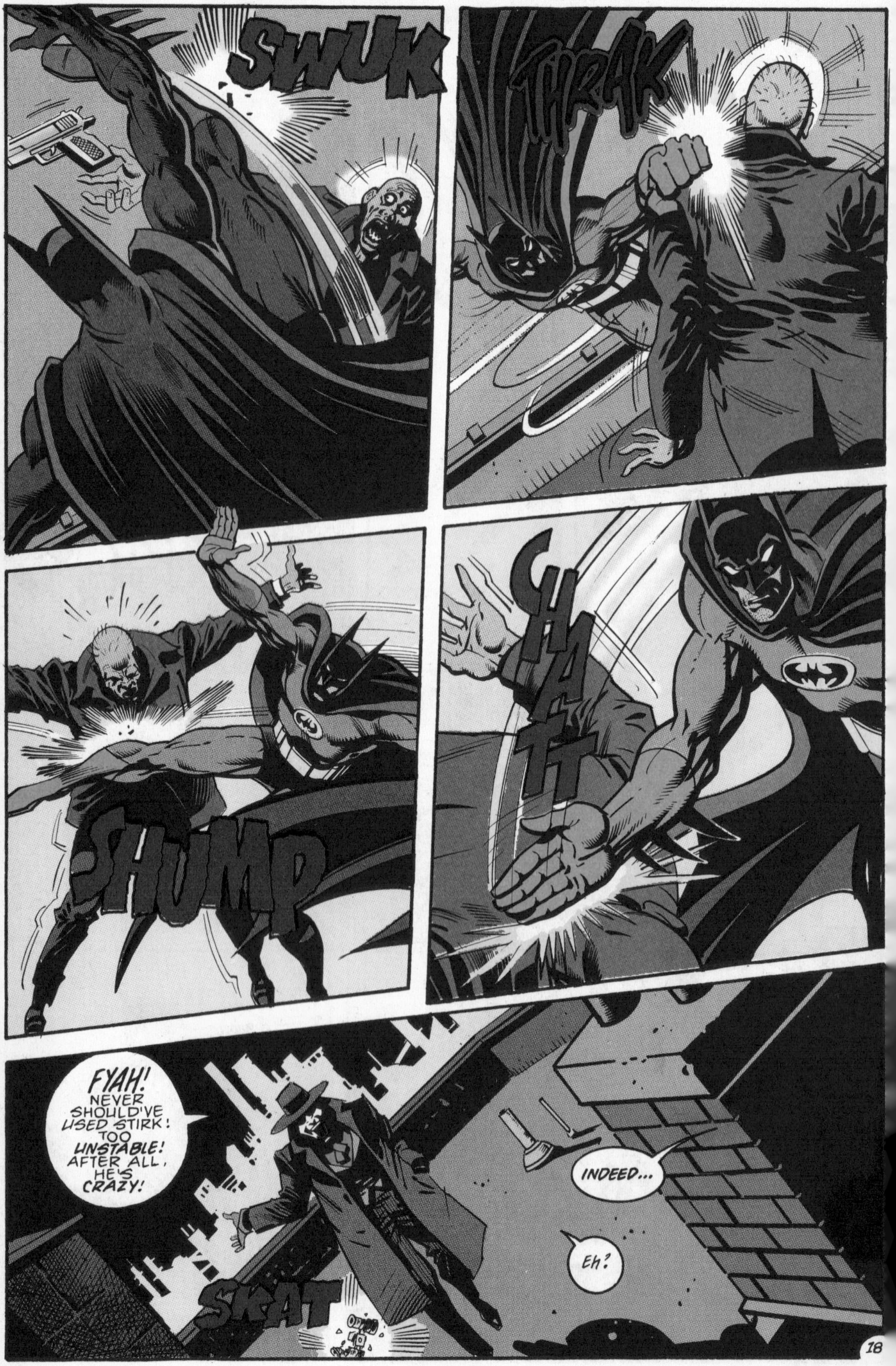
SWUK
THRAK
SHUMP
CHATT
FYAH! NEVER SHOULD'VE USED STIRK! TOO UNSTABLE! AFTER ALL, HE'S CRAZY!
INDEED...
Eh?
SKAT
18

AFTER MY VISIT TO THE *8-BALL,* I *KNEW* I'D FIND YOU SOMEWHERE NEAR *GORDON...*

SCARECROW -- WHAT A *BIZARRE* SURPRISE!

...AND I'M *OFFENDED,* JOKER, BY THE FACT THAT YOU WENT TO A *RANK AMATEUR* IN THE REALM OF FEAR...

...WHEN *THE MASTER* WAS *READILY* AVAILABLE.

MEANING *YOU,* OF COURSE... BUT MAYBE I FIGURED I COULD *CONTROL* STIRK, EH?

AND HOW *WRONG YOU WERE!* BAD CHOICE, JOKER -- AND IT MAKES ME *ANGRY.*

IN FACT, I'M *TEMPTED* TO GIVE *YOU* A DOSE OF MY *FEAR...*

HAHAHA

JUST *TRY IT,* SCARECROW! I'M SURE I'D FIND THE EXPERIENCE *HIGHLY AMUSING!*

I'D PREFER *TAKING STIRK'S PLACE* -- BUT THIS TIME IT MUST BE AN *EQUAL PARTNERSHIP...*

NO ONE CONTROLS ANYONE.

JUST *WHAT DO* YOU HAVE IN *MIND"?* IF ONE MAY USE THE TERM ON *CRANIUM-PACKED STRAW.*

THE POLICE COMMISSIONER IS *PEANUTS!* IF YOU WANT TO BRING *REAL FEAR* AND *CHAOS* TO GOTHAM...

...WHY NOT GO STRAIGHT TO THE *TOP?*

TERRORIZE THE MAYOR?

Hmm... I THINK... I *LIKE* IT!

HAHAHA

19

R-RED GRID... MANDALA... OF B-BLOOD...

EASY, GORDON -- IT'S JUST AN *HYPNOTIC MIND-PLANT...* HIS *PSIONIC POWER* PUT YOU INTO A --

RED GRIIIIIID!! BATMAN K'LLED MEEEE!!

JAMES!

IT... IT WAS *CORNELIUS STIRK...* POSING AS ME...

STIRK? THE *SERIAL KILLER?*

MY GOD, WHAT HAVE YOU *DONE* TO HIM!?!

B-BATMAN... MY F-FRIEND... WITH A *KNIFE...*

IF IT WEREN'T FOR *YOU* --

YOU'RE *WRONG*, MRS. GORDON -- YOUR *HUSBAND* WAS THE TARGET, *NOT ME.*

JUST AS HE WAS IN THE *HEADHUNTER INCIDENT* --

-- WHEN I TOLD YOU TO *LEAVE US ALONE?!*

EVERYTHING EXPLODING... CRUMBLING... COLLAPSING...

...AND THE *BIG* ONES... THE ONES LIKE *TWO-FACE* AND THE *JOKER...*

THEY HAVEN'T EVEN MADE *THEIR* MOVES YET!

20

THE MAYOR'S MANSION, MASTER BEDROOM:

FSSSSSSSSSSSSSSSSSSSSSS

NFFF... MMNN? ?

HAHAHAHAHAHA

BWAMM

?WHA?!

N-NO! C-CAN'T BE REAL--!

M-MUST BE...A N-NIGHTMARE... N-NOT REAL...!

Ah... BUT WE ARE VERY REAL INDEED, MR. MAYOR... HYPER-REAL...

"...AS YOUR BODYGUARDS DOWNSTAIRS COULD READILY ATTEST -- WERE THEY STILL CAPABLE OF SPEECH."

N-NO... P-P-POISONOUS!

WHAT'S POISONOUS, MR. MAYOR? WHAT ARE YOU SEEING? WHAT'S YOUR GREATEST FEAR?

SPIDERS? SNAKES?

BAD SUSHI?

21

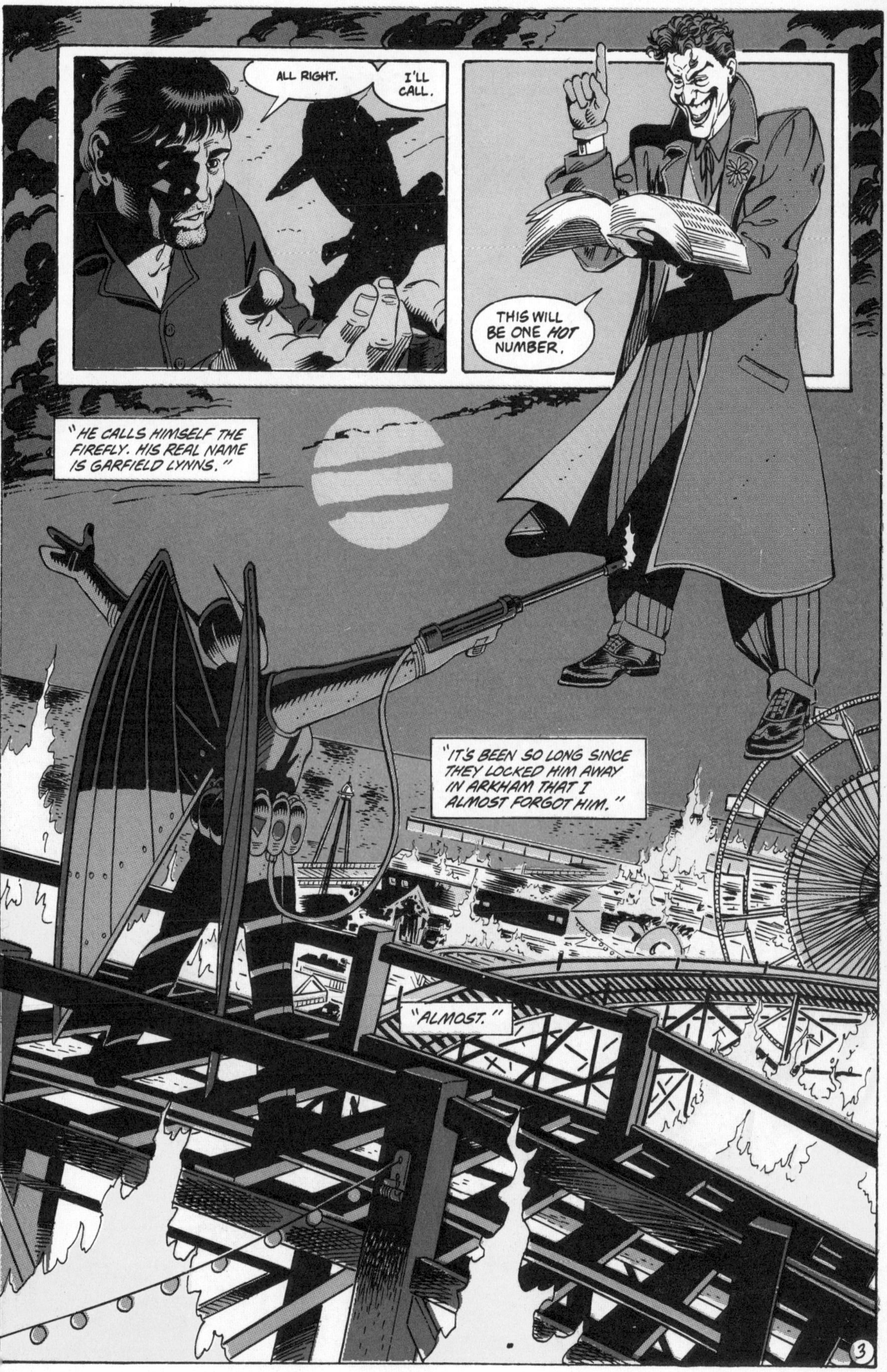
ALL RIGHT.
I'LL CALL.
THIS WILL BE ONE HOT NUMBER.
"HE CALLS HIMSELF THE FIREFLY. HIS REAL NAME IS GARFIELD LYNNS."
"IT'S BEEN SO LONG SINCE THEY LOCKED HIM AWAY IN ARKHAM THAT I ALMOST FORGOT HIM."
"ALMOST."
3

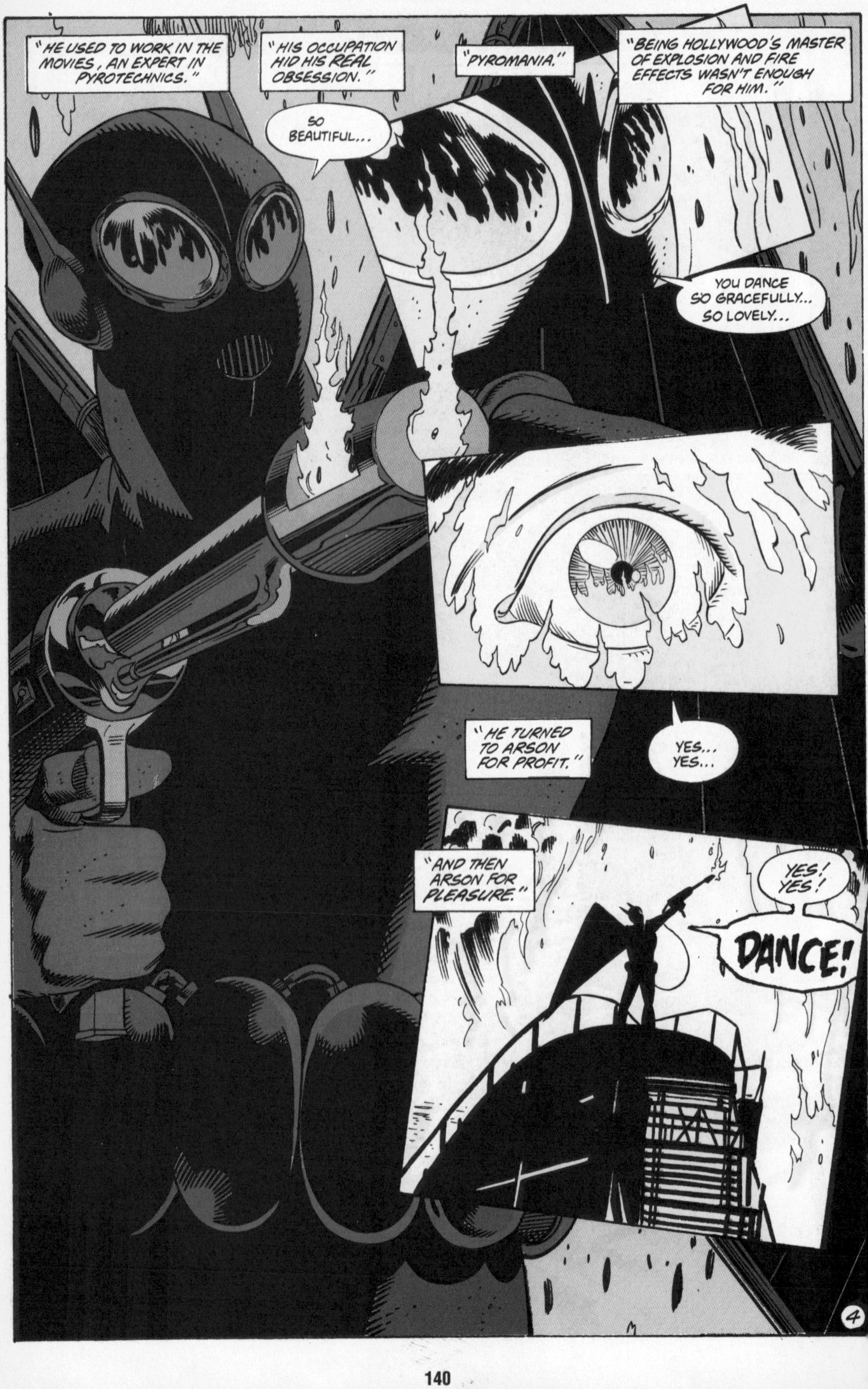
"HE USED TO WORK IN THE MOVIES, AN EXPERT IN PYROTECHNICS."
"HIS OCCUPATION HID HIS REAL OBSESSION."
"PYROMANIA."
"BEING HOLLYWOOD'S MASTER OF EXPLOSION AND FIRE EFFECTS WASN'T ENOUGH FOR HIM."
SO BEAUTIFUL...
YOU DANCE SO GRACEFULLY... SO LOVELY...
"HE TURNED TO ARSON FOR PROFIT."
YES... YES...
"AND THEN ARSON FOR PLEASURE."
YES! YES!
DANCE!
4

I HATE TO SAY WHAT YOU LOOK LIKE.

I CAN MAKE IT. I DON'T *NEED* HELP.

YOU NEED *SOME*THING. YOU'RE PUSHING TOO HARD.

I *HAVE* TO PUSH HARD. GOTHAM IS GOING TO HELL AT THE HANDS OF AN ARMY OF MANIACS LED BY BANE.

LET GORDON AND THE COPS TAKE CARE OF A FEW OF THEM.

THEY *CAN'T*. THEY DON'T KNOW THE NATURE OF THESE BEASTS. NOT THE WAY THAT *I* DO.

GOD HELP ME.

I *KNOW* THEM.

BUT YOU CAN'T JUST *THROW* YOURSELF AFTER THEM. THERE'S SOMETHING TO BE SAID FOR USING OUR BRAINS, RIGHT?

NO TIME. NO TIME. WE HAVE TO REACT WHENEVER THEY SURFACE.

THAT'S NOT WHAT YOU TAUGHT *ME*.

ALL RIGHT.

FIREFLY IS YOURS. DO THE FOOTWORK. DIG INTO THE FILES BACK AT THE CAVE AND TRY TO GET A TWENTY ON HIM.

WHILE THERE'S STILL A CITY LEFT.

8

LOOK, IF I HELP YOU, THEN I'M AN *ACCOMPLICE*.

A MAN OF PRINCIPLES. ARE YOU *SURE* YOU'RE A LAWYER?

LET ME PLUG HIM, SOCKO. *WAAAAUGH!*

CALM DOWN, DUCKMAN. LOOK, YOU AGREE TO HELP US FIND SCARFACE OR MY FOWL PAL HERE IS GOING TO DRILL YOU.

I CAN'T CONTROL HIM. HE'S A *WILD* DUCK, COUNSELOR.

JUST TELL US WHERE TO FIND SCARFACE AND WE'RE *GONE*.

I'M NOT SURE WHERE HE'D BE. I GUESS HE'D BE HELD IN THE EVIDENCE ROOM OF THE PRECINCT WHERE THE VENTRILOQUIST WAS ARRESTED.

BUT YOU'D NEED A COP AND THE LEGIT PAPERWORK TO GET THE PROPERTY ROOM TO RELEASE HIM.

AND YOU COULD HELP US GET AHOLD OF SOME PAPERWORK, RIGHT?

SH-SURE. BUT YOU'LL STILL NEED A *POLICEMAN* TO GET IT RELEASED.

A CINCH, *HUH*, OFFICER O'HARA?

OH, IT 'TIS, IT 'TIS, ME SON. I'M YER MAN, I AM.

9

145

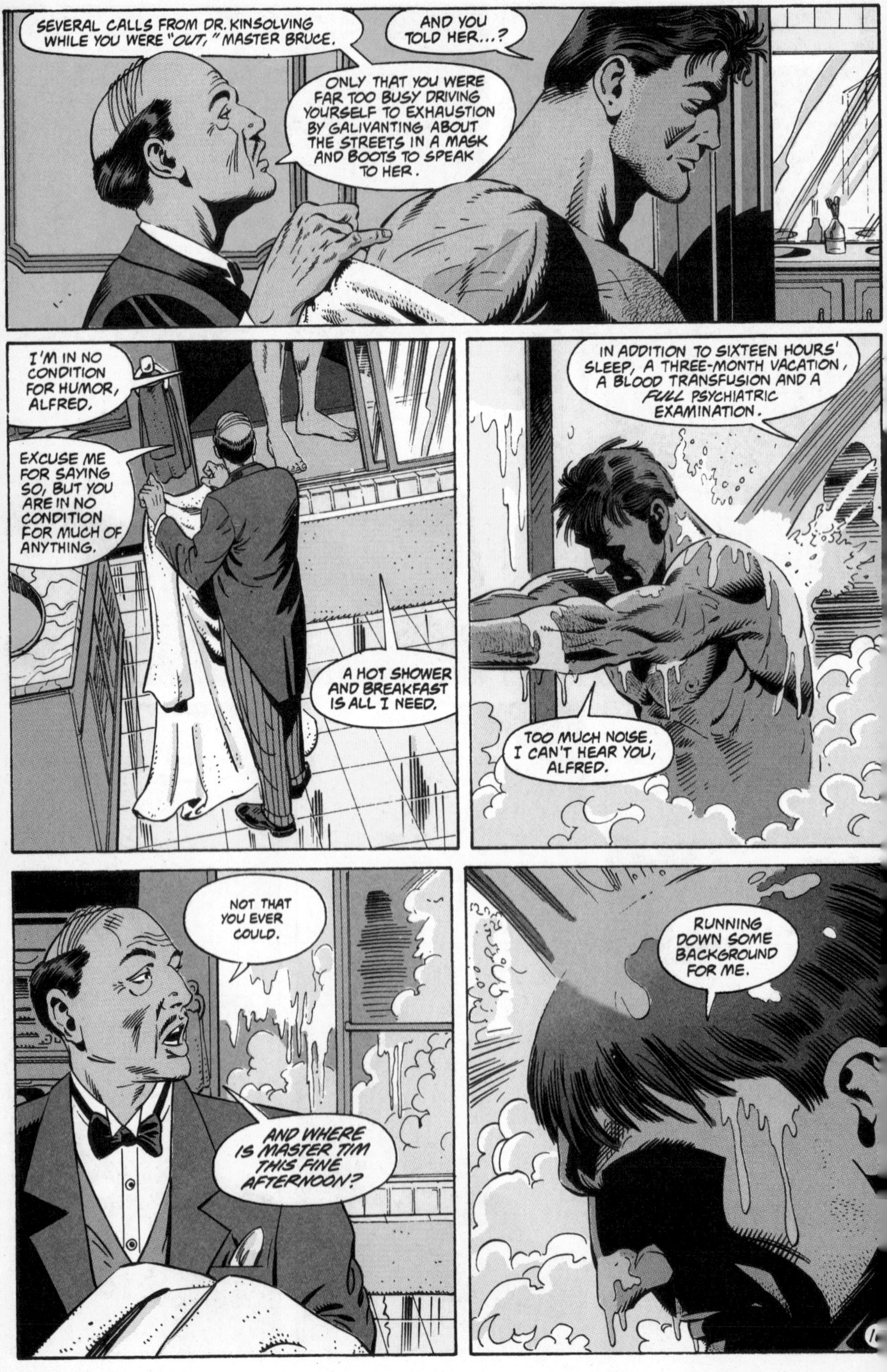
SEVERAL CALLS FROM DR. KINSOLVING WHILE YOU WERE "OUT," MASTER BRUCE.
AND YOU TOLD HER...?
ONLY THAT YOU WERE FAR TOO BUSY DRIVING YOURSELF TO EXHAUSTION BY GALIVANTING ABOUT THE STREETS IN A MASK AND BOOTS TO SPEAK TO HER.
I'M IN NO CONDITION FOR HUMOR, ALFRED.
EXCUSE ME FOR SAYING SO, BUT YOU ARE IN NO CONDITION FOR MUCH OF ANYTHING.
A HOT SHOWER AND BREAKFAST IS ALL I NEED.
IN ADDITION TO SIXTEEN HOURS' SLEEP, A THREE-MONTH VACATION, A BLOOD TRANSFUSION AND A FULL PSYCHIATRIC EXAMINATION.
TOO MUCH NOISE. I CAN'T HEAR YOU, ALFRED.
NOT THAT YOU EVER COULD.
AND WHERE IS MASTER TIM THIS FINE AFTERNOON?
RUNNING DOWN SOME BACKGROUND FOR ME.

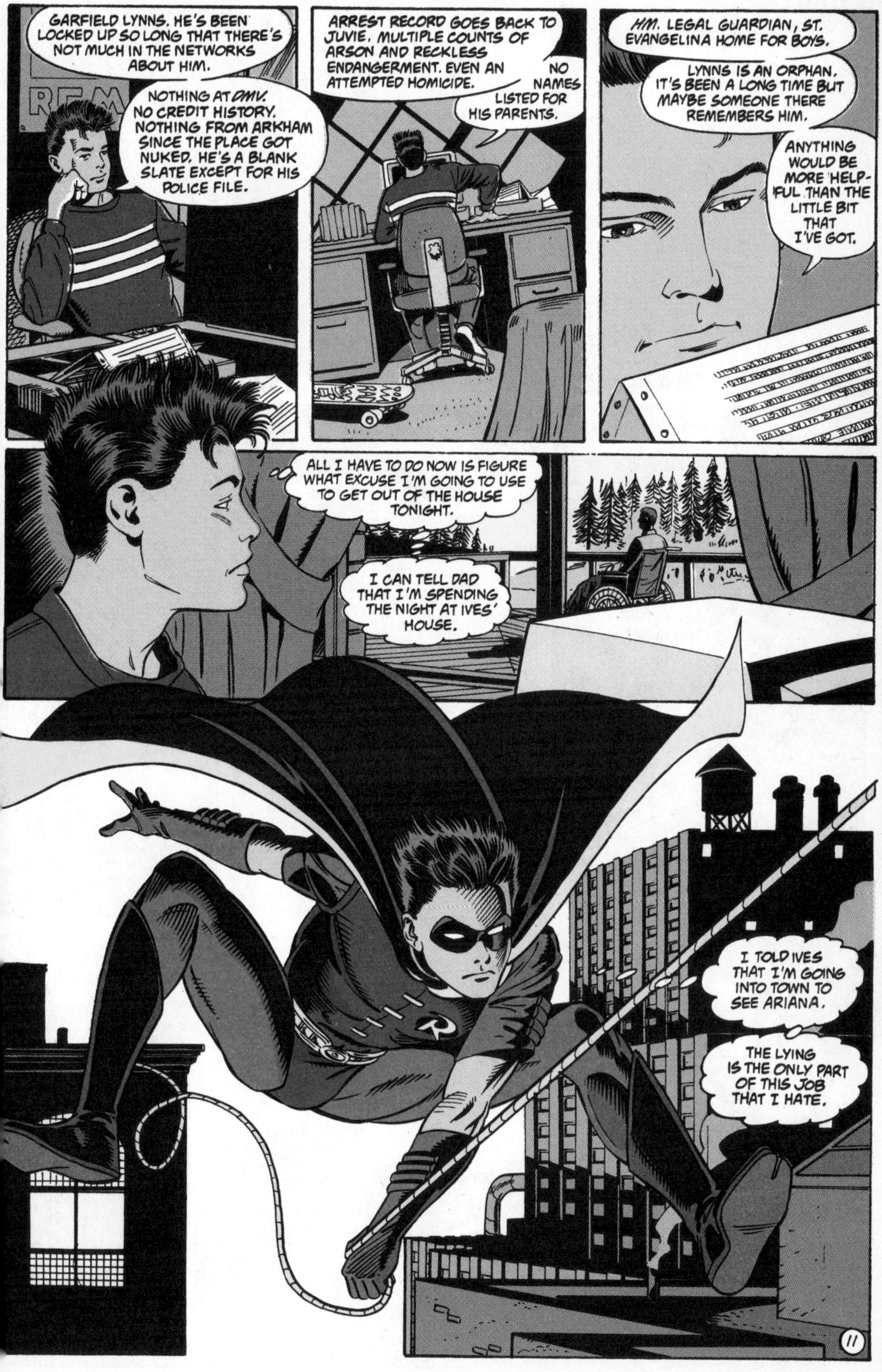
GARFIELD LYNNS. HE'S BEEN LOCKED UP SO LONG THAT THERE'S NOT MUCH IN THE NETWORKS ABOUT HIM.
NOTHING AT DMV. NO CREDIT HISTORY. NOTHING FROM ARKHAM SINCE THE PLACE GOT NUKED. HE'S A BLANK SLATE EXCEPT FOR HIS POLICE FILE.
ARREST RECORD GOES BACK TO JUVIE. MULTIPLE COUNTS OF ARSON AND RECKLESS ENDANGERMENT. EVEN AN ATTEMPTED HOMICIDE.
NO NAMES LISTED FOR HIS PARENTS.
HM. LEGAL GUARDIAN, ST. EVANGELINA HOME FOR BOYS.
LYNNS IS AN ORPHAN. IT'S BEEN A LONG TIME BUT MAYBE SOMEONE THERE REMEMBERS HIM.
ANYTHING WOULD BE MORE HELPFUL THAN THE LITTLE BIT THAT I'VE GOT.
ALL I HAVE TO DO NOW IS FIGURE WHAT EXCUSE I'M GOING TO USE TO GET OUT OF THE HOUSE TONIGHT.
I CAN TELL DAD THAT I'M SPENDING THE NIGHT AT IVES' HOUSE.
I TOLD IVES THAT I'M GOING INTO TOWN TO SEE ARIANA.
THE LYING IS THE ONLY PART OF THIS JOB THAT I HATE.
11

THAT AND THE LONG HOURS.

BUT HOW CAN I COMPLAIN WHEN BATMAN IS PUSHING HIMSELF SO HARD?

NO LUCK.

THIS PLACE HAS BEEN CLOSED FOR AGES.

A DEAD END.

BUT I HAVE TO COME BACK WITH SOMETHING.

QUIET HERE.

MAYBE THE ONLY PEACEFUL PLACE IN ALL OF GOTHAM.

IS SOMEONE THERE?

UH?

UH... I'M SORRY IF I BOTHERED YOU.

NO BOTHER. I'M JUST NOT USED TO SHARING THE COURTYARD WITH ANYONE.

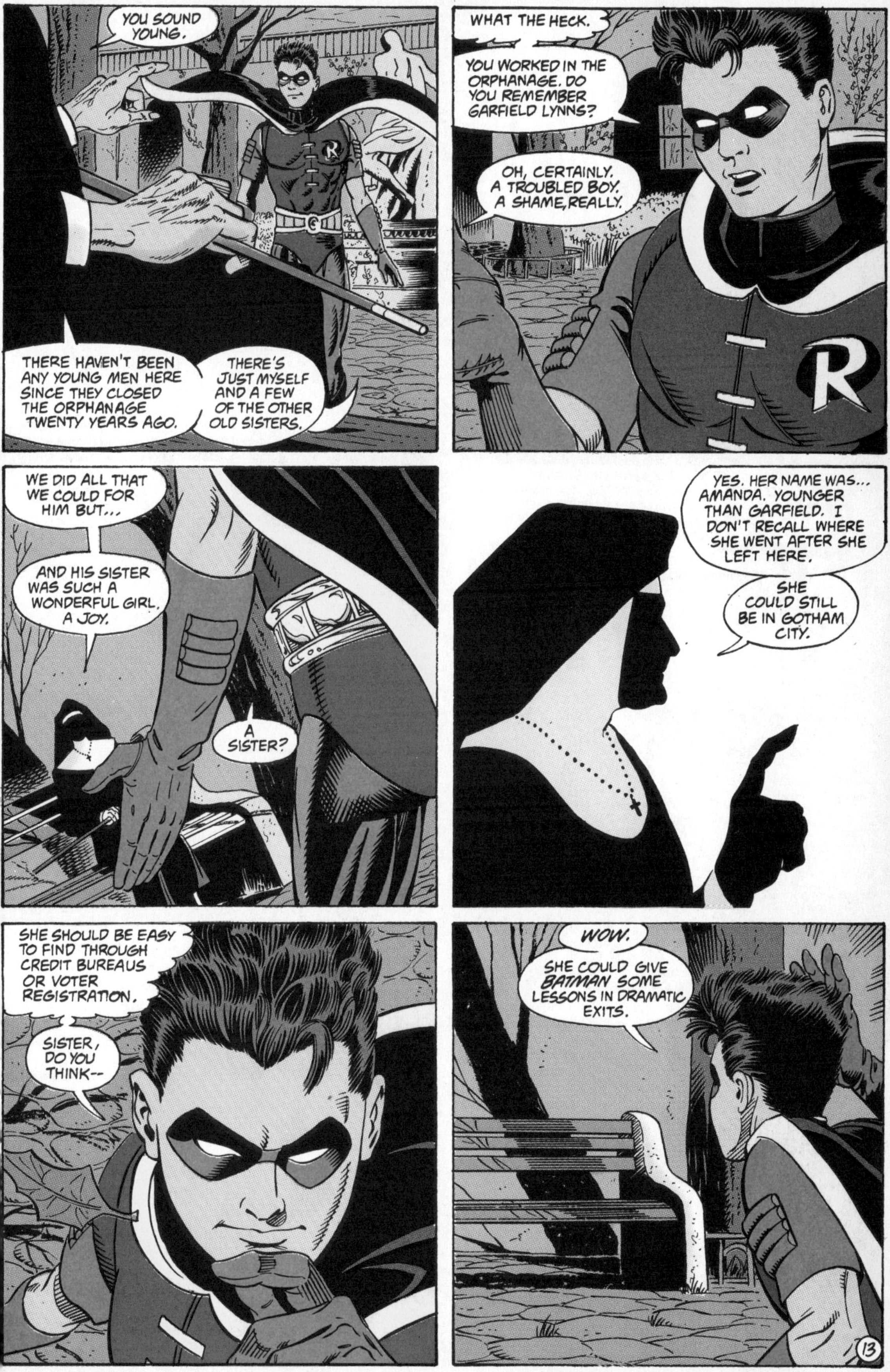
YOU SOUND YOUNG.
THERE HAVEN'T BEEN ANY YOUNG MEN HERE SINCE THEY CLOSED THE ORPHANAGE TWENTY YEARS AGO.
THERE'S JUST MYSELF AND A FEW OF THE OTHER OLD SISTERS.
WHAT THE HECK.
YOU WORKED IN THE ORPHANAGE. DO YOU REMEMBER GARFIELD LYNNS?
OH, CERTAINLY. A TROUBLED BOY. A SHAME, REALLY.
WE DID ALL THAT WE COULD FOR HIM BUT...
AND HIS SISTER WAS SUCH A WONDERFUL GIRL. A JOY.
A SISTER?
YES. HER NAME WAS... AMANDA. YOUNGER THAN GARFIELD. I DON'T RECALL WHERE SHE WENT AFTER SHE LEFT HERE.
SHE COULD STILL BE IN GOTHAM CITY.
SHE SHOULD BE EASY TO FIND THROUGH CREDIT BUREAUS OR VOTER REGISTRATION.
SISTER, DO YOU THINK--
WOW.
SHE COULD GIVE BATMAN SOME LESSONS IN DRAMATIC EXITS.
13

...IT'S ALL YOUR FAULT.

AIN'T THERE A *GAME* ON?

IT'S BLACKED OUT.

JEEZE. I NEVER BEEN SO BORED IN MY *LIFE.*

STAN'S RIGHT, RIDDLER. THIS IS A STONE DRAG. WHEN WE GONNA MAKE OUR *MOVE?*

I *TOLD* YOU DUNCES THAT THESE THINGS TAKE *PLANNING.* YOU HAVE TO CROSS YOUR TEES AND DOT YOUR EYES. EVERYTHING IN ITS PLACE AND A PLACE FOR EVERY-THING.

WHAT'S THE HOLD-UP? WE ALREADY GOT THE TALENT, THE GETAWAY CARS AND THE BUILDING PLANS.

IT'S JUST A *JOB* TO YOU, ISN'T IT, BONEY?

TO ME IT'S THE HIGHEST FORM OF ART.

IT SHOULDN'T BE WORKMANLIKE DRUDGERY. CRIME DEMANDS A CERTAIN AMOUNT OF FLAIR, WIT.

IF BREAKING THE LAW CAN'T BE FUN, THEN WHAT *GOOD* IS IT?

POLICE HEADQUARTERS GOTHAM CENTRAL URGENT

15

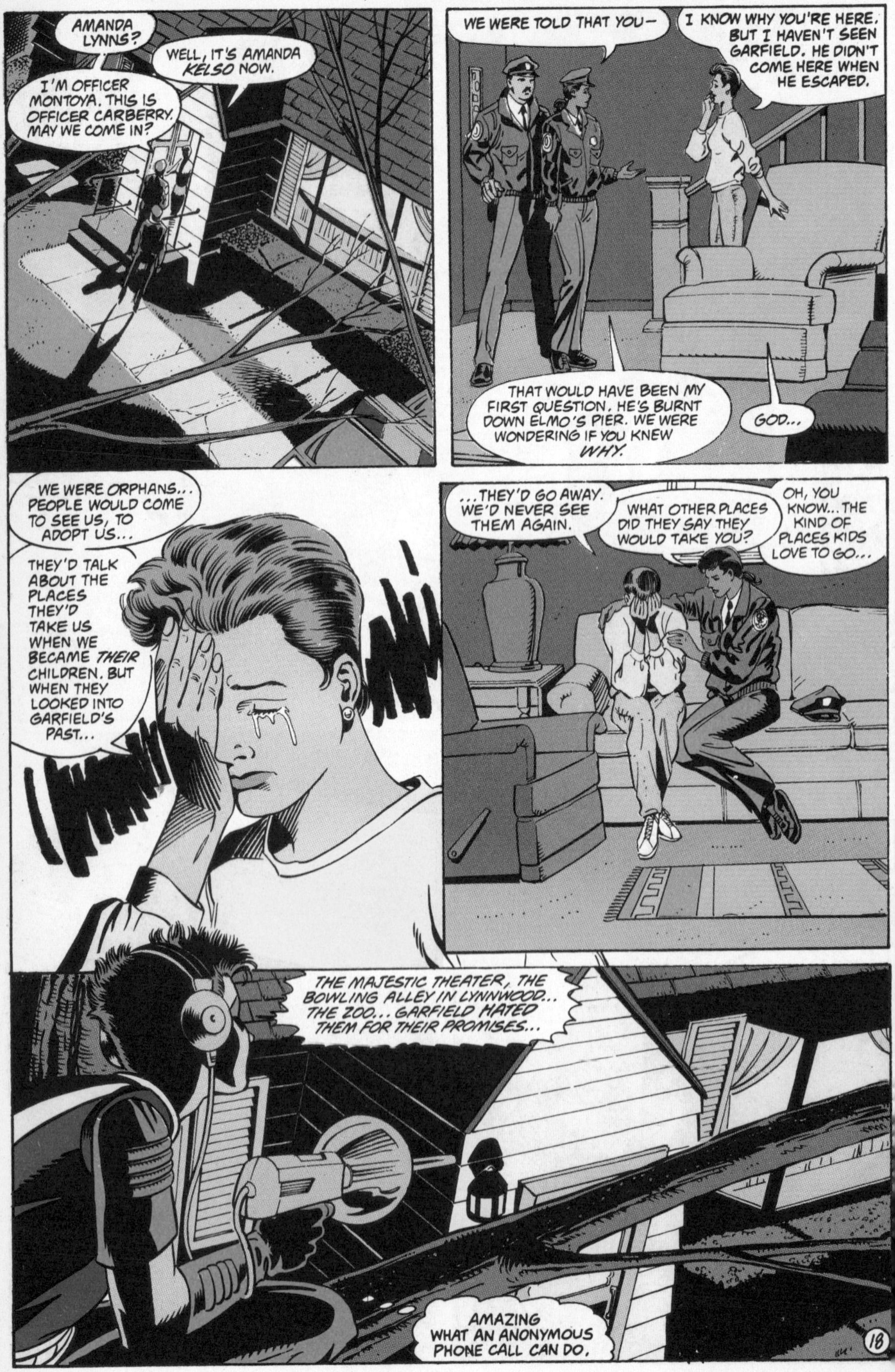
AMANDA LYNNS?
WELL, IT'S AMANDA KELSO NOW.
I'M OFFICER MONTOYA. THIS IS OFFICER CARBERRY. MAY WE COME IN?
WE WERE TOLD THAT YOU—
I KNOW WHY YOU'RE HERE. BUT I HAVEN'T SEEN GARFIELD. HE DIDN'T COME HERE WHEN HE ESCAPED.
THAT WOULD HAVE BEEN MY FIRST QUESTION. HE'S BURNT DOWN ELMO'S PIER. WE WERE WONDERING IF YOU KNEW WHY.
GOD...
WE WERE ORPHANS... PEOPLE WOULD COME TO SEE US, TO ADOPT US...
THEY'D TALK ABOUT THE PLACES THEY'D TAKE US WHEN WE BECAME THEIR CHILDREN. BUT WHEN THEY LOOKED INTO GARFIELD'S PAST...
...THEY'D GO AWAY. WE'D NEVER SEE THEM AGAIN.
WHAT OTHER PLACES DID THEY SAY THEY WOULD TAKE YOU?
OH, YOU KNOW... THE KIND OF PLACES KIDS LOVE TO GO...
THE MAJESTIC THEATER, THE BOWLING ALLEY IN LYNNWOOD... THE ZOO... GARFIELD HATED THEM FOR THEIR PROMISES...
AMAZING WHAT AN ANONYMOUS PHONE CALL CAN DO.
18

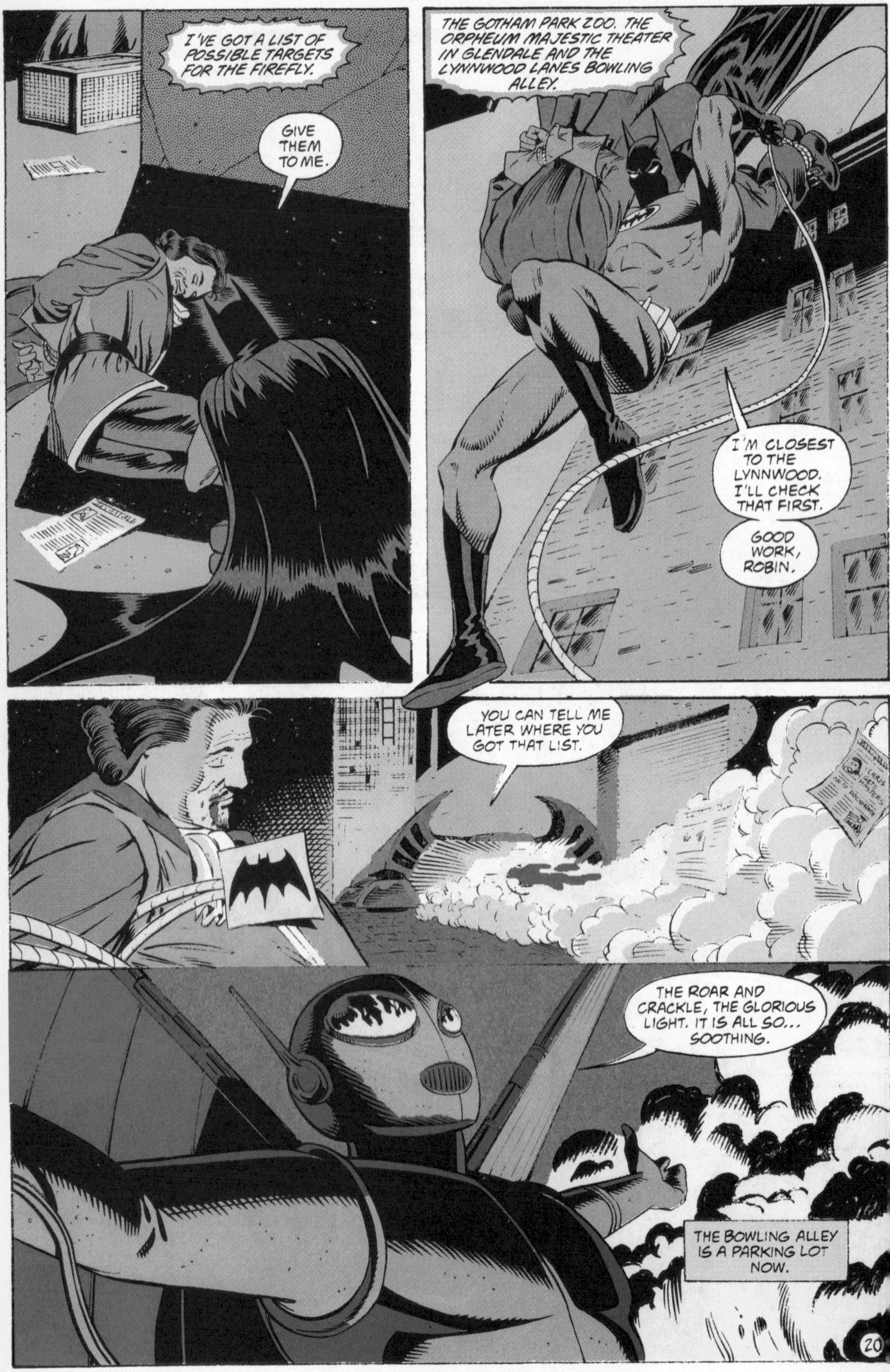
I'VE GOT A LIST OF POSSIBLE TARGETS FOR THE FIREFLY.
GIVE THEM TO ME.
THE GOTHAM PARK ZOO. THE ORPHEUM MAJESTIC THEATER IN GLENDALE AND THE LYNNWOOD LANES BOWLING ALLEY.
I'M CLOSEST TO THE LYNNWOOD. I'LL CHECK THAT FIRST.
GOOD WORK, ROBIN.
YOU CAN TELL ME LATER WHERE YOU GOT THAT LIST.
THE ROAR AND CRACKLE, THE GLORIOUS LIGHT. IT IS ALL SO... SOOTHING.
THE BOWLING ALLEY IS A PARKING LOT NOW.
20

THE MAJESTIC IS NEXT. IT HASN'T BEEN A THEATER FOR YEARS. THESE DAYS IT'S A FURNITURE WAREHOUSE.

BURN... BURN... BURN!

IT DOESN'T SEEM TO MATTER TO LYNNS.

YOU'RE GETTING TO BE A *PEST*, BATMAN.

I'M *NOT* ONE OF THOSE ARKHAM INMATES WHO *OBSESSED* OVER YOU DAY AND NIGHT.

IN FACT, I'LL GET ALONG QUITE NICELY *WITH-OUT* YOUR INTERFERENCE.

BUT IF YOU SPOIL MY FUN ONE MORE TIME I MAY BE FORCED TO CHANGE MY *MIND* ABOUT THAT!

YOU REALLY ARE A WET *BLANKET*, BATTY.

21

158

STRANGE DEADFELLOWS

PULLING US BOTH DOWN -- STRAIGHT INTO HELL.

NO! YOU'LL KILL US BURN US ALIVE!

ANOTHER MADMAN HATCHED FROM SHATTERED ARKHAM -- THE FIREFLY -- PYROMANIAC...

HE DESERVES IT -- MAYBE WE BOTH DO...

...BUT GOT TO LET HIM GO...

THIS END UP

BATMAN CREATED BY BOB KANE

| DOUG MOENCH WRITER | JIM APARO PENCILLER | BOB WIACEK INKER | ADRIENNE ROY COLORIST | RICHARD STARKINGS LETTERER | JORDAN B. GORFINKEL ASST. EDITOR | DENNIS O'NEIL EDITOR |

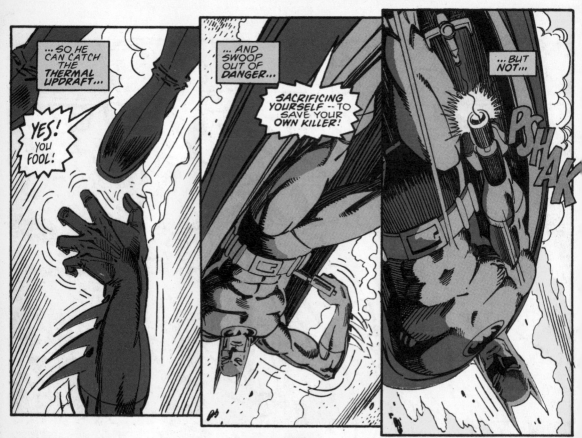

...SO HE CAN CATCH THE THERMAL UPDRAFT...

YES! YOU FOOL!

...AND SWOOP OUT OF DANGER...

SACRIFICING YOURSELF -- TO SAVE YOUR OWN KILLER!

...BUT NOT...

PSHAKAK

...OUT OF REACH.

WHAT THE--?!

SKAKT

GOT TO HOLD ON -- TOUGH OUT THE IMPACT...

...LET MY CAPE PROTECT ME...

SKRASH

3

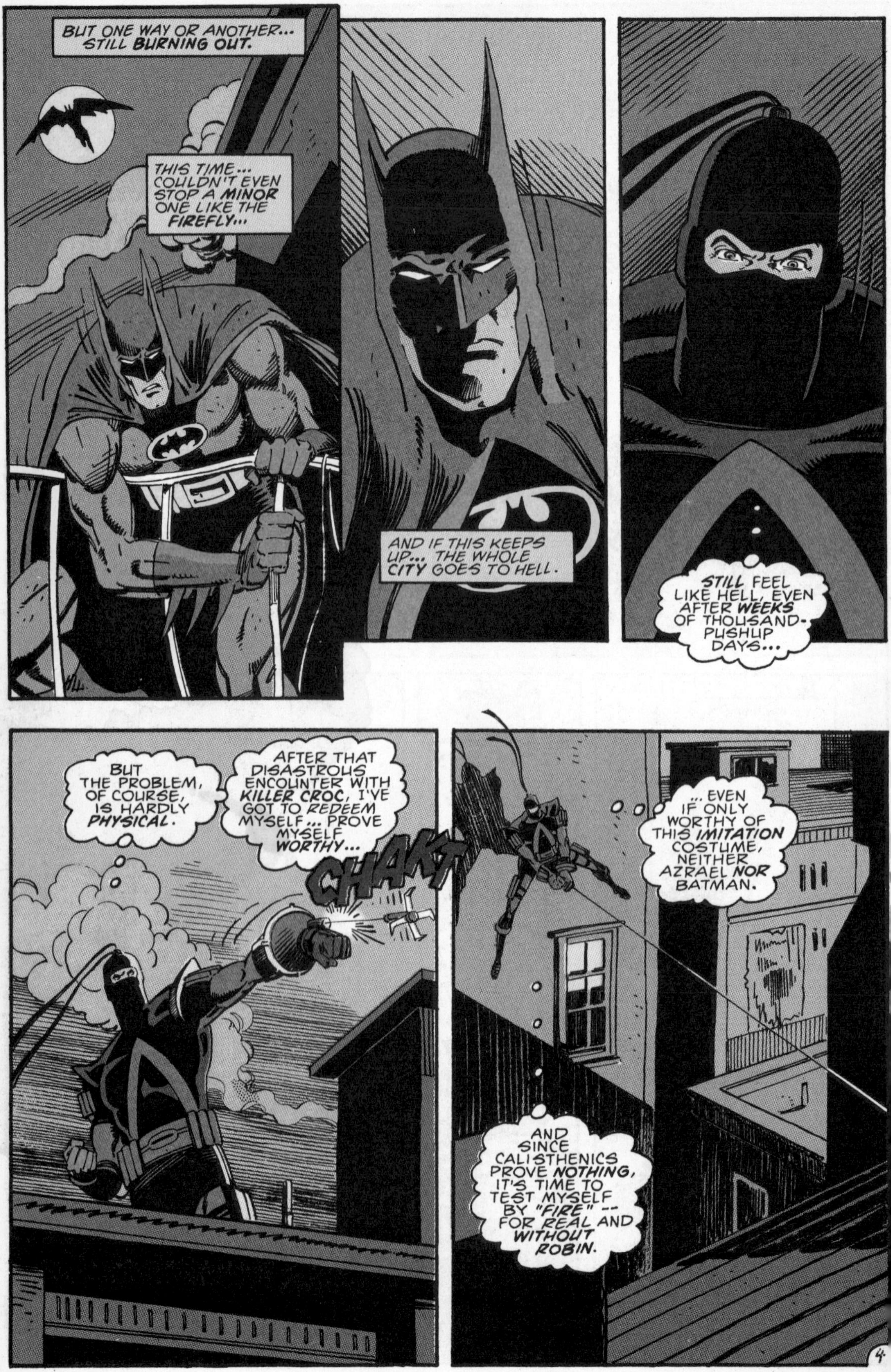
BUT ONE WAY OR ANOTHER... STILL BURNING OUT.
THIS TIME... COULDN'T EVEN STOP A MINOR ONE LIKE THE FIREFLY...
AND IF THIS KEEPS UP... THE WHOLE CITY GOES TO HELL.
STILL FEEL LIKE HELL, EVEN AFTER WEEKS OF THOUSAND-PUSHUP DAYS...
BUT THE PROBLEM, OF COURSE, IS HARDLY PHYSICAL.
AFTER THAT DISASTROUS ENCOUNTER WITH KILLER CROC, I'VE GOT TO REDEEM MYSELF... PROVE MYSELF WORTHY...
CHAKT
... EVEN IF ONLY WORTHY OF THIS IMITATION COSTUME, NEITHER AZRAEL NOR BATMAN.
AND SINCE CALISTHENICS PROVE NOTHING, IT'S TIME TO TEST MYSELF BY "FIRE" -- FOR REAL AND WITHOUT ROBIN.
4

--IT SHOULD PERHAPS BE POINTED OUT THAT THE PUBLIC IS WELL AWARE OF THE BATMAN BEING *RUN RAGGED* OF LATE...

...AND WERE *BRUCE WAYNE* TO CONCURRENTLY DROP FROM SIGHT, FAILING TO APPEAR AT A *WAYNE FOUNDATION DINNER*, PLANNED *MONTHS* IN AD--

ENOUGH, ALFRED...

--*CHARITY FUNCTION* TONIGHT, SIR, AND ALTHOUGH I'M LOATH TO URGE ATTENDANCE IN YOUR *PRESENT* CONDITION --

AT THIS POINT, I COULDN'T CARE *LESS* ABOUT SUCH CONSIDERATIONS ... BUT I *WILL* ATTEND.

YOU *WILL*, SIR?!

WITH SO MANY MANIACS STILL LOOSE IN GOTHAM... TONIGHT'S GATHERING MAKES FOR A *RIPE TARGET*.

IN ONE MASK OR THE *OTHER*...

...I *HAVE* TO BE THERE.

WHATEVER GETS YOU THROUGH THE *DAY*, SIR, AND TO THAT DINNER *TONIGHT*.

I SHALL AWAKEN YOU AS *LATE* AS POSSIBLE.

5

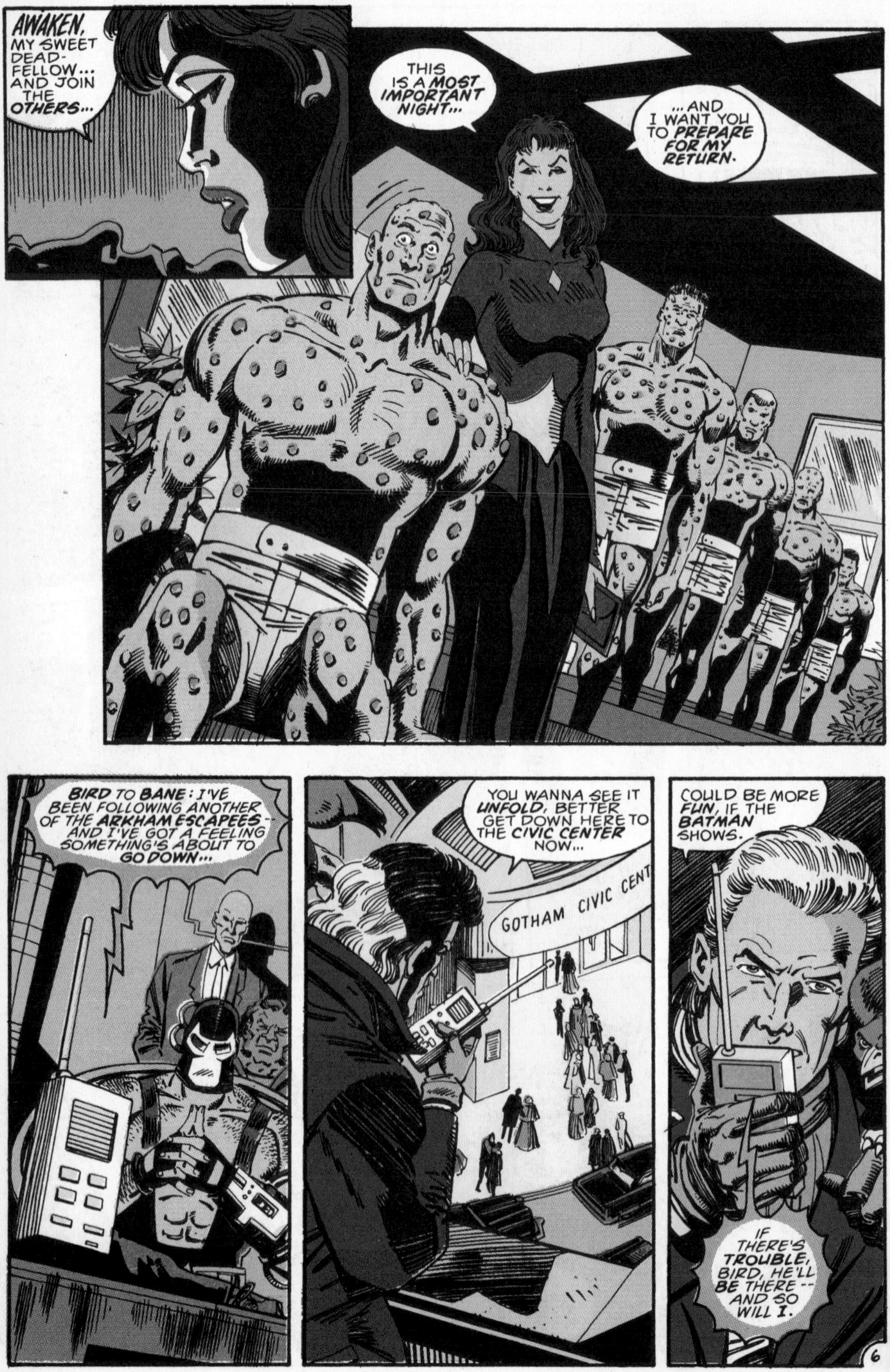
AWAKEN, MY SWEET DEAD-FELLOW... AND JOIN THE OTHERS...
THIS IS A MOST IMPORTANT NIGHT...
...AND I WANT YOU TO PREPARE FOR MY RETURN.
BIRD TO BANE: I'VE BEEN FOLLOWING ANOTHER OF THE ARKHAM ESCAPEES-- AND I'VE GOT A FEELING SOMETHING'S ABOUT TO GO DOWN...
YOU WANNA SEE IT UNFOLD, BETTER GET DOWN HERE TO THE CIVIC CENTER NOW...
GOTHAM CIVIC CENT
COULD BE MORE FUN, IF THE BATMAN SHOWS.
IF THERE'S TROUBLE, BIRD, HE'LL BE THERE -- AND SO WILL I.
6

YOU KNOW, BEFORE ARKHAM, I GOT *L-WOPPED* **BIG TIME.**

L-WOPPED.

"EL WOPPED?"

LIFE -- WITHOUT POSSIBILITY OF PAROLE.

POTATO CHIPS

AHAH -- THAT IS BIG TIME, SCARECROW -- THE **BIGGEST** TIME YOU CAN **DO.**

ALL IN ALL, I'D SAY BEING *CRAZY* IS **BETTER.**

BUT, BEST OF ALL IS *THIS*, SCARECROW -- BEING *BUSTED* OUT -- WITHOUT **GETTING** BETTER!

INDEED, JOKER -- ANY TIME YOU CAN BE *CURED* OF CONFINEMENT, IT'S **BETTER.**

HA HAHAHA

BUT *NOW*... IT'S **PHONE-TIME** AGAIN!

FEAR-GAS TIME TOO!

SKSH

YOU'RE GOING TO SEND EVERY COP IN THIS CITY ON A *WILD GOOSE CHASE,* MAYOR KROL -- TO GET THEIR GOOSES COOKED!

HAHA

7

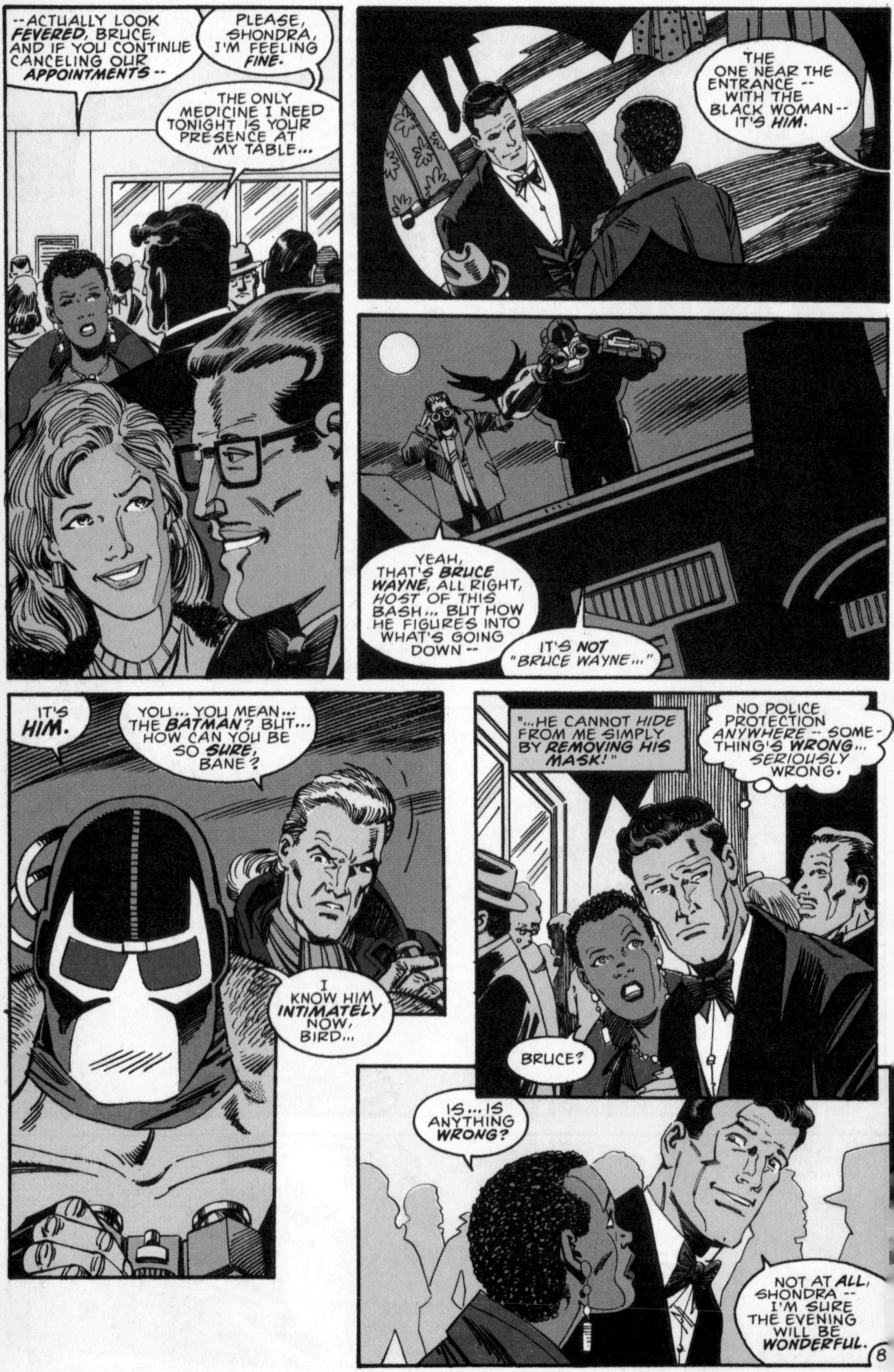
--ACTUALLY LOOK FEVERED, BRUCE, AND IF YOU CONTINUE CANCELING OUR APPOINTMENTS--
PLEASE, SHONDRA, I'M FEELING FINE.
THE ONLY MEDICINE I NEED TONIGHT IS YOUR PRESENCE AT MY TABLE...
THE ONE NEAR THE ENTRANCE -- WITH THE BLACK WOMAN -- IT'S HIM.
YEAH, THAT'S BRUCE WAYNE, ALL RIGHT, HOST OF THIS BASH... BUT HOW HE FIGURES INTO WHAT'S GOING DOWN --
IT'S NOT "BRUCE WAYNE..."
IT'S HIM.
YOU... YOU MEAN... THE BATMAN? BUT... HOW CAN YOU BE SO SURE, BANE?
I KNOW HIM INTIMATELY NOW, BIRD...
"...HE CANNOT HIDE FROM ME SIMPLY BY REMOVING HIS MASK!"
NO POLICE PROTECTION ANYWHERE -- SOMETHING'S WRONG... SERIOUSLY WRONG.
BRUCE?
IS... IS ANYTHING WRONG?
NOT AT ALL, SHONDRA -- I'M SURE THE EVENING WILL BE WONDERFUL.
8

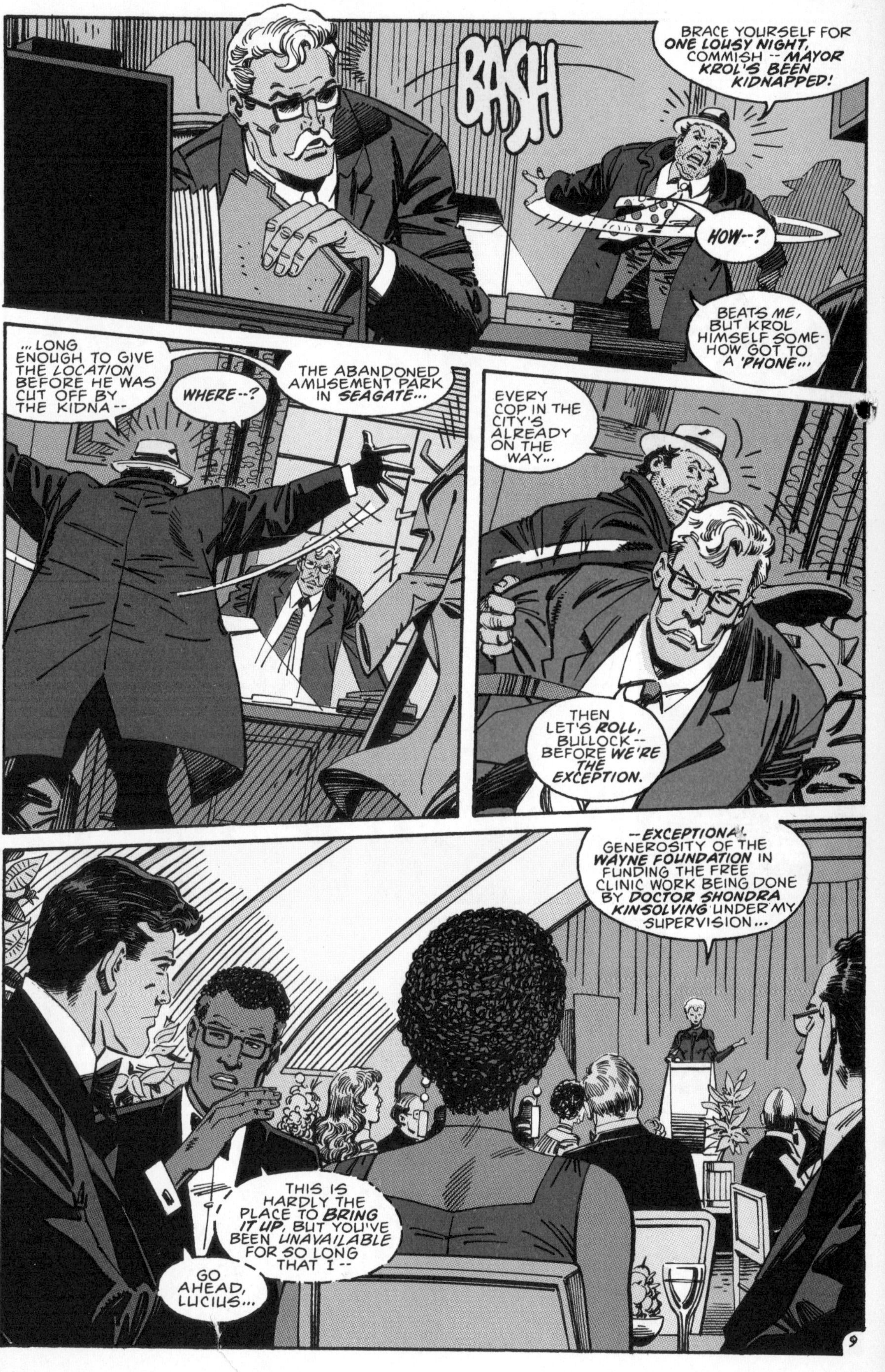
BASH
BRACE YOURSELF FOR ONE LOUSY NIGHT, COMMISH -- MAYOR KROL'S BEEN KIDNAPPED!
HOW--?
BEATS ME, BUT KROL HIMSELF SOME-HOW GOT TO A 'PHONE...
...LONG ENOUGH TO GIVE THE LOCATION BEFORE HE WAS CUT OFF BY THE KIDNA--
WHERE--?
THE ABANDONED AMUSEMENT PARK IN SEAGATE...
EVERY COP IN THE CITY'S ALREADY ON THE WAY...
THEN LET'S ROLL, BULLOCK-- BEFORE WE'RE THE EXCEPTION.
--EXCEPTIONAL GENEROSITY OF THE WAYNE FOUNDATION IN FUNDING THE FREE CLINIC WORK BEING DONE BY DOCTOR SHONDRA KINSOLVING UNDER MY SUPERVISION...
THIS IS HARDLY THE PLACE TO BRING IT UP, BUT YOU'VE BEEN UNAVAILABLE FOR SO LONG THAT I --
GO AHEAD, LUCIUS...
9

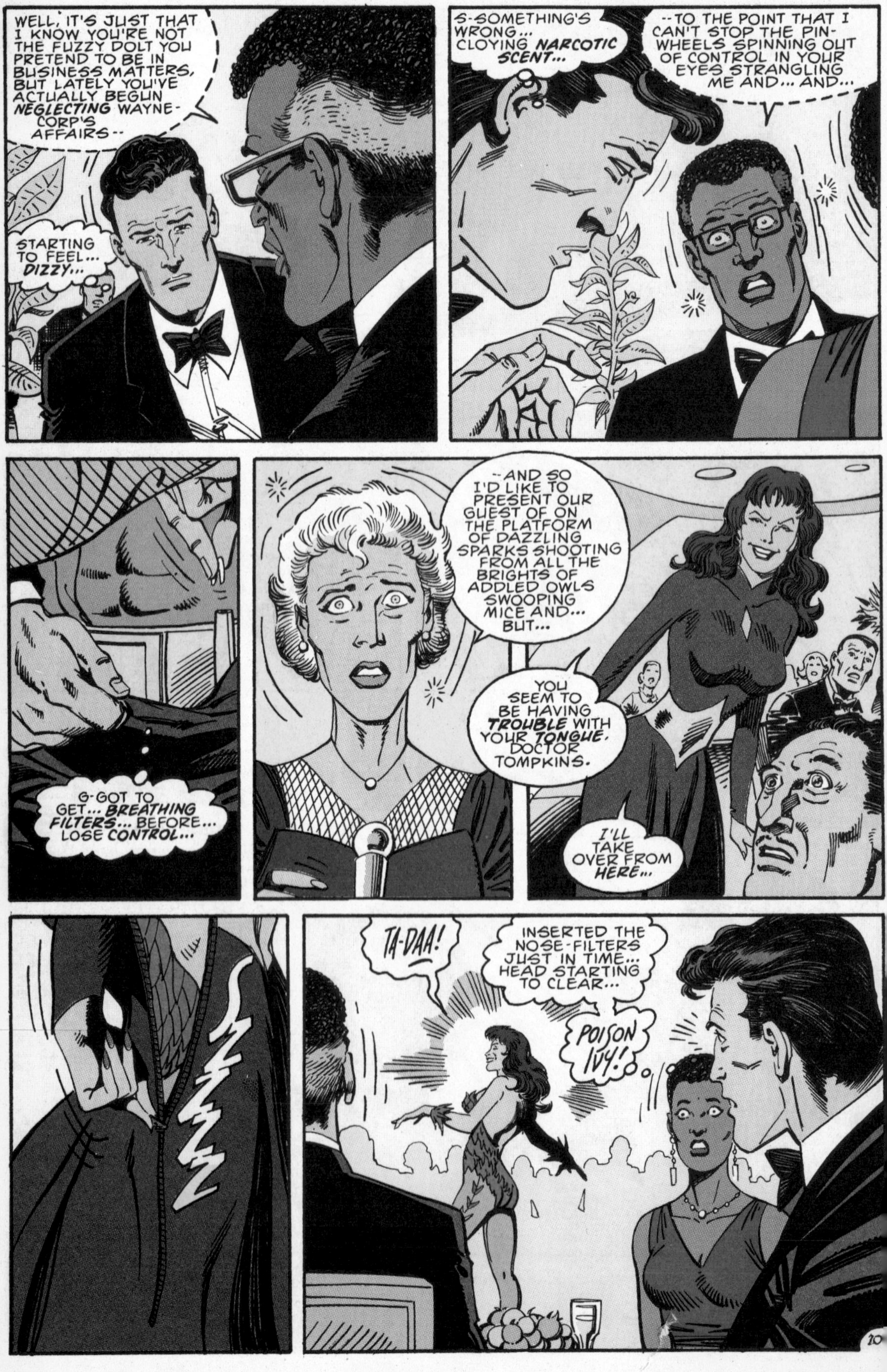
WELL, IT'S JUST THAT I KNOW YOU'RE NOT THE FUZZY DOLT YOU PRETEND TO BE IN BUSINESS MATTERS, BUT LATELY YOU'VE ACTUALLY BEGUN NEGLECTING WAYNE-CORP'S AFFAIRS--
STARTING TO FEEL... DIZZY...
S-SOMETHING'S WRONG... CLOYING NARCOTIC SCENT...
--TO THE POINT THAT I CAN'T STOP THE PIN-WHEELS SPINNING OUT OF CONTROL IN YOUR EYES STRANGLING ME AND... AND...
G-GOT TO GET... BREATHING FILTERS... BEFORE... LOSE CONTROL...
--AND SO I'D LIKE TO PRESENT OUR GUEST OF ON THE PLATFORM OF DAZZLING SPARKS SHOOTING FROM ALL THE BRIGHTS OF ADDLED OWLS SWOOPING MICE AND... BUT...
YOU SEEM TO BE HAVING TROUBLE WITH YOUR TONGUE, DOCTOR TOMPKINS.
I'LL TAKE OVER FROM HERE...
TA-DAA!
INSERTED THE NOSE-FILTERS JUST IN TIME... HEAD STARTING TO CLEAR...
POISON IVY!
10

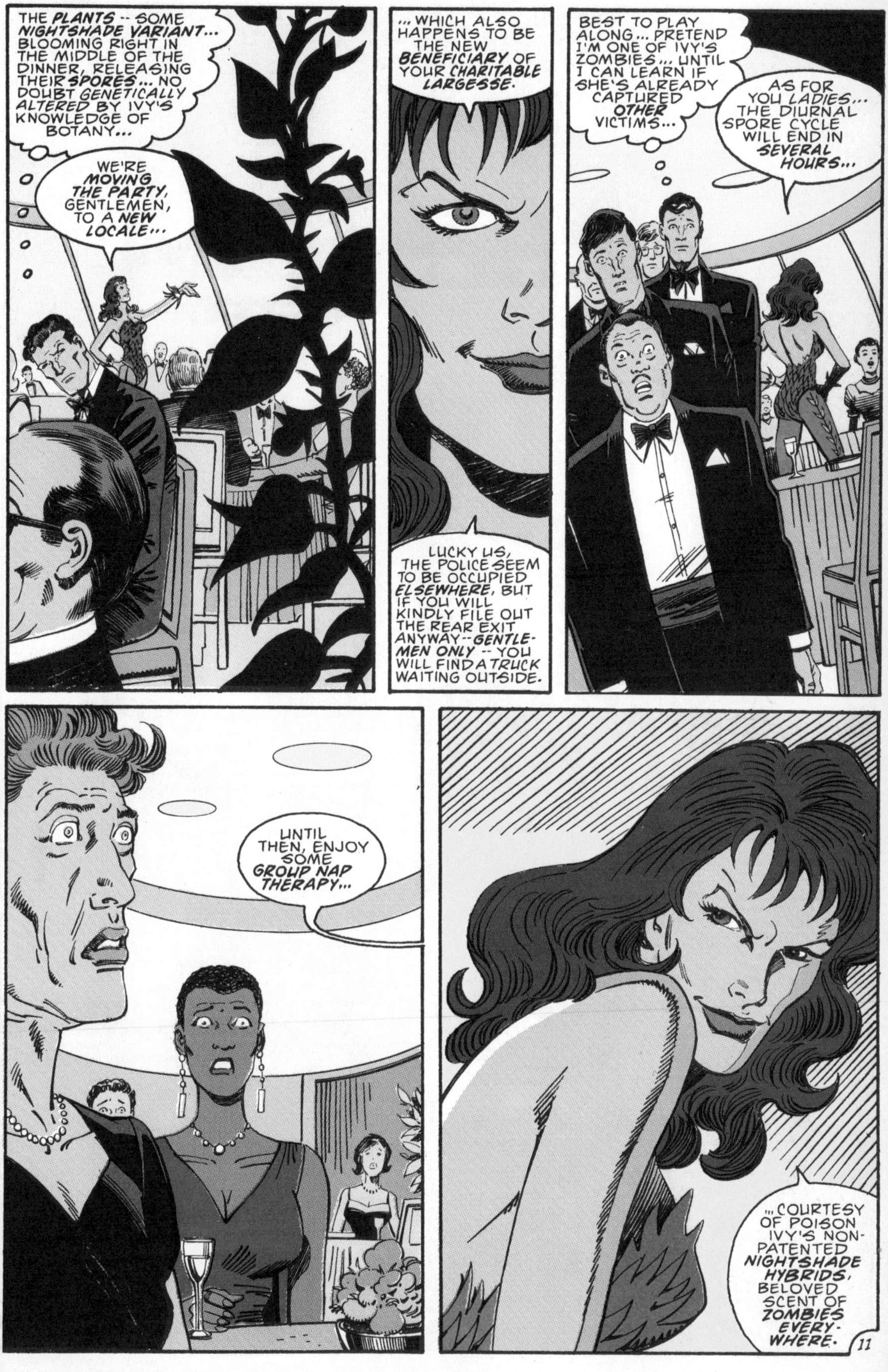
THE PLANTS -- SOME NIGHTSHADE VARIANT... BLOOMING RIGHT IN THE MIDDLE OF THE DINNER, RELEASING THEIR SPORES... NO DOUBT GENETICALLY ALTERED BY IVY'S KNOWLEDGE OF BOTANY...
WE'RE MOVING THE PARTY, GENTLEMEN, TO A NEW LOCALE...
...WHICH ALSO HAPPENS TO BE THE NEW BENEFICIARY OF YOUR CHARITABLE LARGESSE.
LUCKY US, THE POLICE SEEM TO BE OCCUPIED ELSEWHERE, BUT IF YOU WILL KINDLY FILE OUT THE REAR EXIT ANYWAY -- GENTLEMEN ONLY -- YOU WILL FIND A TRUCK WAITING OUTSIDE.
BEST TO PLAY ALONG... PRETEND I'M ONE OF IVY'S ZOMBIES... UNTIL I CAN LEARN IF SHE'S ALREADY CAPTURED OTHER VICTIMS...
AS FOR YOU LADIES... THE DIURNAL SPORE CYCLE WILL END IN SEVERAL HOURS...
UNTIL THEN, ENJOY SOME GROUP NAP THERAPY...
...COURTESY OF POISON IVY'S NON-PATENTED NIGHTSHADE HYBRIDS, BELOVED SCENT OF ZOMBIES EVERYWHERE.
11

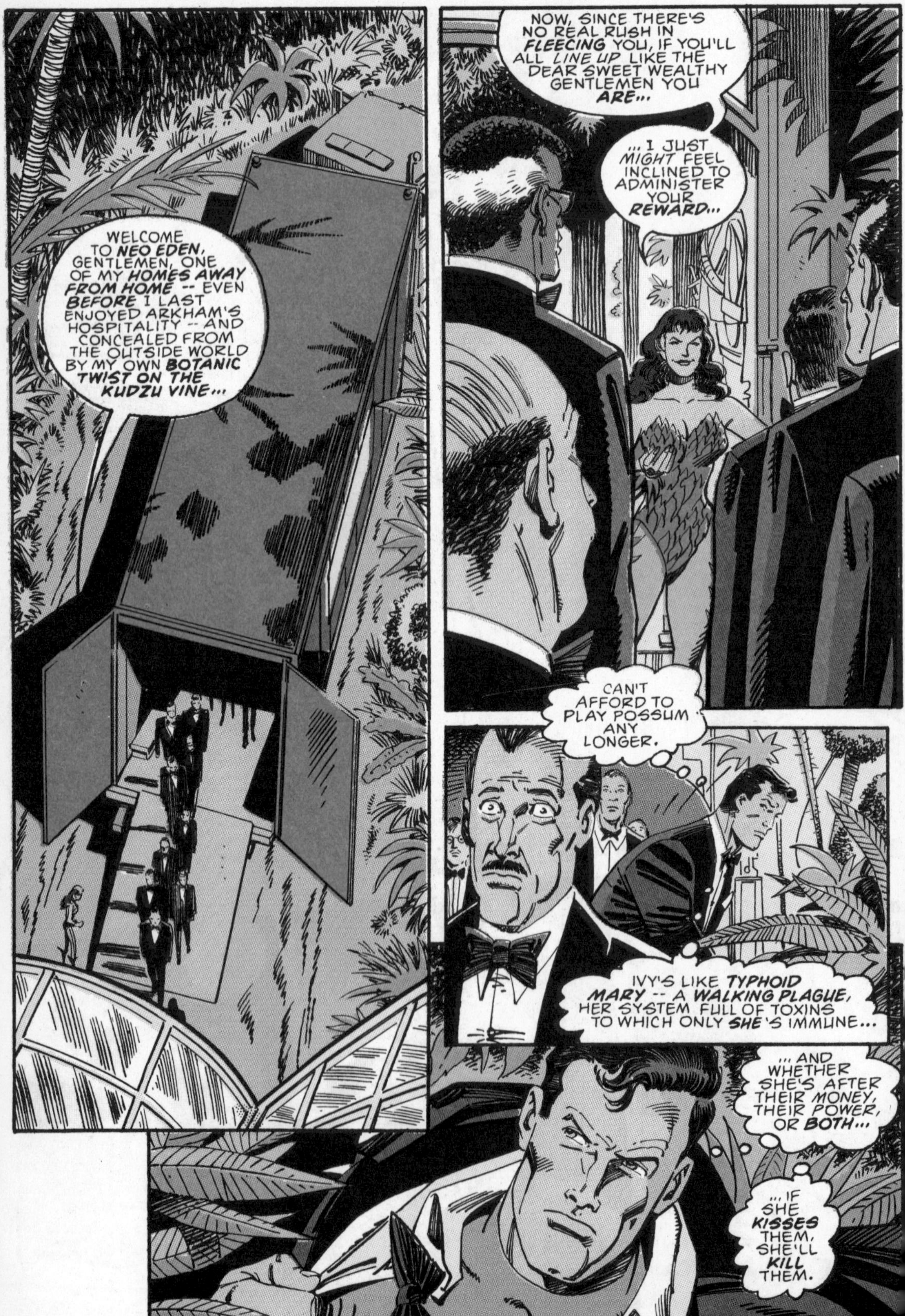
WELCOME TO NEO EDEN, GENTLEMEN, ONE OF MY HOMES AWAY FROM HOME -- EVEN BEFORE I LAST ENJOYED ARKHAM'S HOSPITALITY -- AND CONCEALED FROM THE OUTSIDE WORLD BY MY OWN BOTANIC TWIST ON THE KUDZU VINE...
NOW, SINCE THERE'S NO REAL RUSH IN FLEECING YOU, IF YOU'LL ALL LINE UP LIKE THE DEAR SWEET WEALTHY GENTLEMEN YOU ARE...
...I JUST MIGHT FEEL INCLINED TO ADMINISTER YOUR REWARD...
CAN'T AFFORD TO PLAY POSSUM ANY LONGER.
IVY'S LIKE TYPHOID MARY -- A WALKING PLAGUE, HER SYSTEM FULL OF TOXINS TO WHICH ONLY SHE'S IMMUNE...
...AND WHETHER SHE'S AFTER THEIR MONEY, THEIR POWER, OR BOTH...
...IF SHE KISSES THEM, SHE'LL KILL THEM.
14

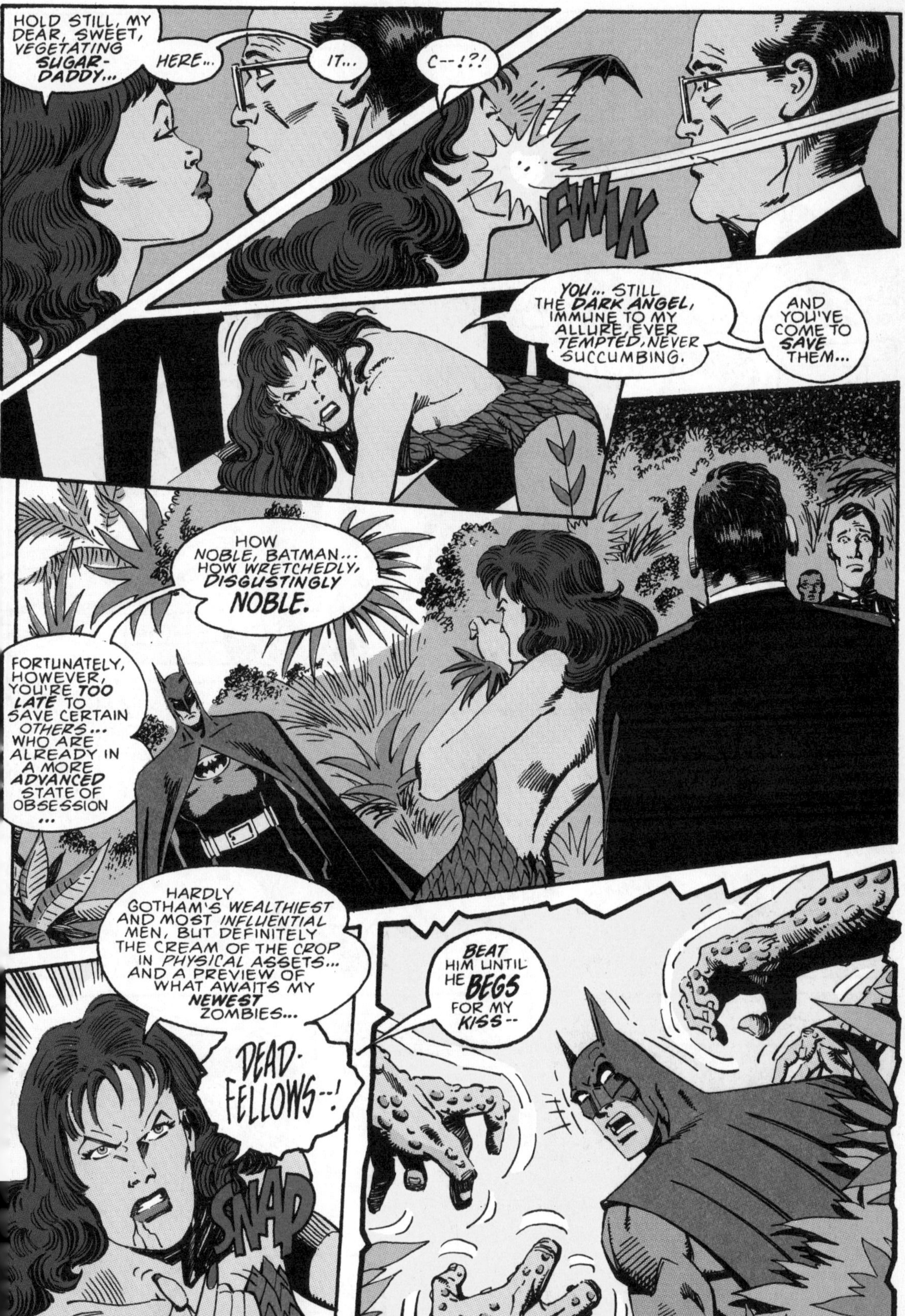
HOLD STILL, MY DEAR, SWEET, VEGETATING SUGAR-DADDY...
HERE...
IT...
C--!?!
FWIK
YOU... STILL THE DARK ANGEL, IMMUNE TO MY ALLURE, EVER TEMPTED, NEVER SUCCUMBING.
AND YOU'VE COME TO SAVE THEM...
HOW NOBLE, BATMAN... HOW WRETCHEDLY, DISGUSTINGLY NOBLE.
FORTUNATELY, HOWEVER, YOU'RE TOO LATE TO SAVE CERTAIN OTHERS... WHO ARE ALREADY IN A MORE ADVANCED STATE OF OBSESSION...
HARDLY GOTHAM'S WEALTHIEST AND MOST INFLUENTIAL MEN, BUT DEFINITELY THE CREAM OF THE CROP IN PHYSICAL ASSETS... AND A PREVIEW OF WHAT AWAITS MY NEWEST ZOMBIES...
DEAD-FELLOWS--!
SNAP
BEAT HIM UNTIL HE BEGS FOR MY KISS--
15

FIVE OF THEM...

NYAHRR

...ALL INFECTED.

CAN'T RISK OPEN WOUNDS.

SWUT

WUKT

ON ME.

AND I CAN'T WASTE ANY TIME...

...NOT WITH IVY'S BLOODY MOUTH STILL BREATHING...

KISSSSS....

...STILL THREATENING TO POISON HER NEW PUPPETS...

LUCIUS!

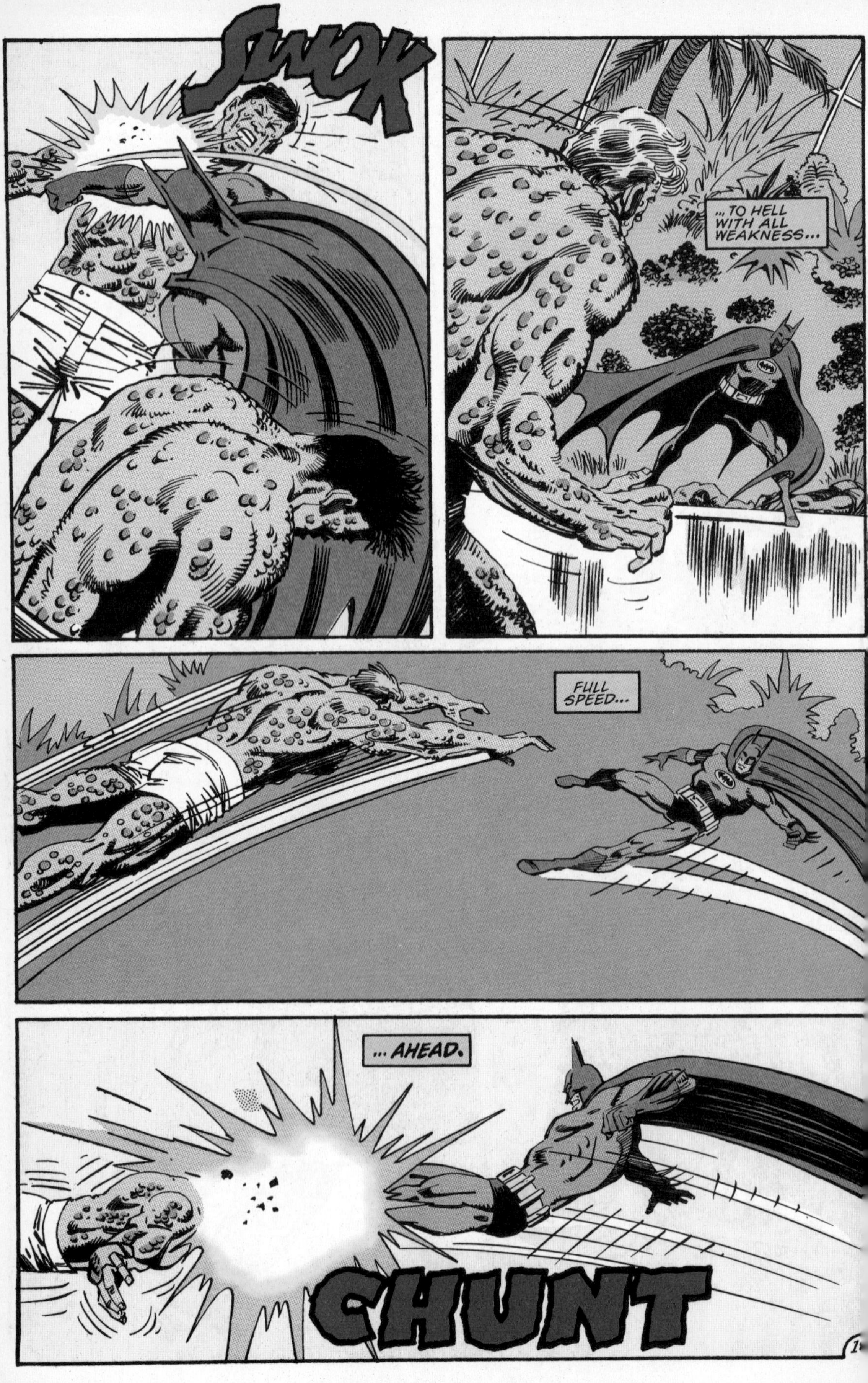
SWOK
...TO HELL WITH ALL WEAKNESS...
FULL SPEED...
...AHEAD.
CHUNT

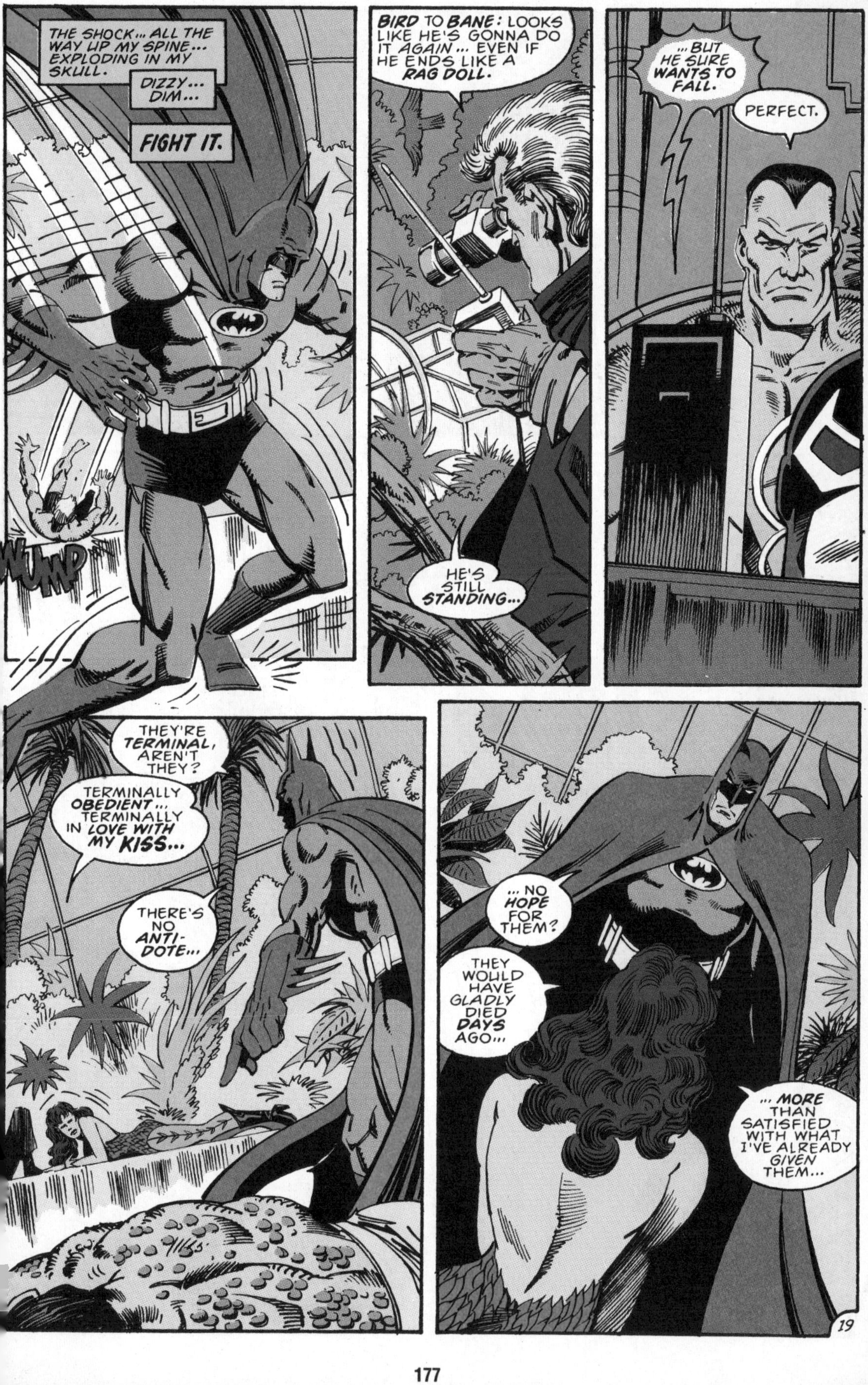
THE SHOCK... ALL THE WAY UP MY SPINE... EXPLODING IN MY SKULL.
DIZZY... DIM...
FIGHT IT.
WUMP
BIRD TO BANE: LOOKS LIKE HE'S GONNA DO IT AGAIN... EVEN IF HE ENDS LIKE A RAG DOLL.
HE'S STILL STANDING...
...BUT HE SURE WANTS TO FALL.
PERFECT.
THEY'RE TERMINAL, AREN'T THEY?
TERMINALLY OBEDIENT... TERMINALLY IN LOVE WITH MY KISS...
THERE'S NO ANTI-DOTE...
...NO HOPE FOR THEM?
THEY WOULD HAVE GLADLY DIED DAYS AGO...
...MORE THAN SATISFIED WITH WHAT I'VE ALREADY GIVEN THEM...
19

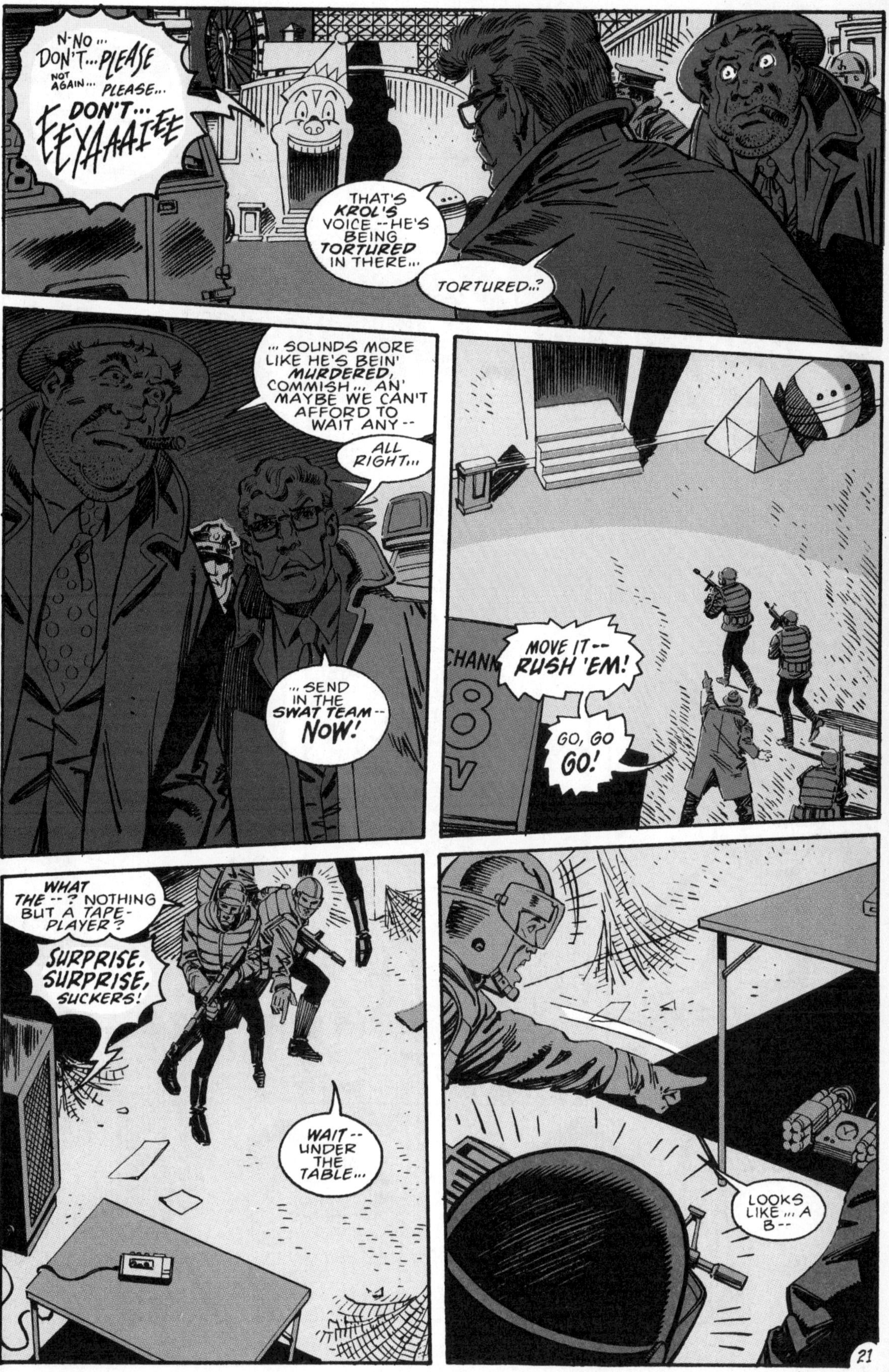
N-NO... DON'T...PLEASE NOT AGAIN... PLEASE... DON'T... EEYAAAIEE
THAT'S KROL'S VOICE--HE'S BEING TORTURED IN THERE...
TORTURED..?
...SOUNDS MORE LIKE HE'S BEIN' MURDERED, COMMISH... AN' MAYBE WE CAN'T AFFORD TO WAIT ANY--
ALL RIGHT...
...SEND IN THE SWAT TEAM--NOW!
CHANN
8
MOVE IT--RUSH 'EM!
GO, GO GO!
WHAT THE--? NOTHING BUT A TAPE-PLAYER?
SURPRISE, SURPRISE, SUCKERS!
WAIT--UNDER THE TABLE...
LOOKS LIKE... A B--
21

BONEY! STAN! PHIL! PLEASE!

WE PLANNED THIS JOB TO A "T" AND WE'RE READY TO GO, EVERYTHING IN PLACE.

WE GOTTA WAIT UNTIL YOU SEND OUT YOUR STUPID *RIDDLES!*

WELL, WE'RE PULLIN' THIS JOB *TONIGHT* AND IF IT HAS TO BE OVER YOUR DEAD BODY...

BLAM BLAM

BUT DO WE MAKE OUR MOVE? *NO!*

BLAM BOOM

...THEN THAT'S THE WAY IT'S GONNA BE!

BLAM

BLAM

BLAM

BLAM

THAT'S IT! RUN BACK TO ARKHAM! THEY GOT A WARM BED AND A COZY STRAIT-JACKET WAITIN'!

EMERGENCY EXIT

MEBBE WE SHUNNA LET HIM *GO,* BONEY. THE CREEP MIGHT RAT US OUT.

IF YOU THINK HE MIGHT GO TO THE COPS AND TELL HIM FLAT-OUT WHAT WE WAS PLANNIN' THEN YOU DON'T UNDER-STAND THE RIDDLER.

②

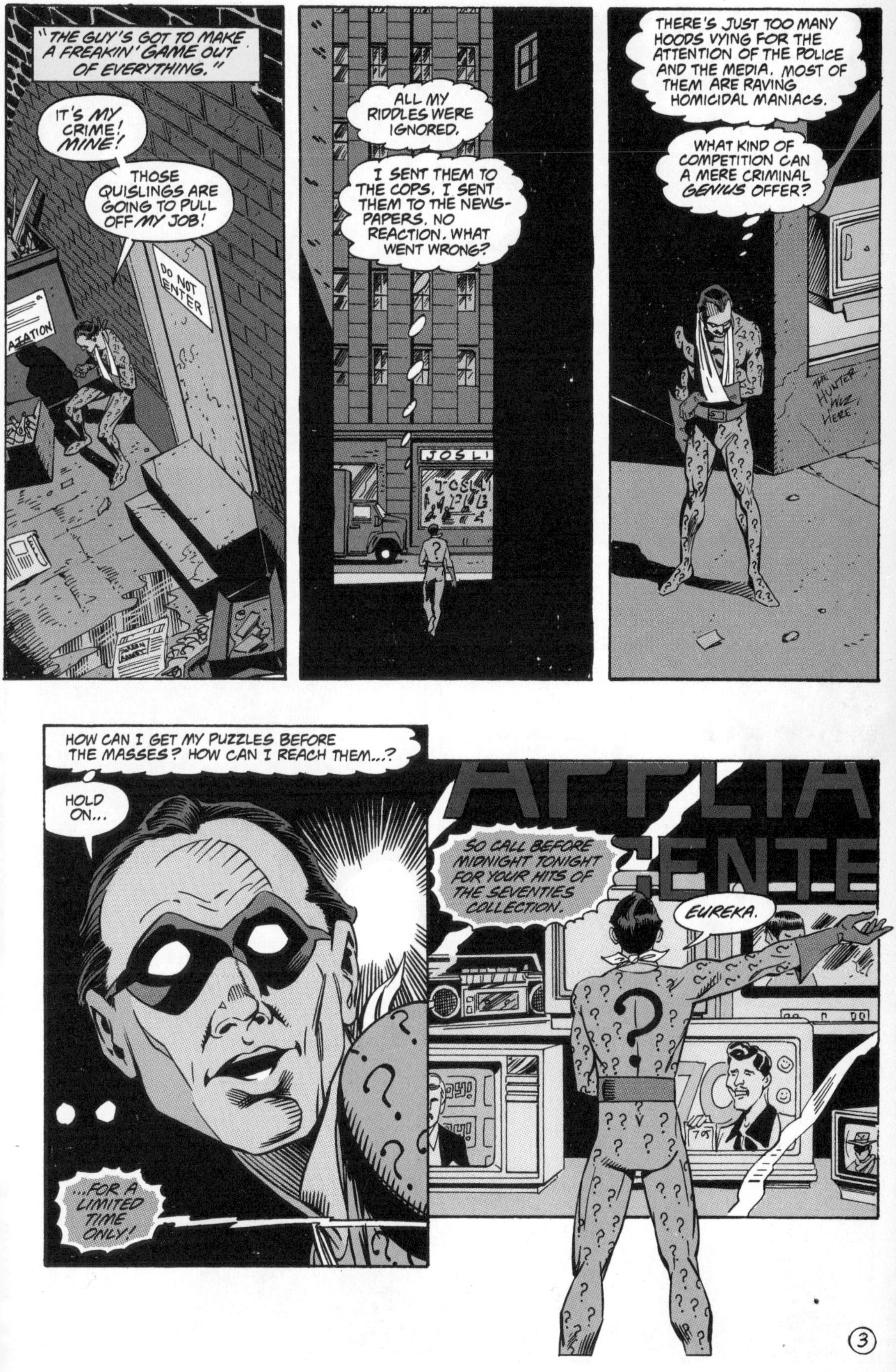
"THE GUY'S GOT TO MAKE A FREAKIN' GAME OUT OF EVERYTHING."
IT'S MY CRIME! MINE!
THOSE QUISLINGS ARE GOING TO PULL OFF MY JOB!
DO NOT ENTER
ALL MY RIDDLES WERE IGNORED.
I SENT THEM TO THE COPS. I SENT THEM TO THE NEWS-PAPERS. NO REACTION. WHAT WENT WRONG?
THERE'S JUST TOO MANY HOODS VYING FOR THE ATTENTION OF THE POLICE AND THE MEDIA. MOST OF THEM ARE RAVING HOMICIDAL MANIACS.
WHAT KIND OF COMPETITION CAN A MERE CRIMINAL GENIUS OFFER?
THE HUNTER WUZ HERE.
HOW CAN I GET MY PUZZLES BEFORE THE MASSES? HOW CAN I REACH THEM...?
HOLD ON...
SO CALL BEFORE MIDNIGHT TONIGHT FOR YOUR HITS OF THE SEVENTIES COLLECTION.
...FOR A LIMITED TIME ONLY!
EUREKA.
3

IS THIS HOW YOU PLAN ON SPENDING YOUR ENTIRE SUMMER VACATION?

THUP THUP THUP THUP

I'M JUST, WORKING OUT, A LITTLE *FRUSTRATION*.

THROPH THUD! WHUD!

...I GET TO WATCH IT ALL ON THE TUBE.

I DID ALL THE FOOTWORK ON THE FIREFLY CASE AND BATMAN'S MAKING ME SIT OUT THE BUST.

DENIED THE OPPOR- TUNITY TO CONFRONT A PSYCHOTIC ARSONIST. I CAN ONLY *IMAGINE* YOUR DISAPPOINTMENT.

SO WHILE HE GOES FOR THE GLORY...

AND WHERE DID YOUR INVESTIGATIONS LEAD YOU?

THE GOTHAM PARK ZOO.

IT WAS LAST ON THE FIREFLY'S LIST.

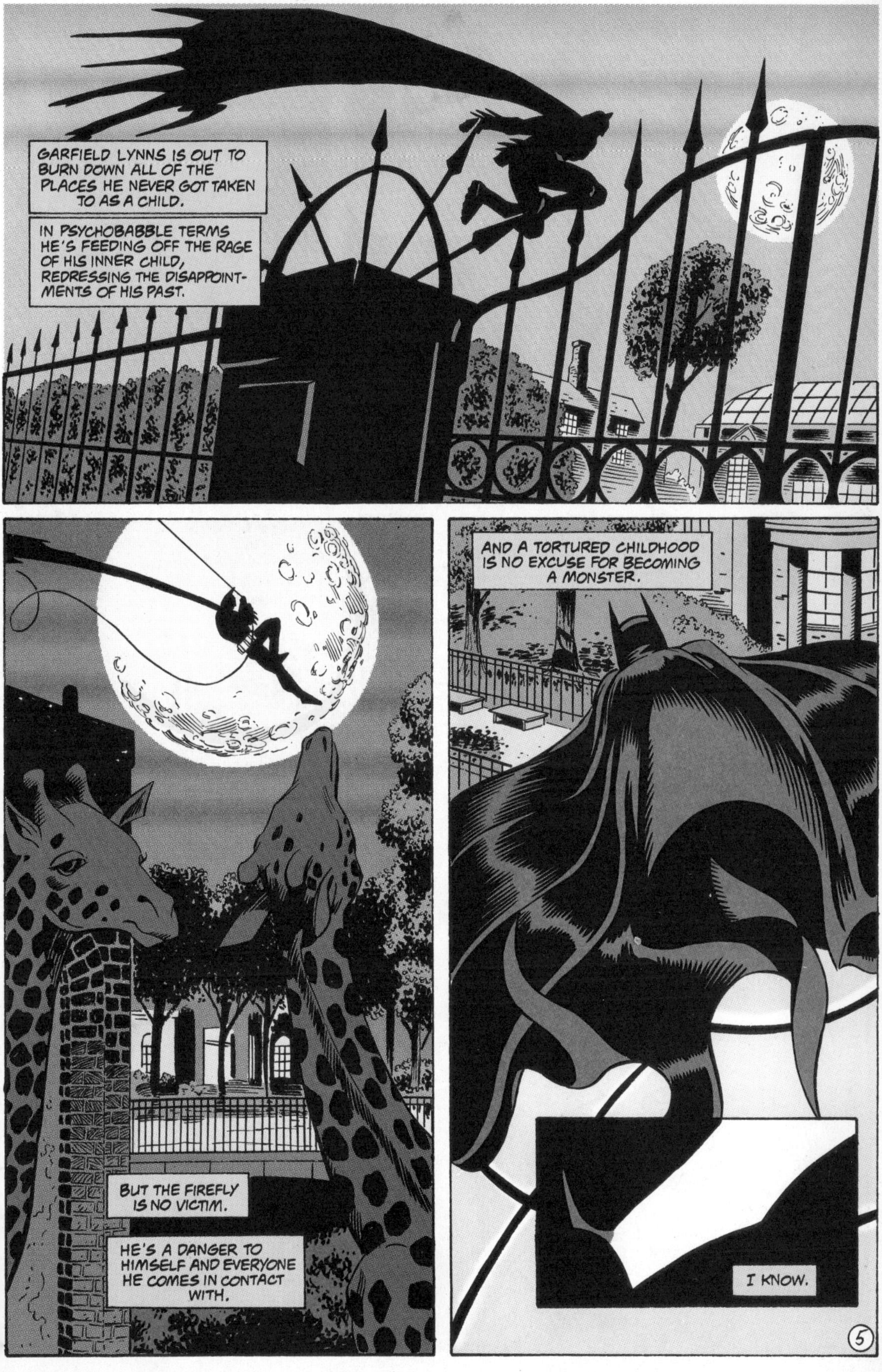
GARFIELD LYNNS IS OUT TO BURN DOWN ALL OF THE PLACES HE NEVER GOT TAKEN TO AS A CHILD.
IN PSYCHOBABBLE TERMS HE'S FEEDING OFF THE RAGE OF HIS INNER CHILD, REDRESSING THE DISAPPOINT-MENTS OF HIS PAST.
BUT THE FIREFLY IS NO VICTIM.
HE'S A DANGER TO HIMSELF AND EVERYONE HE COMES IN CONTACT WITH.
AND A TORTURED CHILDHOOD IS NO EXCUSE FOR BECOMING A MONSTER.
I KNOW.
5

WELL, LET'S GIVE OUR AUDIENCE A CHANCE TO QUESTION DR. FLANDERS.

DO ANY OF YOU HAVE ANYTHING TO ASK OUR GUEST?

ACTUALLY, CASSIE, I HAD A *NUMBER* OF QUESTIONS.

GO AHEAD, SIR. THIS IS AN OPEN FORUM.

WHAT LETTER IS NEVER FOUND IN THE ALPHABET?

WHAT DOES THE BALLPLAYER LIKE TO BE CALLED AT HOME?

I'M NOT SURE I--

OH MY GOD!

WHAT TRAVELS AROUND THE WORLD BUT NEVER LEAVES ITS CORNER?

WHY WAS THE LETTER DAMP?

LET'S GET TO THE *VAN*, ALFRED! THAT SHOW ORIGINATES IN GOTHAM.

BUT...

COME ON, IT AIRS LIVE!

THE FIRST SIGN OF DANGER IS THE ANIMALS.

THEY'RE REACTING TO A THREAT.

THEN THE GLOW OF FIRE.

THEN THAT MADDENING LAUGHTER ON THE SUMMER WIND.

IT RISES EVEN OVER THE HOWL OF THE TERRIFIED ANIMALS.

HA HA HA HOO HA HA!

BEAUTIFUL! BEAUTIFUL!

BY FAR MY BEST EFFORT!

YOU!

NOT AGAIN!

8

188

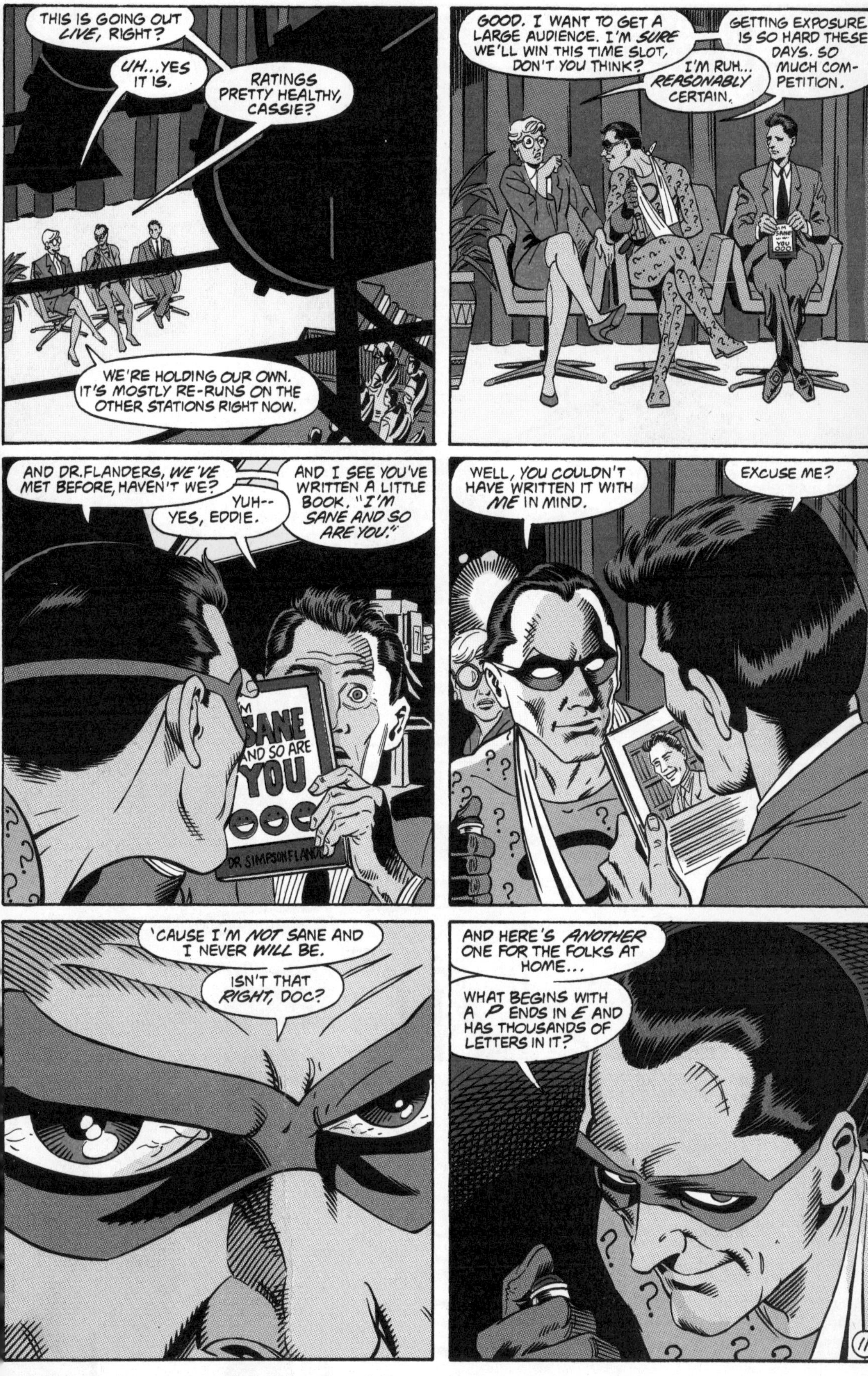
THIS IS GOING OUT LIVE, RIGHT?
UH...YES IT IS.
RATINGS PRETTY HEALTHY, CASSIE?
WE'RE HOLDING OUR OWN. IT'S MOSTLY RE-RUNS ON THE OTHER STATIONS RIGHT NOW.
GOOD. I WANT TO GET A LARGE AUDIENCE. I'M SURE WE'LL WIN THIS TIME SLOT, DON'T YOU THINK?
I'M RUH... REASONABLY CERTAIN.
GETTING EXPOSURE IS SO HARD THESE DAYS. SO MUCH COMPETITION.
AND DR. FLANDERS, WE'VE MET BEFORE, HAVEN'T WE?
YUH-- YES, EDDIE.
AND I SEE YOU'VE WRITTEN A LITTLE BOOK. "I'M SANE AND SO ARE YOU."
I'M SANE AND SO ARE YOU
DR SIMPSON FLANDERS
WELL, YOU COULDN'T HAVE WRITTEN IT WITH ME IN MIND.
EXCUSE ME?
'CAUSE I'M NOT SANE AND I NEVER WILL BE.
ISN'T THAT RIGHT, DOC?
AND HERE'S ANOTHER ONE FOR THE FOLKS AT HOME...
WHAT BEGINS WITH A P ENDS IN E AND HAS THOUSANDS OF LETTERS IN IT?
11

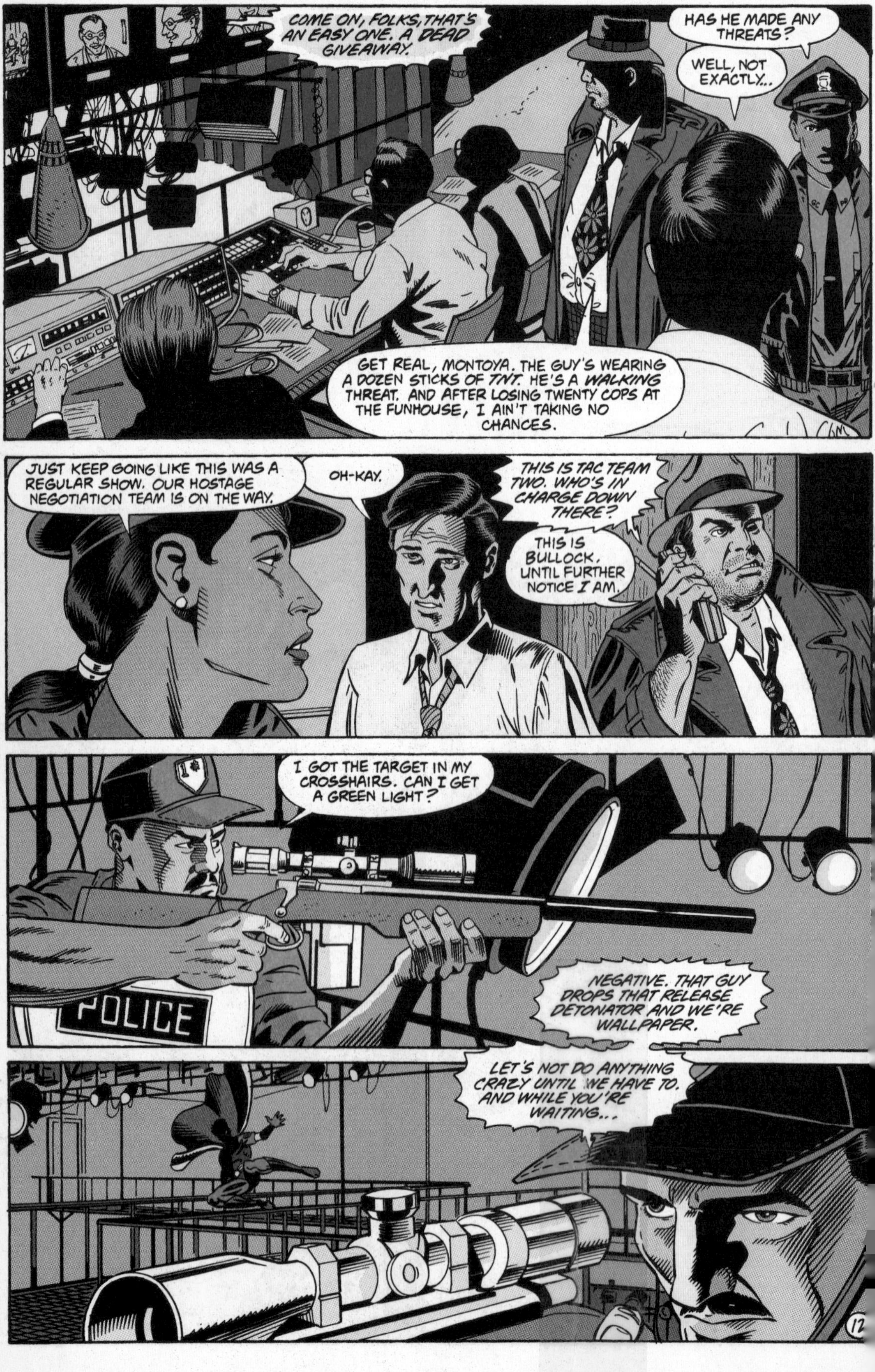
COME ON, FOLKS, THAT'S AN EASY ONE. A DEAD GIVEAWAY.
HAS HE MADE ANY THREATS?
WELL, NOT EXACTLY...
GET REAL, MONTOYA. THE GUY'S WEARING A DOZEN STICKS OF TNT. HE'S A WALKING THREAT. AND AFTER LOSING TWENTY COPS AT THE FUNHOUSE, I AIN'T TAKING NO CHANCES.
JUST KEEP GOING LIKE THIS WAS A REGULAR SHOW. OUR HOSTAGE NEGOTIATION TEAM IS ON THE WAY.
OH-KAY.
THIS IS TAC TEAM TWO. WHO'S IN CHARGE DOWN THERE?
THIS IS BULLOCK. UNTIL FURTHER NOTICE I AM.
I GOT THE TARGET IN MY CROSSHAIRS. CAN I GET A GREEN LIGHT?
POLICE
NEGATIVE. THAT GUY DROPS THAT RELEASE DETONATOR AND WE'RE WALLPAPER.
LET'S NOT DO ANYTHING CRAZY UNTIL WE HAVE TO. AND WHILE YOU'RE WAITING...
12

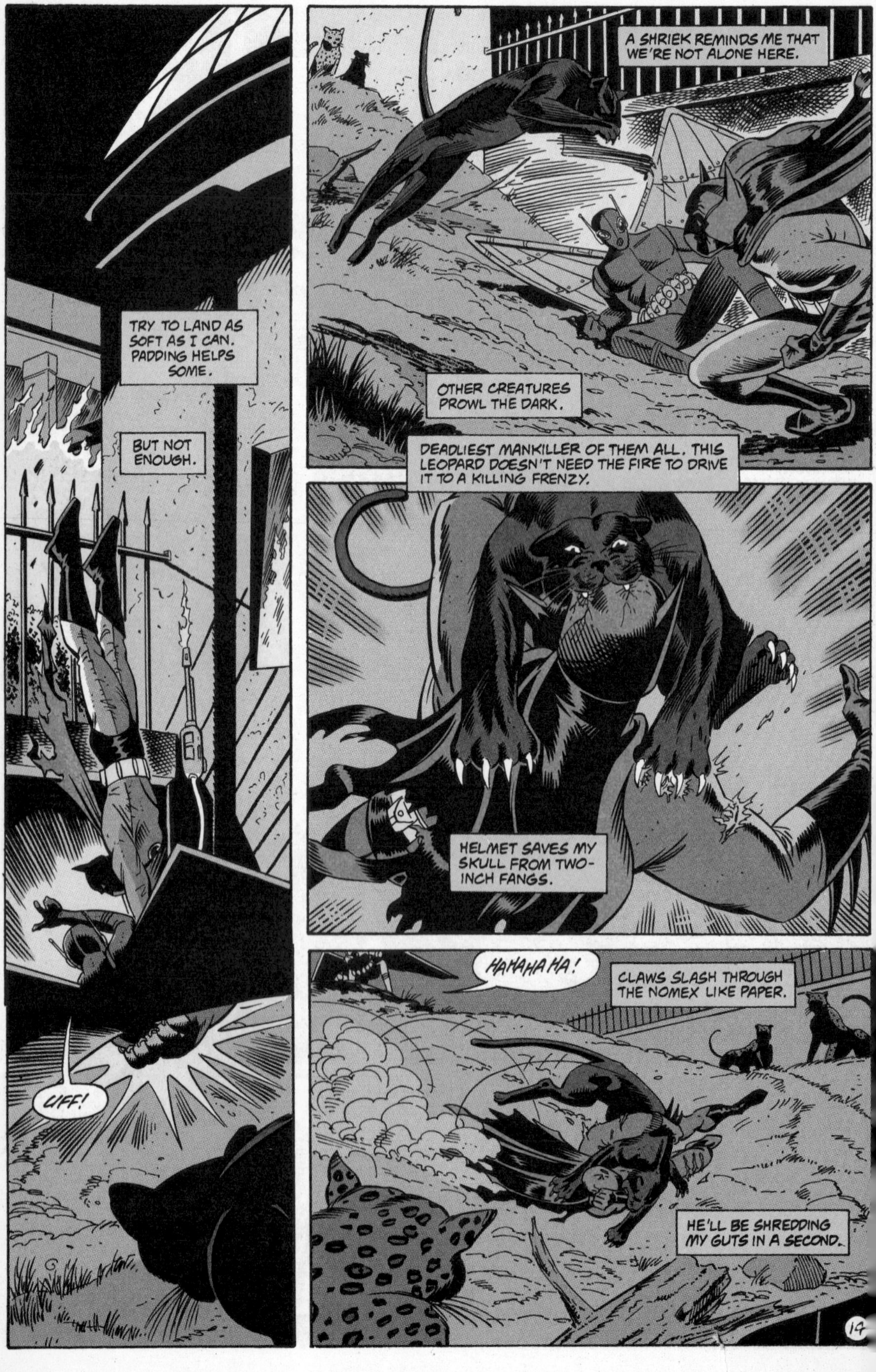

TRY TO LAND AS SOFT AS I CAN. PADDING HELPS SOME.
BUT NOT ENOUGH.
UFF!
A SHRIEK REMINDS ME THAT WE'RE NOT ALONE HERE.
OTHER CREATURES PROWL THE DARK.
DEADLIEST MANKILLER OF THEM ALL. THIS LEOPARD DOESN'T NEED THE FIRE TO DRIVE IT TO A KILLING FRENZY.
HELMET SAVES MY SKULL FROM TWO-INCH FANGS.
HAHAHAHA!
CLAWS SLASH THROUGH THE NOMEX LIKE PAPER.
HE'LL BE SHREDDING MY GUTS IN A SECOND.
17

♪ All the animals in the zoo are jumping up and down on you! ♪

I'D MUCH RATHER YOU'D *BURNED*, BATMAN. BUT A FLYING RODENT BEING EATEN BY A CAT IS SO MUCH MORE...

...POETIC.

HAVE TO BREAK AWAY BEFORE THE OTHERS JOIN IN.

MEANT THE FIRE RETARDANT OPTION FOR FIREFLY.

RUN FOR THE FENCE BEFORE THEY RECOVER.

KITTY DOESN'T LIKE HALON.

IT'S A MILLION MILES AWAY.

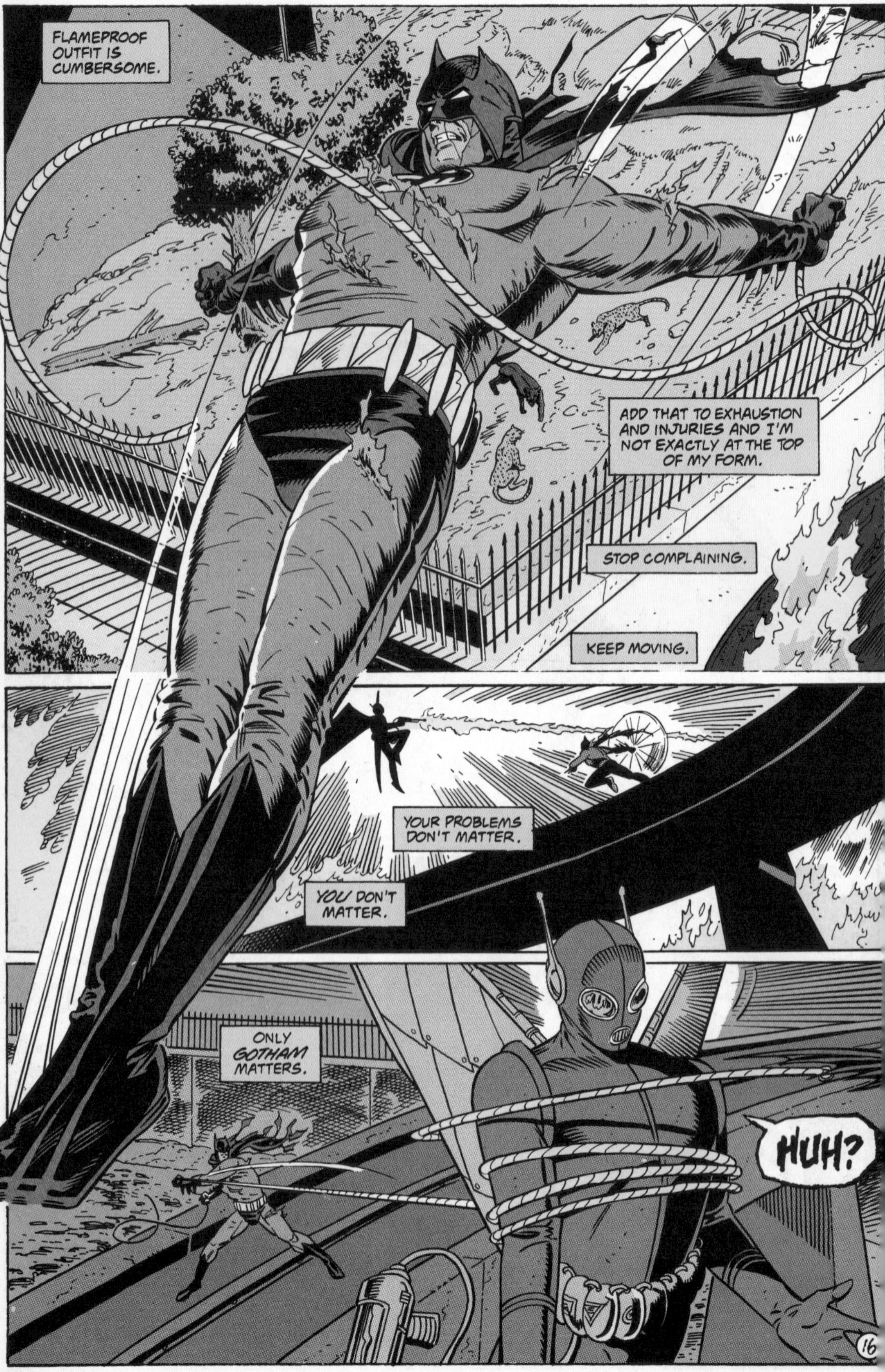
FLAMEPROOF OUTFIT IS CUMBERSOME.
ADD THAT TO EXHAUSTION AND INJURIES AND I'M NOT EXACTLY AT THE TOP OF MY FORM.
STOP COMPLAINING.
KEEP MOVING.
YOUR PROBLEMS DON'T MATTER.
YOU DON'T MATTER.
ONLY GOTHAM MATTERS.
HUH?
16

YOU PUNK KID, HE COULD HAVE BLOWN THIS WHOLE BUILDING INTO NEXT *YEAR!*

BATMAN AND I HAVE DEALT WITH HIM BEFORE. I JUST THOUGHT...

YOU *DIDN'T* THINK!

AND IF I KNOW THE BAT-FREAK LIKE I *THINK* I DO, HE'LL HAVE A FEW WORDS ON THE SUBJECT HIMSELF.

WE HAD THIS PSYCHO COVERED.

BUT...

YO, HARV...

THE BOMB'S A FAKE. JUST WOODEN CHAIR RAILS WRAPPED IN ELECTRIC TAPE.

HEY, WATCH THE ARM, OKAY?

THAT DON'T CHANGE A THING, KID. THAT WAS STILL--

... A BONEHEAD PLAY.

MAN, I *HATE* THAT.

MY GOD, HOW AM I GOING TO FOLLOW *THIS* SHOW? DO *YOU* HAVE ANY IDEAS, DR. FLANDERS?

YES.

A CHANGE IN CAREERS.

SO WHAT WAS WITH ALL THE CRAZY RIDDLES? WHERE'S THE SCORE YOU'RE PULLING DOWN?

FIGURE IT OUT FOR YOURSELF.

⑲

199

OR MAYBE YOU'RE JUST *REAL* SERIOUS STAMP COLLECTORS.

WHO *ARE* YOU? BATLADY?

I DON'T *LIKE* IT WHEN THEY ASK WHO I AM!

BATMAN'S NOT THE *ONLY* ROOFRAT IN TOWN.

UNGH!

BET NOBODY EVER ASKS WHO *HE* IS.

HE'D GET TIRED OF *THAT* REAL QUICK.

NAW...

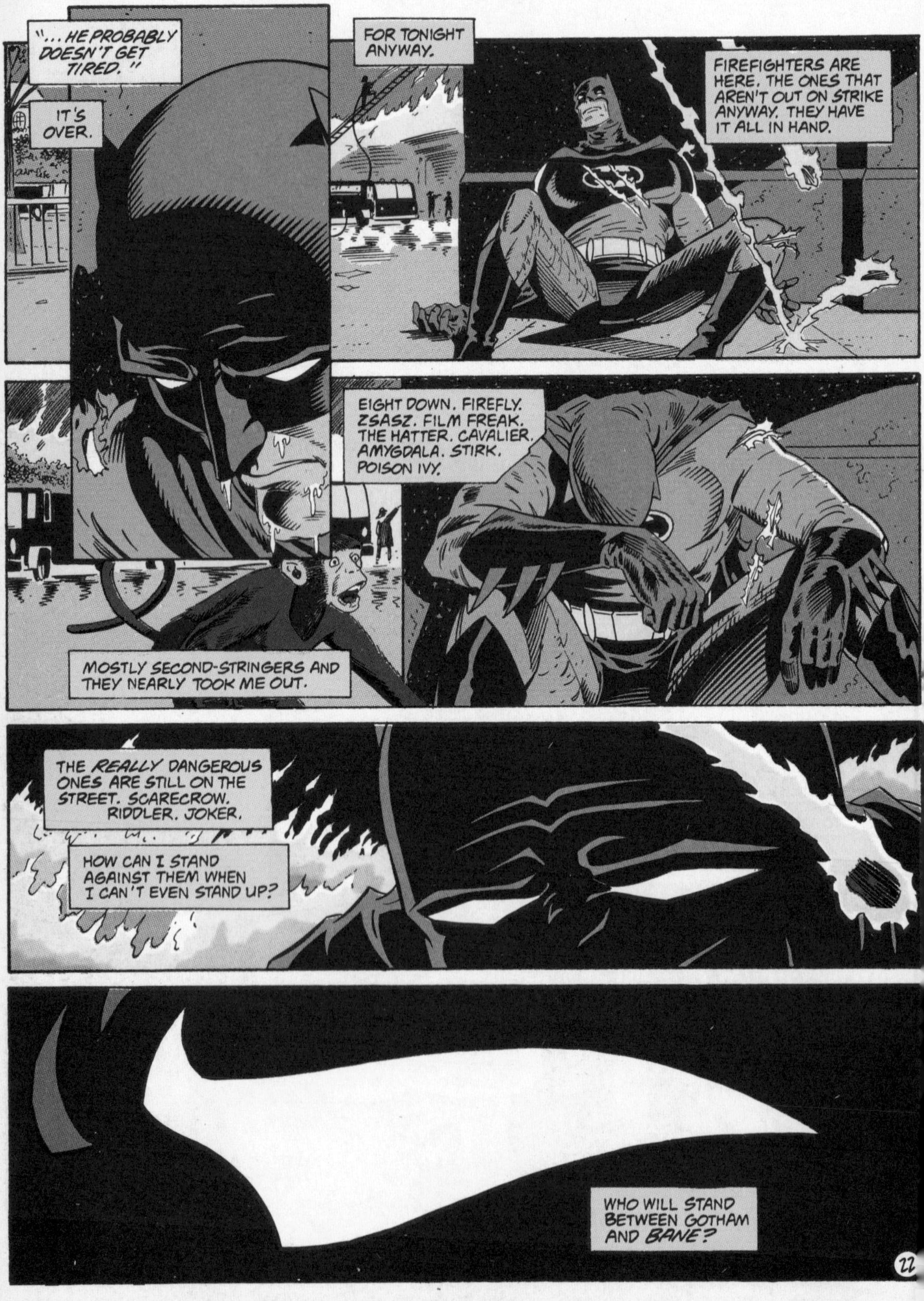
"... HE PROBABLY DOESN'T GET TIRED."
IT'S OVER.
FOR TONIGHT ANYWAY.
FIREFIGHTERS ARE HERE. THE ONES THAT AREN'T OUT ON STRIKE ANYWAY. THEY HAVE IT ALL IN HAND.
EIGHT DOWN. FIREFLY. ZSASZ. FILM FREAK. THE HATTER. CAVALIER. AMYGDALA. STIRK. POISON IVY.
MOSTLY SECOND-STRINGERS AND THEY NEARLY TOOK ME OUT.
THE REALLY DANGEROUS ONES ARE STILL ON THE STREET. SCARECROW. RIDDLER. JOKER.
HOW CAN I STAND AGAINST THEM WHEN I CAN'T EVEN STAND UP?
WHO WILL STAND BETWEEN GOTHAM AND BANE?
22

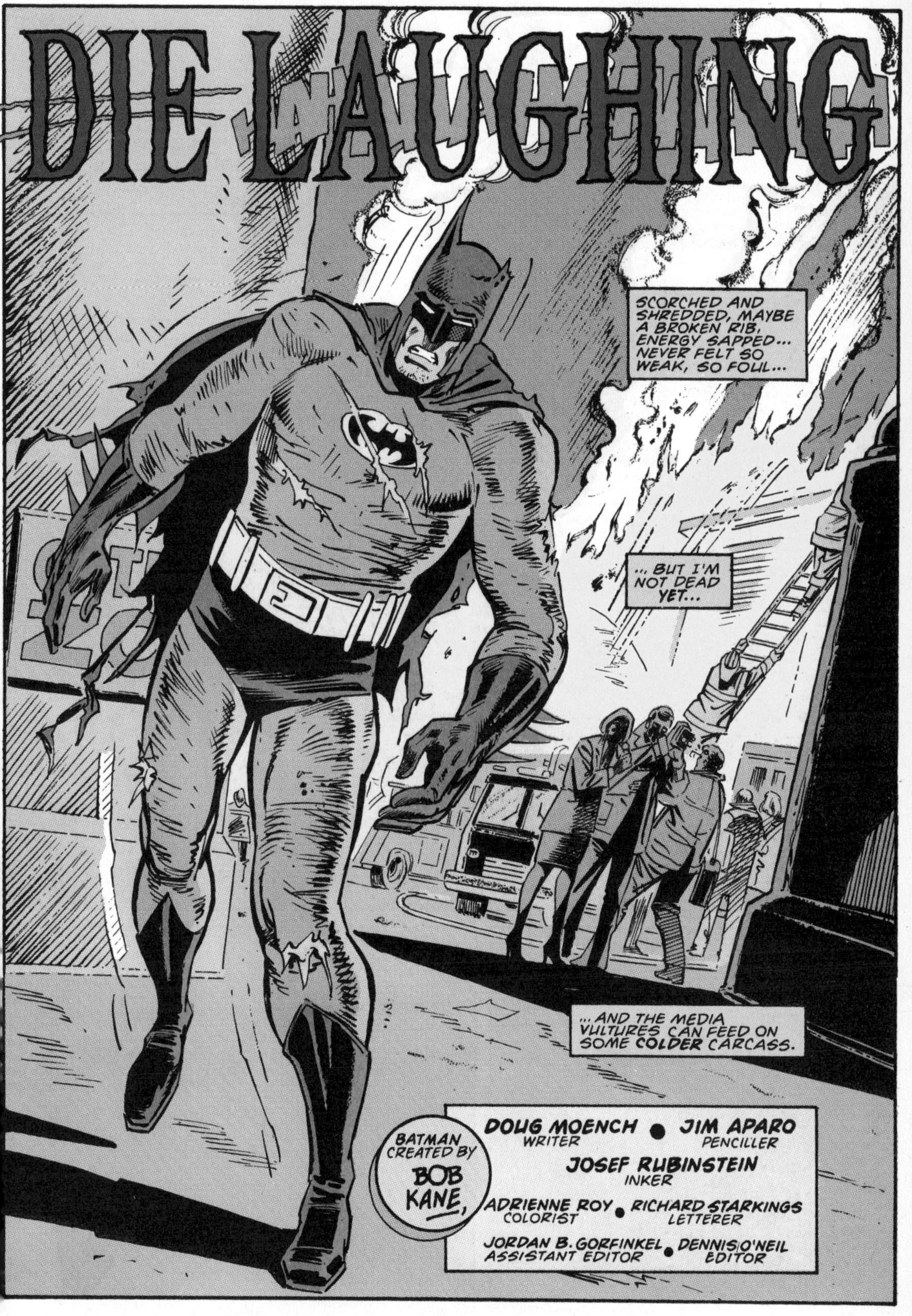
DIE LAUGHING
SCORCHED AND SHREDDED, MAYBE A BROKEN RIB. ENERGY SAPPED... NEVER FELT SO WEAK, SO FOUL...
... BUT I'M NOT DEAD YET...
... AND THE MEDIA VULTURES CAN FEED ON SOME COLDER CARCASS.
BATMAN CREATED BY BOB KANE,
DOUG MOENCH WRITER • JIM APARO PENCILLER
JOSEF RUBINSTEIN INKER
ADRIENNE ROY COLORIST • RICHARD STARKINGS LETTERER
JORDAN B. GORFINKEL ASSISTANT EDITOR • DENNIS O'NEIL EDITOR

BUT THE *CITY*, YOU STRAW-STUFFED *SIMPLETON*, IS *HIS* -- AND ONCE WE TAKE HIM OUT, GOTHAM BECOMES *OURS!*

BESIDES, WE'VE *GOT* TO DO IT, FOR THE *NOVELTY ALONE* -- I'VE *NEVER KILLED BATS* BEFORE...

GOT HIS SNOT-SNIVELING *PARTNER* ONCE...

... ALTHOUGH HE SEEMS TO BE *BACK* SOMEHOW...

SNAP OUT OF IT, YOU *CLOWN!*

I DECIDE HOW WE USE THIS *FEAR-GAS*, AND I SAID *NO WAY!*

OH...

YOU DID, DID YOU?

BLSH

BAD MOVE...

... WHEN I COULD *SQUISH* THIS *ANY TIME* I WANT.

YOUR *FEAR-GAS?!*

I'M LOOKING FORWARD TO IT!

HA HA HA HA!

3

NEW SUIT BUT NO SLEEP.

NO TIME -- KROL'S BEEN ABDUCTED BY THE JOKER -- BY JASON'S KILLER.

VRACOW

GOT TO LOOK FOR CLUES...

...IN THE MAYOR'S MANSION.

YOU... YOU WANT ME TO J-JUST GO IN THERE? I MEAN, AFTER WHAT HAPPENED AT THE AMUSEMENT PARK?

DO I DUST FOR FINGERPRINTS BEFORE OR AFTER I GET BLOWN TO RED MIST?

MONTOYA, YOU CAN STAND HERE AN' BASK IN THE GLOW O' THESE HEARTS O' FIRE --

-- OR YOU CAN COVER ME.

NO TIME TO WAIT ON THE BOMB SQUAD.

I'M GOIN' IN.

4

206

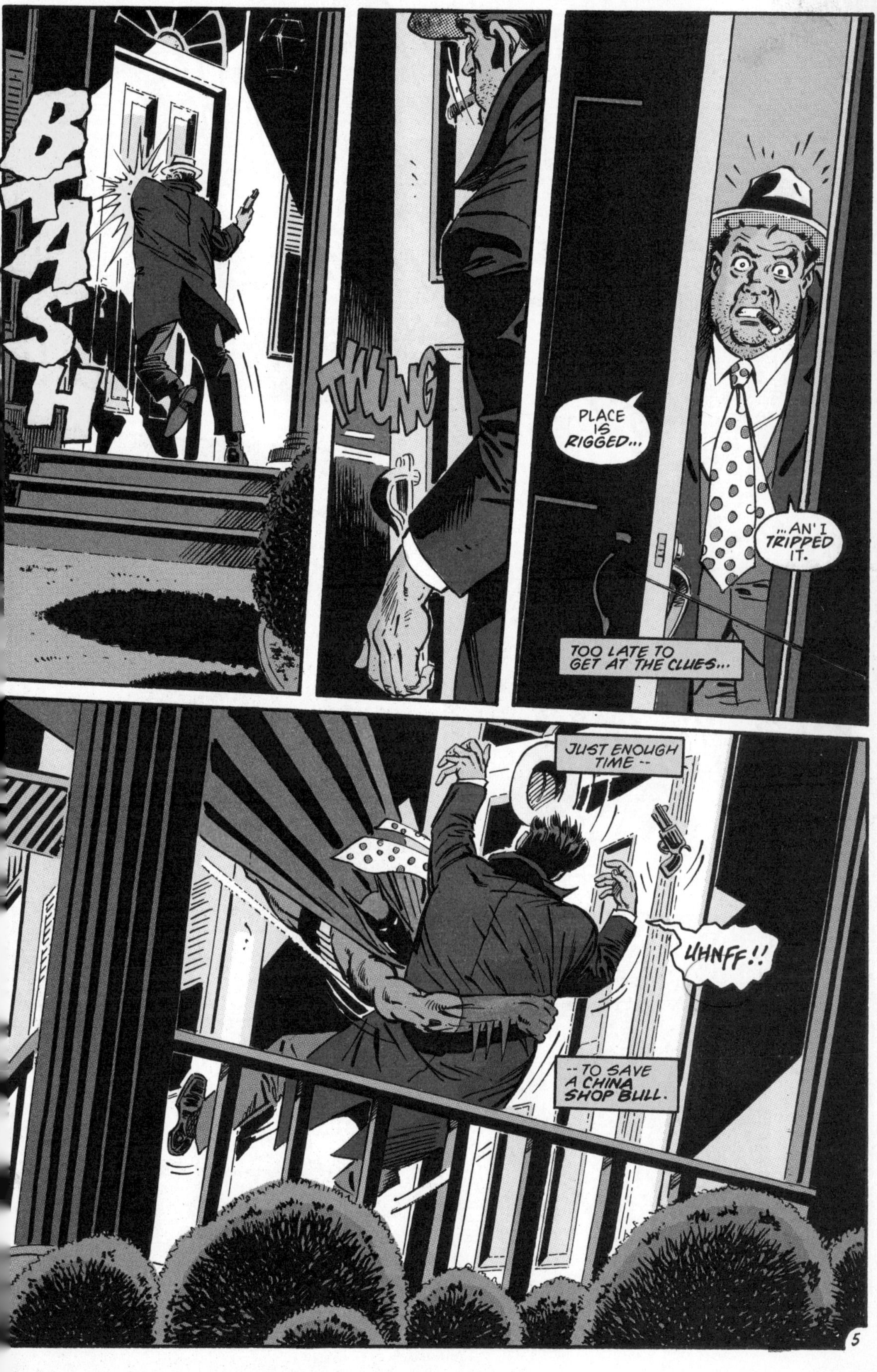
BASH
THUNG
PLACE IS RIGGED...
...AN' I TRIPPED IT.
TOO LATE TO GET AT THE CLUES...
JUST ENOUGH TIME --
UHNFF!!
-- TO SAVE A CHINA SHOP BULL.
5

TWO-FIFTY.

SETTLE FOR ONE?

WHAT THE --

HA HA HA HA HA HA HA HA

YECH

SPLOTCH

BAOOM

GOT

TOLL

7

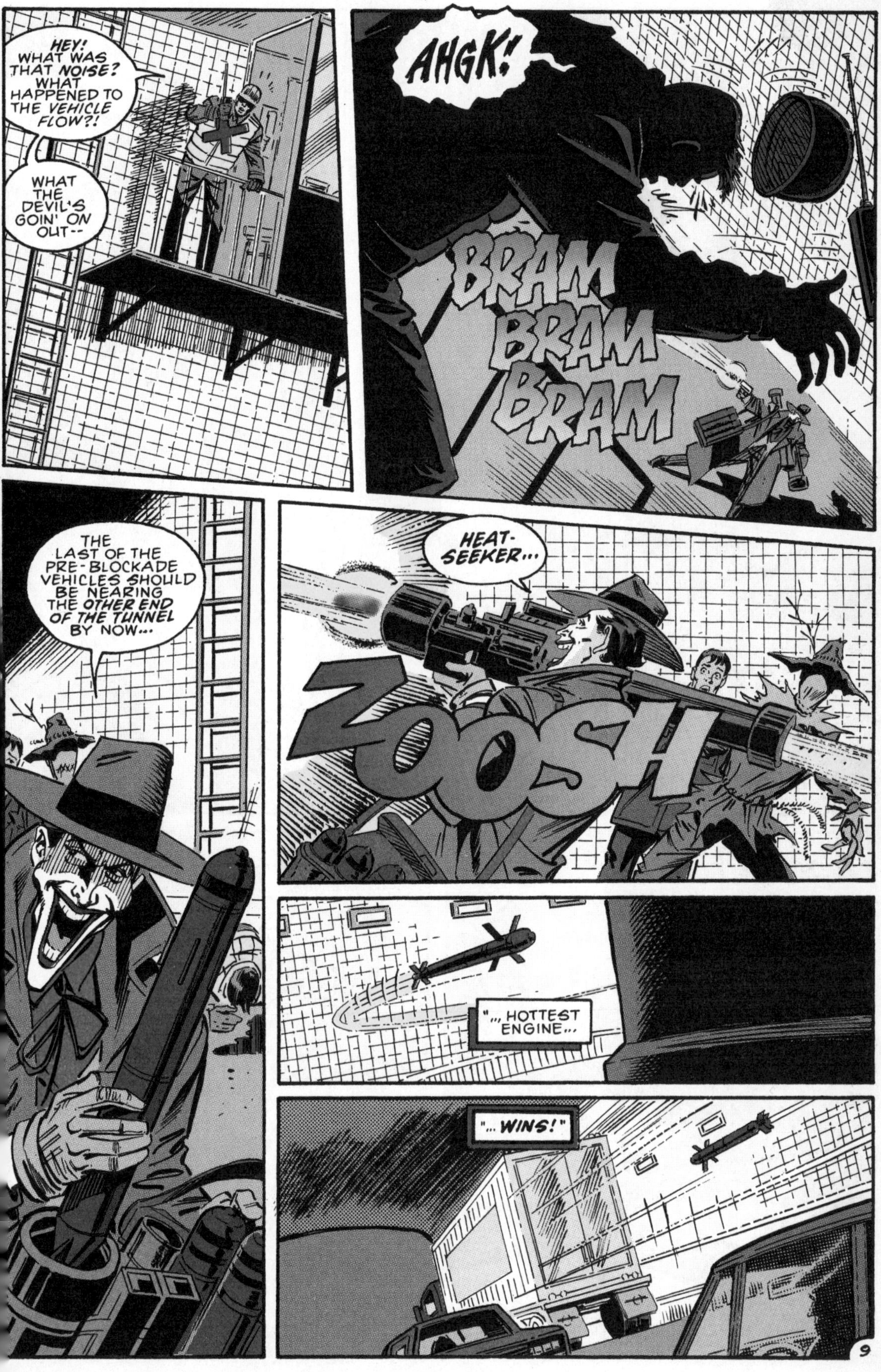
HEY! WHAT WAS THAT NOISE? WHAT HAPPENED TO THE VEHICLE FLOW?!
WHAT THE DEVIL'S GOIN' ON OUT--
AHGK!
BRAM BRAM BRAM
THE LAST OF THE PRE-BLOCKADE VEHICLES SHOULD BE NEARING THE OTHER END OF THE TUNNEL BY NOW...
HEAT-SEEKER...
ZOOSH
"...HOTTEST ENGINE..."
"...WINS!"
9

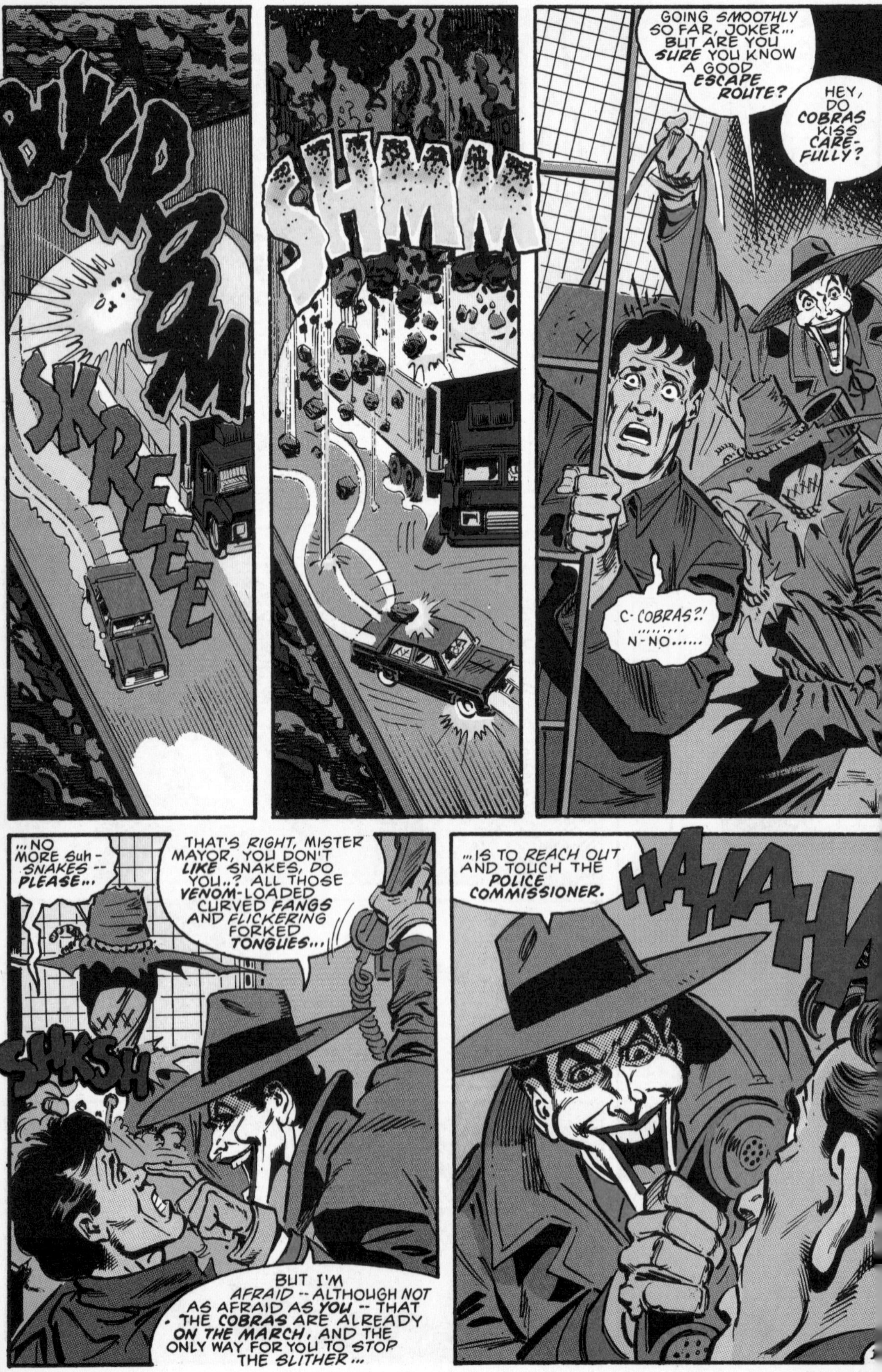
BUKROOM
SKREEEE
SHMM
GOING SMOOTHLY SO FAR, JOKER... BUT ARE YOU SURE YOU KNOW A GOOD ESCAPE ROUTE?
HEY, DO COBRAS KISS CARE-FULLY?
C-COBRAS?! N-NO......
...NO MORE Suh-SNAKES--PLEASE...
THAT'S RIGHT, MISTER MAYOR, YOU DON'T LIKE SNAKES, DO YOU..? ALL THOSE VENOM-LOADED CURVED FANGS AND FLICKERING FORKED TONGUES...
SHKSH
BUT I'M AFRAID -- ALTHOUGH NOT AS AFRAID AS YOU -- THAT THE COBRAS ARE ALREADY ON THE MARCH, AND THE ONLY WAY FOR YOU TO STOP THE SLITHER...
...IS TO REACH OUT AND TOUCH THE POLICE COMMISSIONER.
HAHAHA

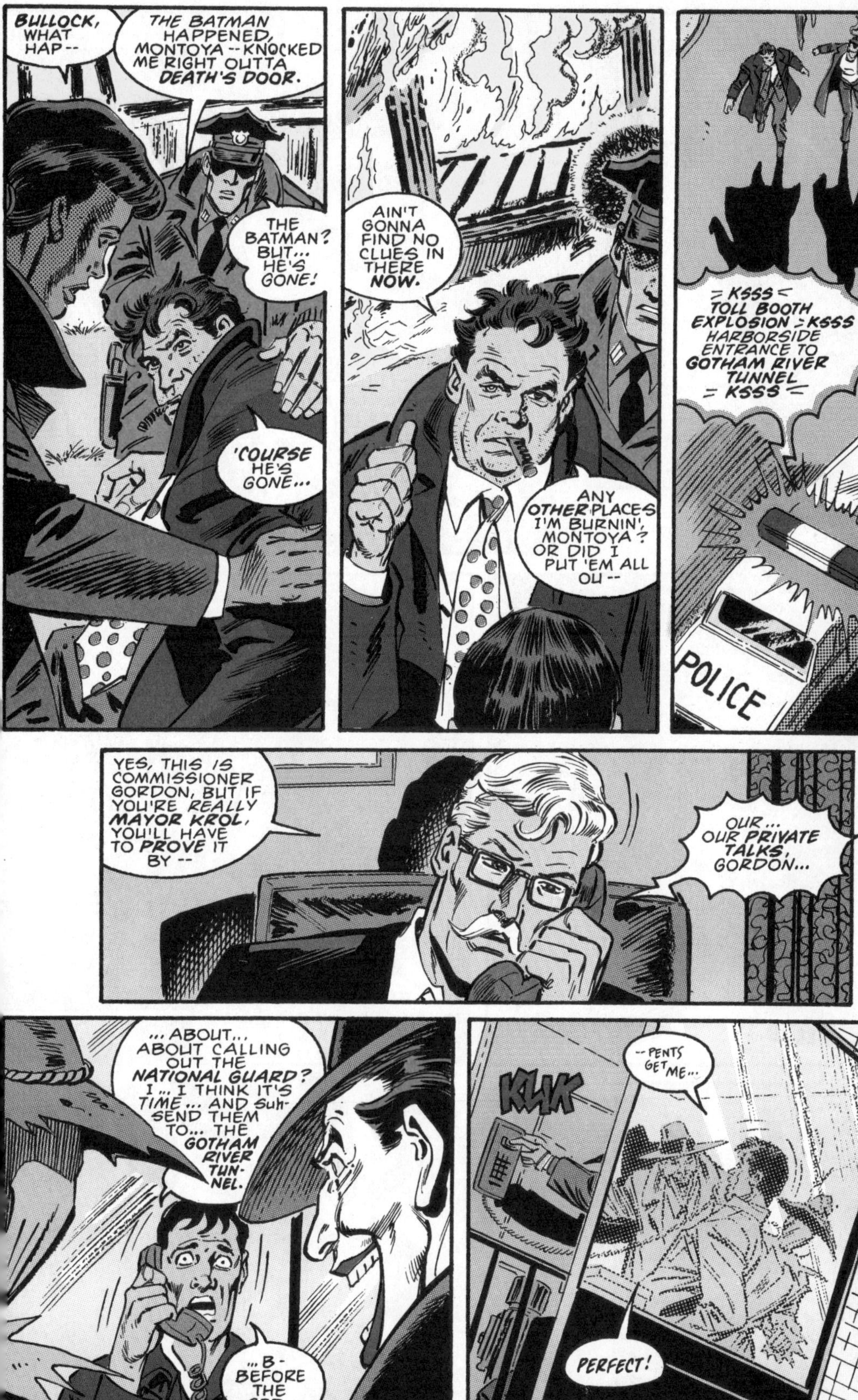
BULLOCK, WHAT HAP--
THE BATMAN HAPPENED, MONTOYA--KNOCKED ME RIGHT OUTTA DEATH'S DOOR.
THE BATMAN? BUT... HE'S GONE!
'COURSE HE'S GONE...
AIN'T GONNA FIND NO CLUES IN THERE NOW.
ANY OTHER PLACES I'M BURNIN', MONTOYA? OR DID I PUT 'EM ALL OU--
=KSSS= TOLL BOOTH EXPLOSION =KSSS= HARBORSIDE ENTRANCE TO GOTHAM RIVER TUNNEL =KSSS=
POLICE
POLICE
YES, THIS IS COMMISSIONER GORDON, BUT IF YOU'RE REALLY MAYOR KROL, YOU'LL HAVE TO PROVE IT BY --
OUR... OUR PRIVATE TALKS, GORDON...
...ABOUT... ABOUT CALLING OUT THE NATIONAL GUARD? I... I THINK IT'S TIME... AND SUH-SEND THEM TO... THE GOTHAM RIVER TUN-NEL.
...B-BEFORE THE SER--
--PENTS GET ME...
KLIK
PERFECT!
11

DID WE GET THE TRACE?!

CLAK

NO WAY THE NATIONAL GUARD -- OR ANYONE ELSE -- WILL BEAT BATS TO THE SCENE!

HA HA HA HA

SKSH

=SKSS= THIS IS GORDON -- EMERGENCY OVERRIDE =SKSS= WE'VE JUST TRACED A PHONE CALL FROM MAYOR KROL AT A SERVICE BOOTH INSIDE GOTHAM RIVER TUNNEL =SKSS=

ALL UNITS CONVERGE ON THE TUNNEL -- BOTH ENDS -- BAYSIDE AND CENTER CITY =SKSS=

THIS'S BULLOCK, COMMISH -- HALF THE UNITS ARE ALREADY ON THEIR WAY -- RESPONDIN' TO THE EXPLOSIONS...

=SKSS= WE'LL MEET YA THERE... =SKSS=

SKREEEOW

BANE -- IT'S BEEN BANE FROM THE BEGINNING -- BUT HE'S USING THE JOKER AGAIN...

214

--TRAFFIC NOW BACKED UP FOR *SIX MILES* ON THE BAY SIDE OF THE TUNNEL, AS POLICE TRY TO DETERMINE THE *CAUSE* OF THE MULTIPLE EXPLOSIONS...

NOT *BAD*, EH, BANE?

I ADMIT, BIRD, THAT THE JOKER AND THE SCARE-CROW *DO* COMBINE WELL FOR *CHAOS.*

WITH MORE *DISCIPLINE,* THEY COULD TAKE THE *CITY.*

BUT YOU STILL FIGURE THE BATMAN WILL *STOP* THEM?

HE'D BETTER -- BECAUSE ONCE HE GETS THROUGH *THAT* TUNNEL...

... HE RUNS *OUR* GAUNT-LET.

SO WHADDA WE *DO,* COMMISH? WE CAN'T JUST *RUSH* IN THERE --

-- NOT AFTER LOSIN' A WHOLE *TACTICAL TEAM* IN THAT *FUN-HOUSE...*

I'M *AWARE* OF THAT, SERGEANT BULLOCK, BUT IF MAYOR KROL REALLY *IS* IN THE TUNNEL --

I'LL FIND HIM

13

AND I'LL BRING HIM *OUT.*

YOU *REALIZE* IT'S *PROBABLY* JUST ANOTHER *TRAP...*

A *TRAP,* GORDON, THAT COULD *END* THE MAYOR'S *LIFE!*

BHK

BUT--

JUST *HOLD TIGHT,* GORDON.

I'VE BEEN IN *TRAPS BEFORE.*

--FRESH *RUMORS* OF THE BATMAN'S *PRESENCE* ON THE SCENE...

AND I'M *STUCK HERE* IN THE *NOWHERE* CAVE...

EASY, TIMOTHY...

AT LEAST YOU STOPPED *THE RIDDLER.*

YEAH, AND WHEN BAT-MAN FINDS OUT *HOW,* I'VE *REALLY* HAD IT.

Nmm, THERE *IS* THAT, ISN'T THERE?

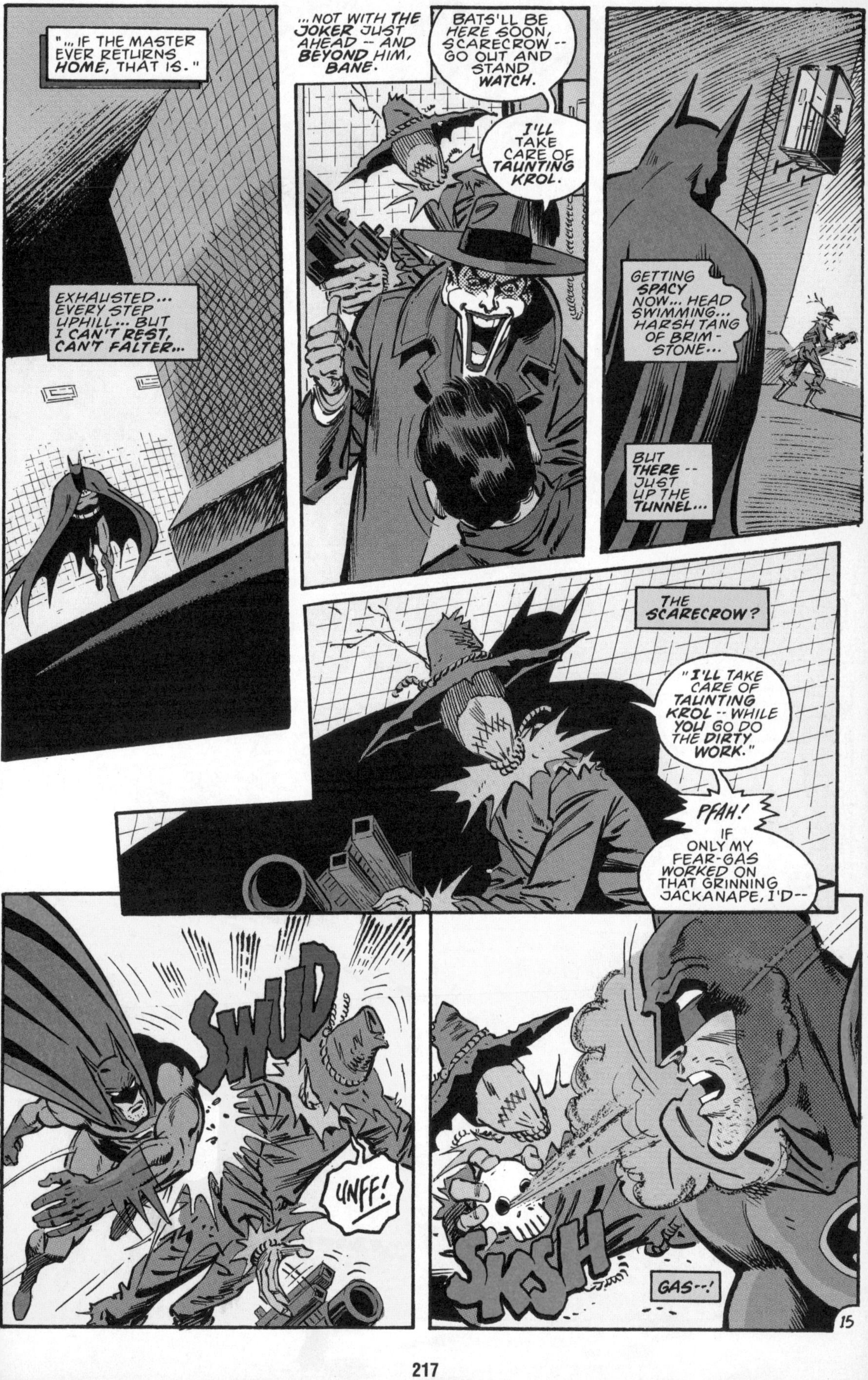
"... IF THE MASTER EVER RETURNS HOME, THAT IS."
EXHAUSTED... EVERY STEP UPHILL... BUT I CAN'T REST, CAN'T FALTER...
...NOT WITH THE JOKER JUST AHEAD -- AND BEYOND HIM, BANE.
BATS'LL BE HERE SOON, SCARECROW -- GO OUT AND STAND WATCH.
I'LL TAKE CARE OF TAUNTING KROL.
GETTING SPACY NOW... HEAD SWIMMING... HARSH TANG OF BRIM-STONE...
BUT THERE -- JUST UP THE TUNNEL...
THE SCARECROW?
"I'LL TAKE CARE OF TAUNTING KROL -- WHILE YOU GO DO THE DIRTY WORK."
PFAH! IF ONLY MY FEAR-GAS WORKED ON THAT GRINNING JACKANAPE, I'D--
SWUD
UNFF!
SKSH
GAS--!
15

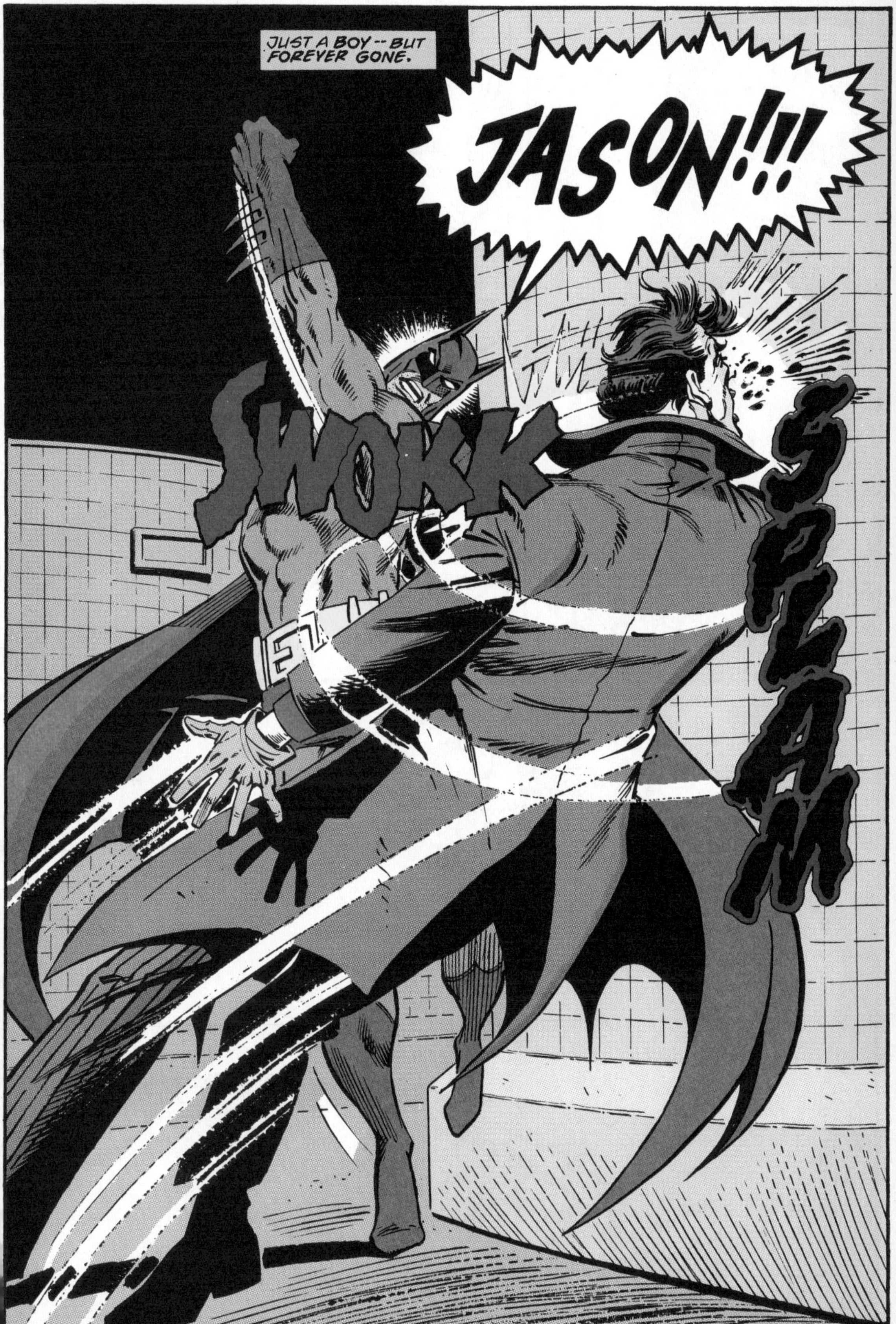
JUST A BOY -- BUT FOREVER GONE.
JASON!!!
SWOKK
SPPLAM
19

G-GAS MADE HIM SEE... HIS GREATEST FEAR... BUT ONLY MADE HIM... MAD...

M-MISSILE... LAUNCHER...

USE IT, SCARE-CROW...

B-BLAST HIM TO GUANO.

NOOSH

KROOM

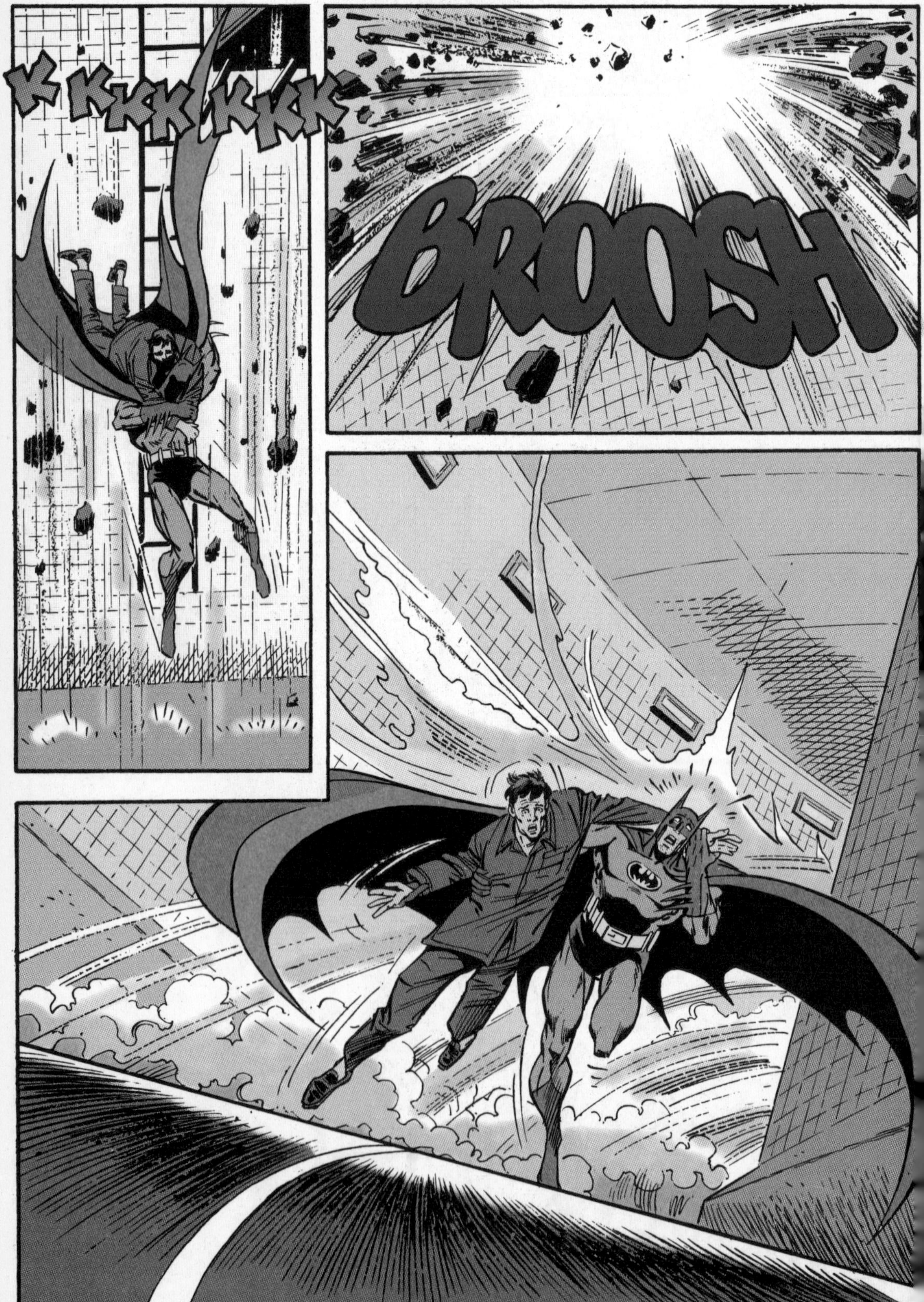
K KKK KKK
BROOSH

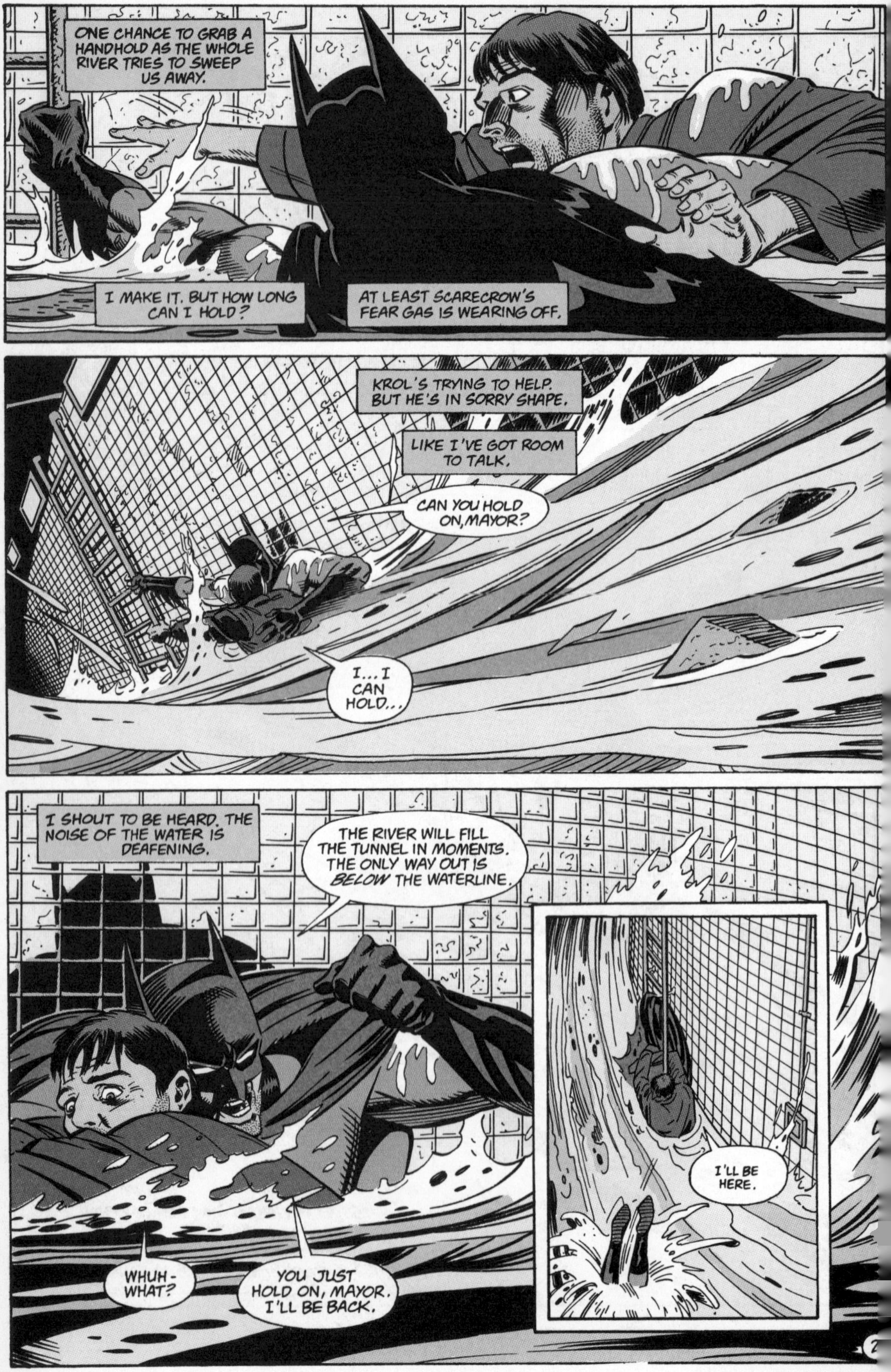
ONE CHANCE TO GRAB A HANDHOLD AS THE WHOLE RIVER TRIES TO SWEEP US AWAY.
I MAKE IT. BUT HOW LONG CAN I HOLD?
AT LEAST SCARECROW'S FEAR GAS IS WEARING OFF.
KROL'S TRYING TO HELP. BUT HE'S IN SORRY SHAPE.
LIKE I'VE GOT ROOM TO TALK.
CAN YOU HOLD ON, MAYOR?
I... I CAN HOLD...
I SHOUT TO BE HEARD. THE NOISE OF THE WATER IS DEAFENING.
THE RIVER WILL FILL THE TUNNEL IN MOMENTS. THE ONLY WAY OUT IS *BELOW* THE WATERLINE.
WHUH-WHAT?
YOU JUST HOLD ON, MAYOR. I'LL BE BACK.
I'LL BE HERE.

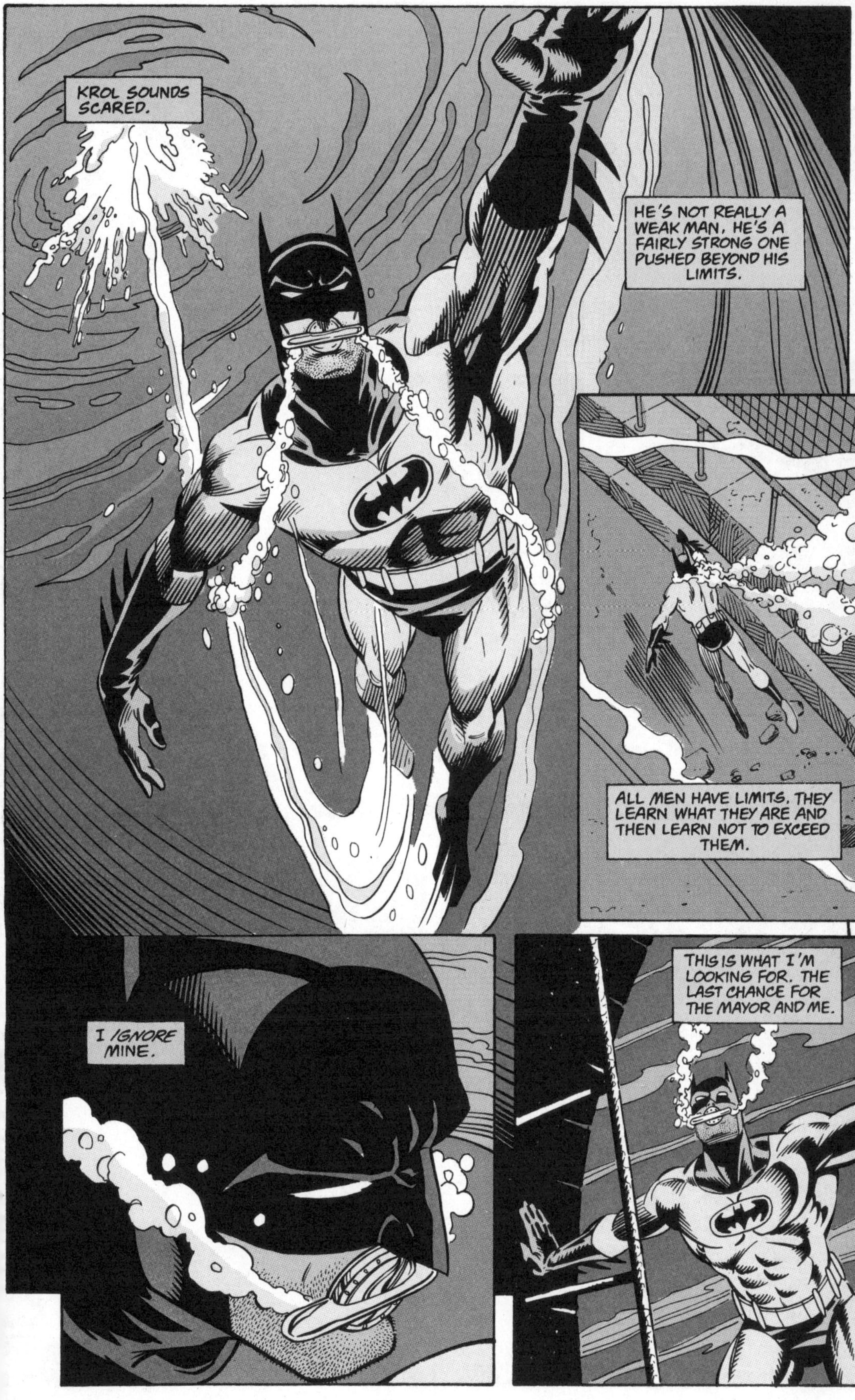
KROL SOUNDS SCARED.
HE'S NOT REALLY A WEAK MAN, HE'S A FAIRLY STRONG ONE PUSHED BEYOND HIS LIMITS.
ALL MEN HAVE LIMITS. THEY LEARN WHAT THEY ARE AND THEN LEARN NOT TO EXCEED THEM.
I IGNORE MINE.
THIS IS WHAT I'M LOOKING FOR. THE LAST CHANCE FOR THE MAYOR AND ME.
3

WE HAVE TO SWIM DOWN TO THE TUNNEL WALKWAY. IT'S ABOUT THIRTY FEET BELOW US.

CAN YOU DO IT?

I DON'T KNOW. I'M SO TIRED. IT'S ALL I CAN DO TO HANG ON TO...

I DIDN'T THINK SO. A SHOT OF VER-SED RENDERS HIM UNCONSCIOUS.

THHHH...

THANK GOD!

THIS WAY HE CAN'T PANIC. THE CAPE WILL HOLD A FEW MINUTES OF AIR AROUND HIM.

IF I FAIL THEN HE'LL JUST NEVER WAKE UP.

REBREATHER'S EXHAUSTED. DOWN TO THE FOUR MINUTES OF AIR I CAN HOLD IN MY LUNGS.

4

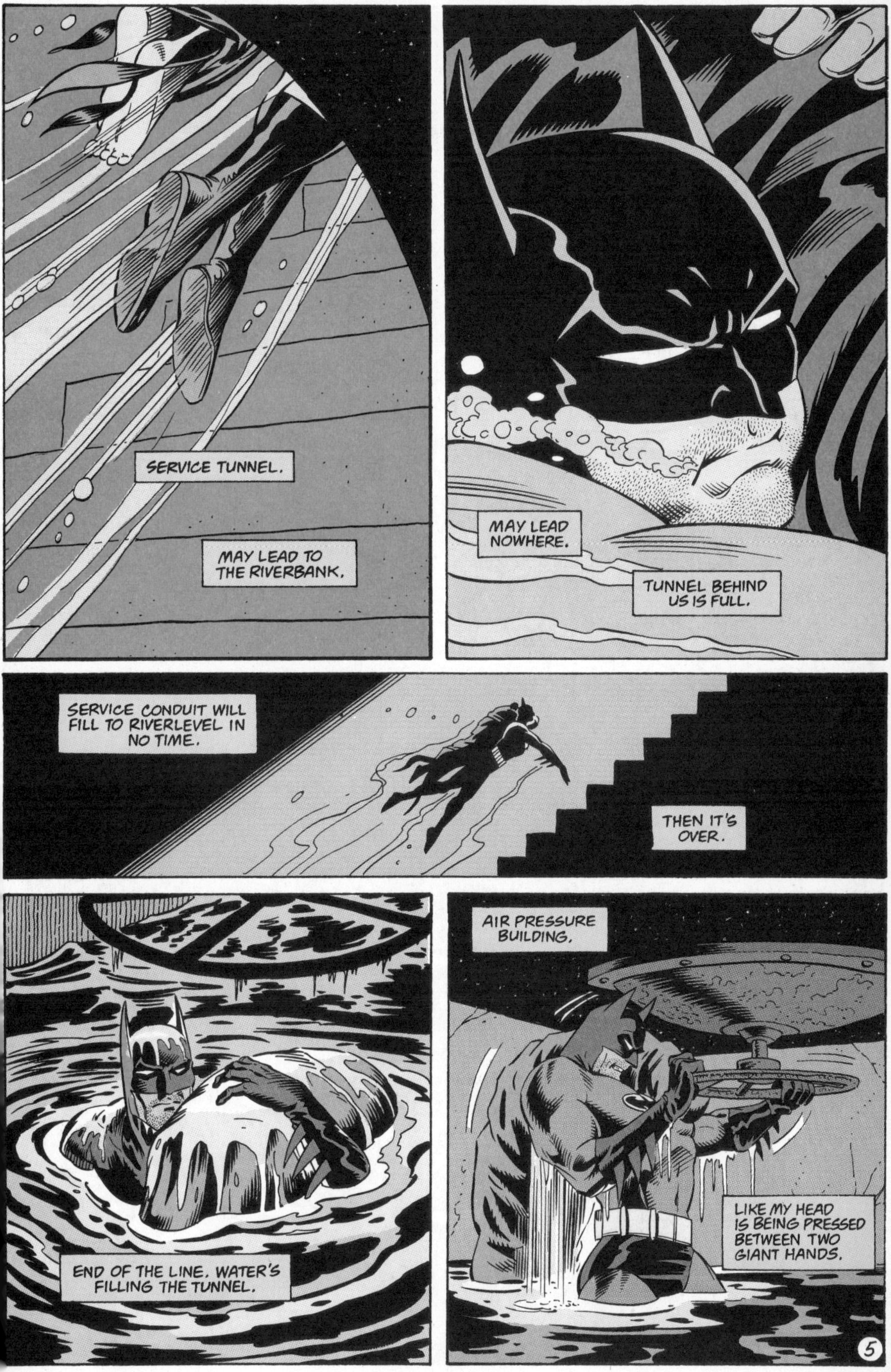
SERVICE TUNNEL.
MAY LEAD TO THE RIVERBANK.
MAY LEAD NOWHERE.
TUNNEL BEHIND US IS FULL.
SERVICE CONDUIT WILL FILL TO RIVERLEVEL IN NO TIME.
THEN IT'S OVER.
END OF THE LINE. WATER'S FILLING THE TUNNEL.
AIR PRESSURE BUILDING.
LIKE MY HEAD IS BEING PRESSED BETWEEN TWO GIANT HANDS.
5

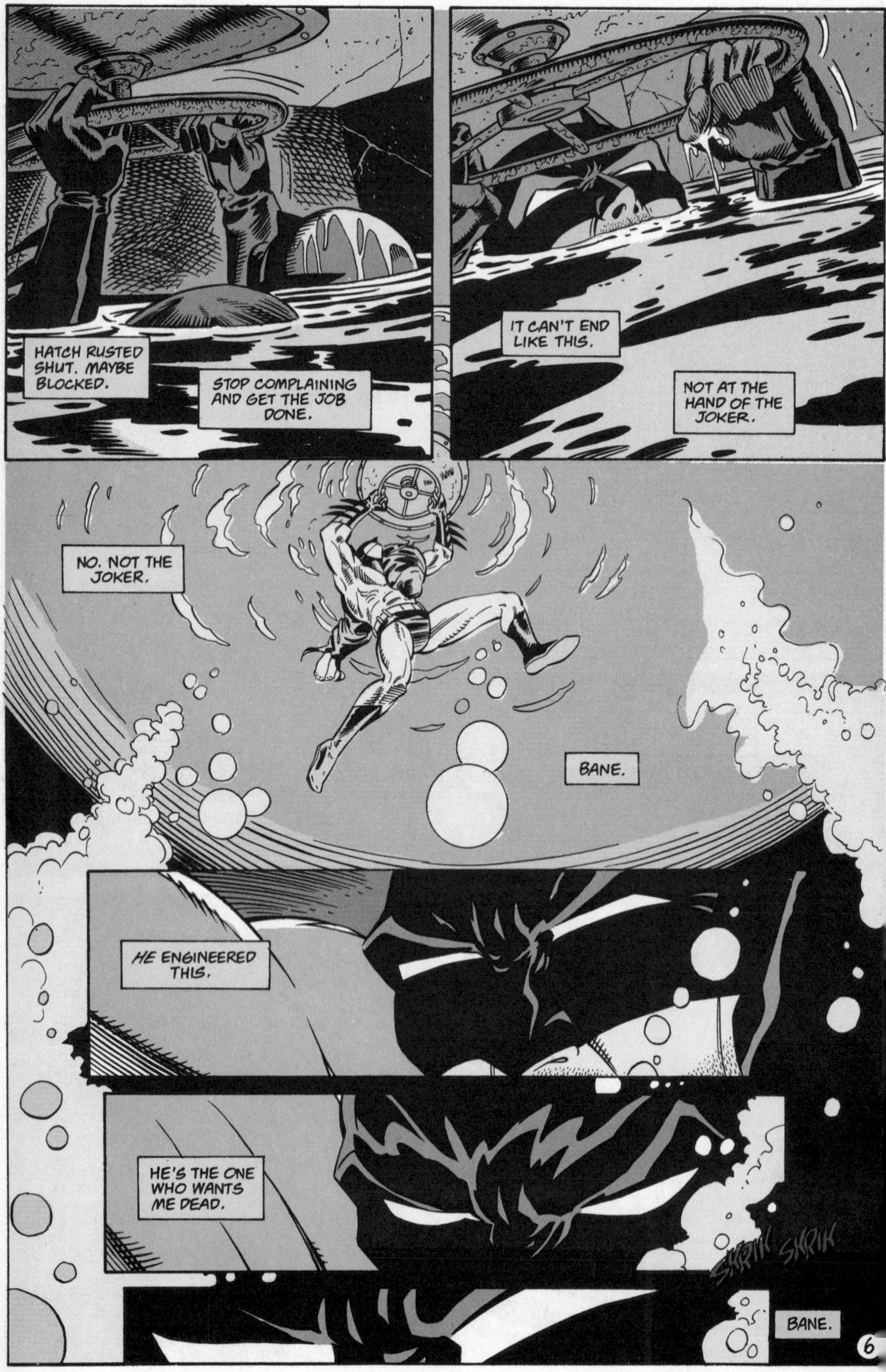
HATCH RUSTED SHUT. MAYBE BLOCKED.
STOP COMPLAINING AND GET THE JOB DONE.
IT CAN'T END LIKE THIS.
NOT AT THE HAND OF THE JOKER.
NO. NOT THE JOKER.
BANE.
HE ENGINEERED THIS.
HE'S THE ONE WHO WANTS ME DEAD.
SKRIK SKRIK
BANE.
6

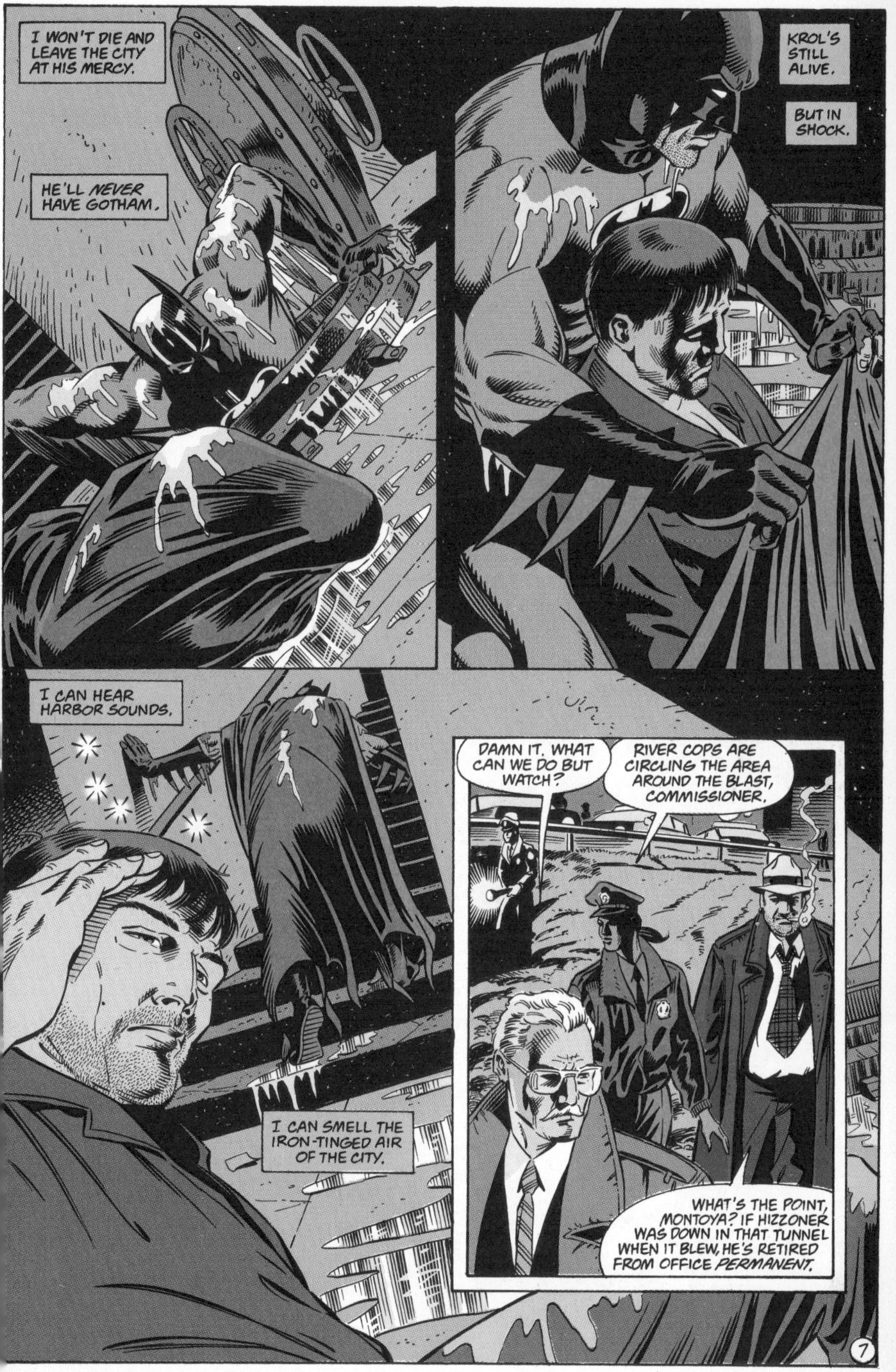
I WON'T DIE AND LEAVE THE CITY AT HIS MERCY.
HE'LL *NEVER* HAVE GOTHAM.
KROL'S STILL ALIVE.
BUT IN SHOCK.
I CAN HEAR HARBOR SOUNDS.
I CAN SMELL THE IRON-TINGED AIR OF THE CITY.
DAMN IT. WHAT CAN WE DO BUT WATCH?
RIVER COPS ARE CIRCLING THE AREA AROUND THE BLAST, COMMISSIONER.
WHAT'S THE POINT, MONTOYA? IF HIZZONER WAS DOWN IN THAT TUNNEL WHEN IT BLEW, HE'S RETIRED FROM OFFICE *PERMANENT*.
7

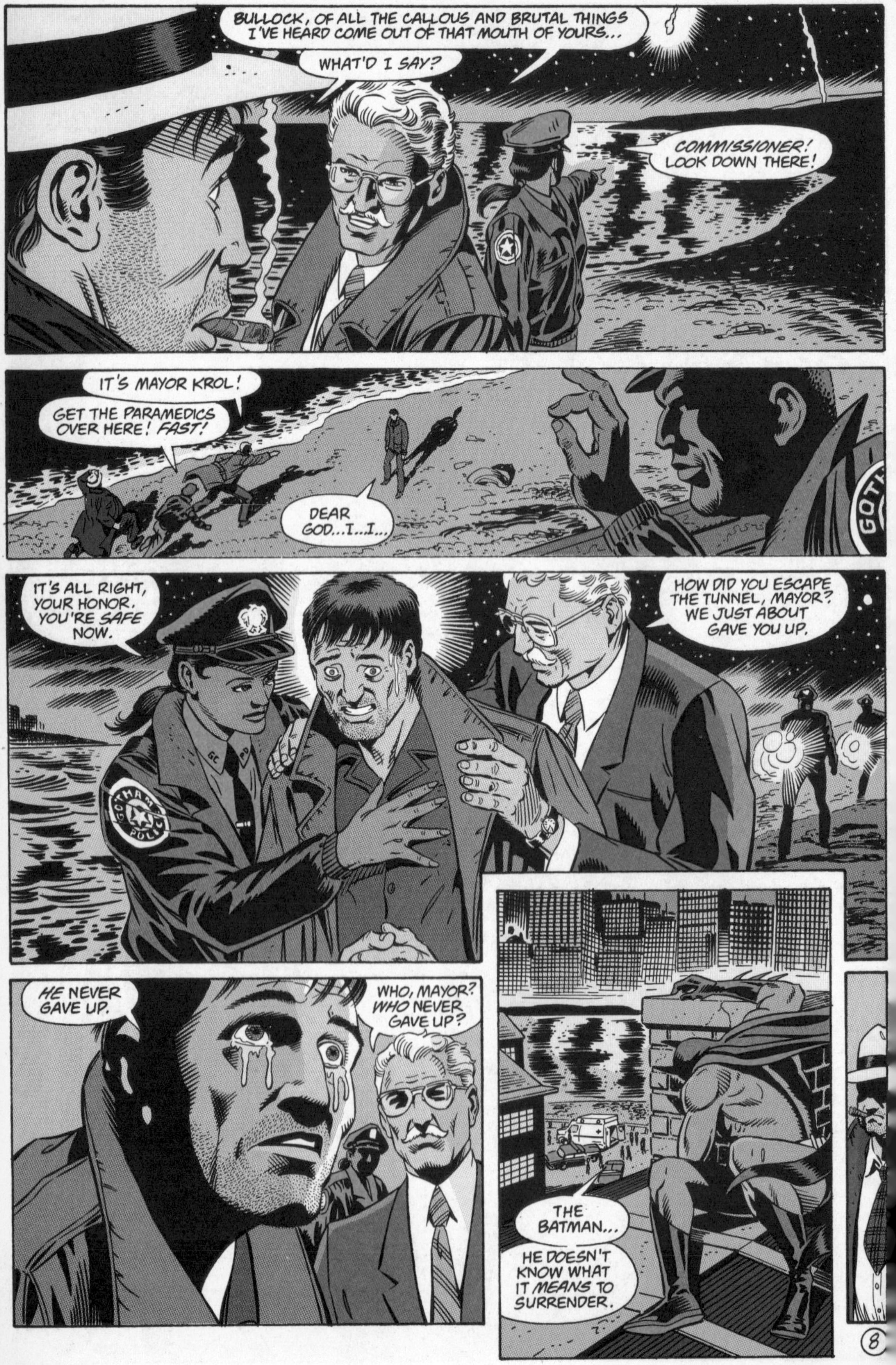
BULLOCK, OF ALL THE CALLOUS AND BRUTAL THINGS I'VE HEARD COME OUT OF THAT MOUTH OF YOURS...
WHAT'D I SAY?
COMMISSIONER! LOOK DOWN THERE!
IT'S MAYOR KROL!
GET THE PARAMEDICS OVER HERE! FAST!
DEAR GOD...I...I...
IT'S ALL RIGHT, YOUR HONOR. YOU'RE SAFE NOW.
HOW DID YOU ESCAPE THE TUNNEL, MAYOR? WE JUST ABOUT GAVE YOU UP.
HE NEVER GAVE UP.
WHO, MAYOR? WHO NEVER GAVE UP?
THE BATMAN...
HE DOESN'T KNOW WHAT IT MEANS TO SURRENDER.
8

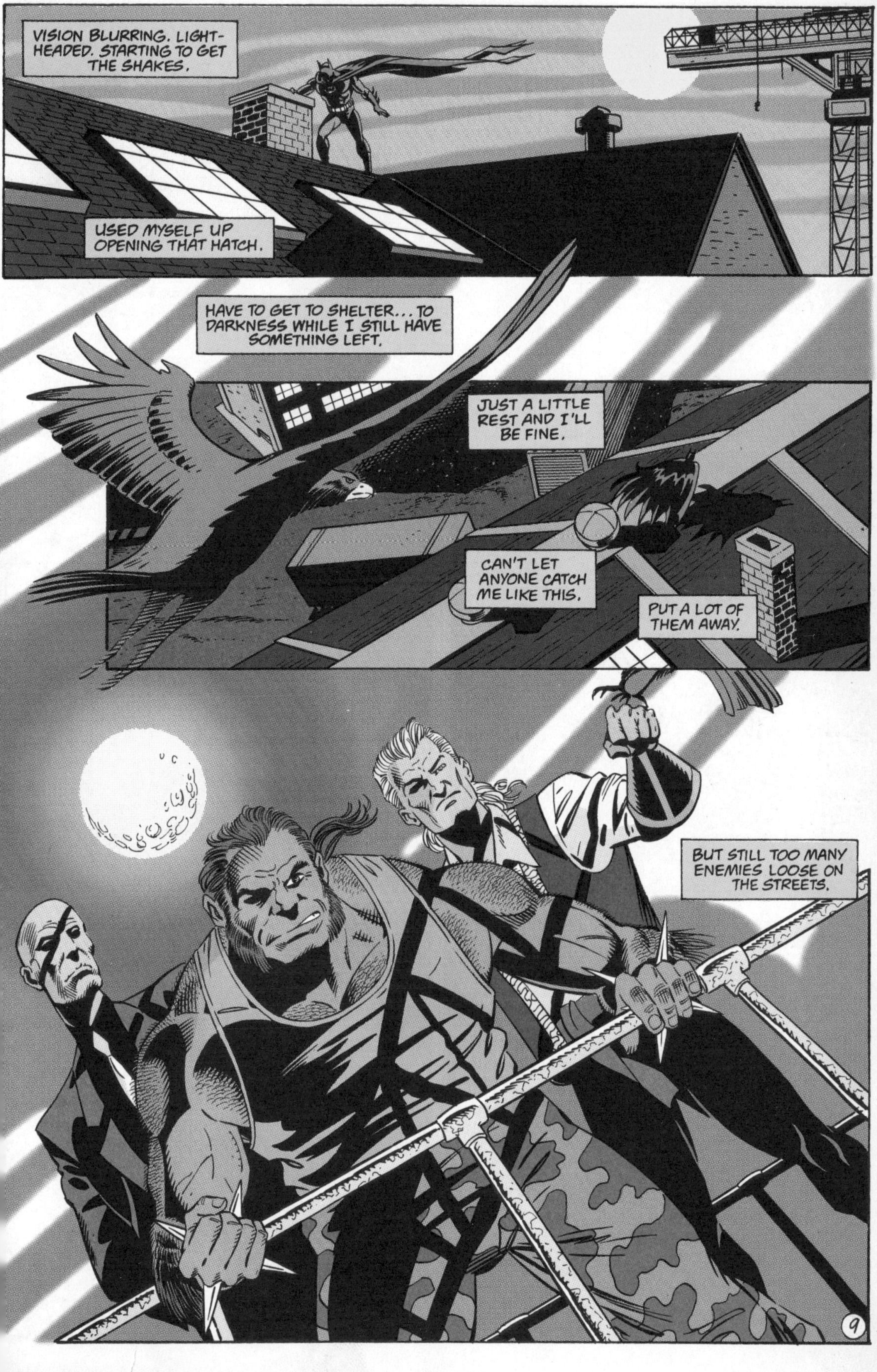
VISION BLURRING. LIGHT-HEADED. STARTING TO GET THE SHAKES.
USED MYSELF UP OPENING THAT HATCH.
HAVE TO GET TO SHELTER... TO DARKNESS WHILE I STILL HAVE SOMETHING LEFT.
JUST A LITTLE REST AND I'LL BE FINE.
CAN'T LET ANYONE CATCH ME LIKE THIS.
PUT A LOT OF THEM AWAY.
BUT STILL TOO MANY ENEMIES LOOSE ON THE STREETS.
9

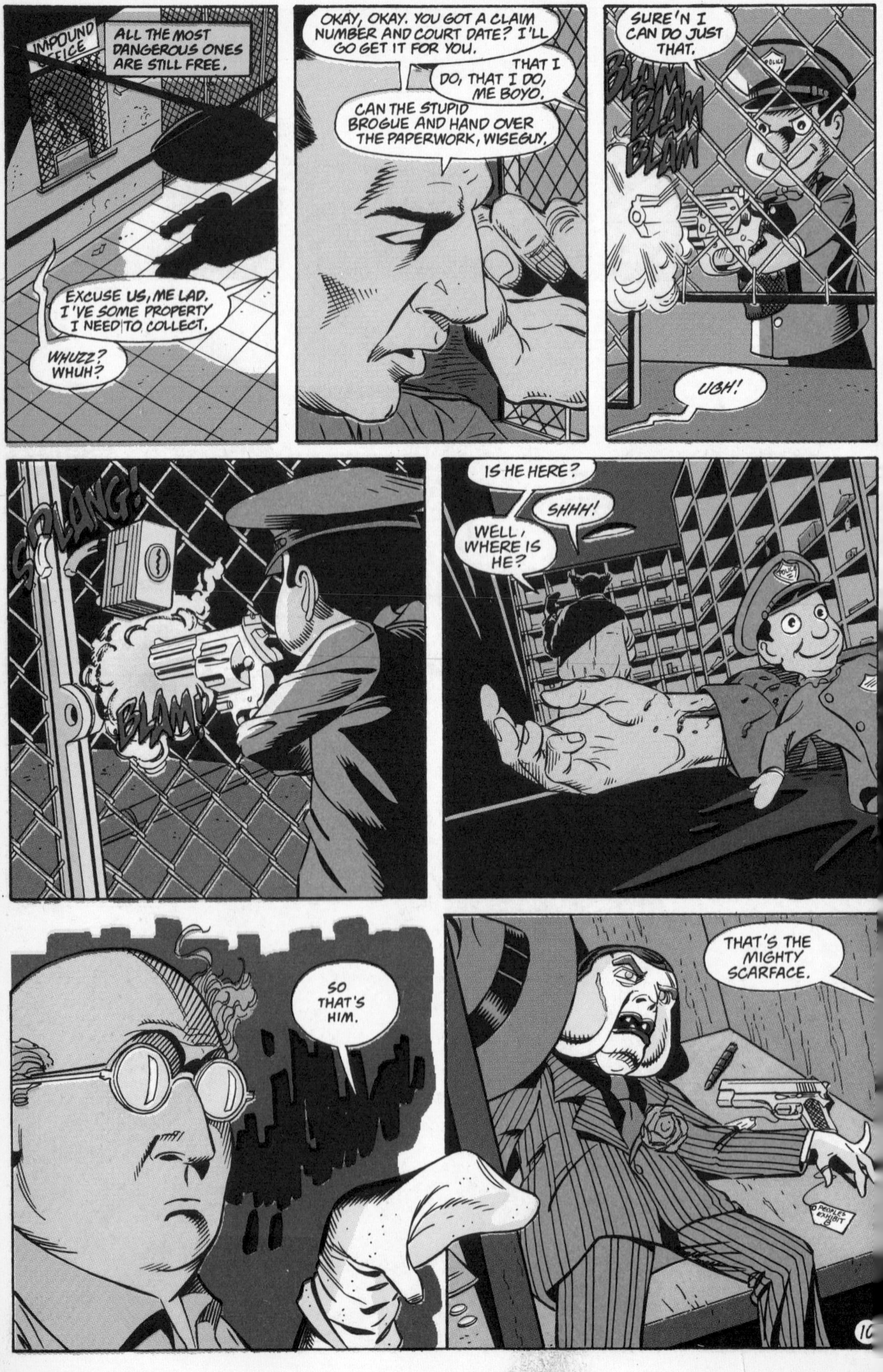
IMPOUND OFFICE
ALL THE MOST DANGEROUS ONES ARE STILL FREE.
EXCUSE US, ME LAD. I'VE SOME PROPERTY I NEED TO COLLECT.
WHUZZ? WHUH?
OKAY, OKAY. YOU GOT A CLAIM NUMBER AND COURT DATE? I'LL GO GET IT FOR YOU.
THAT I DO, THAT I DO, ME BOYO.
CAN THE STUPID BROGUE AND HAND OVER THE PAPERWORK, WISEGUY.
SURE'N I CAN DO JUST THAT.
BLAM BLAM BLAM
UGH!
SPLANG!
BLAM!
IS HE HERE?
SHHH!
WELL, WHERE IS HE?
SO THAT'S HIM.
THAT'S THE MIGHTY SCARFACE.

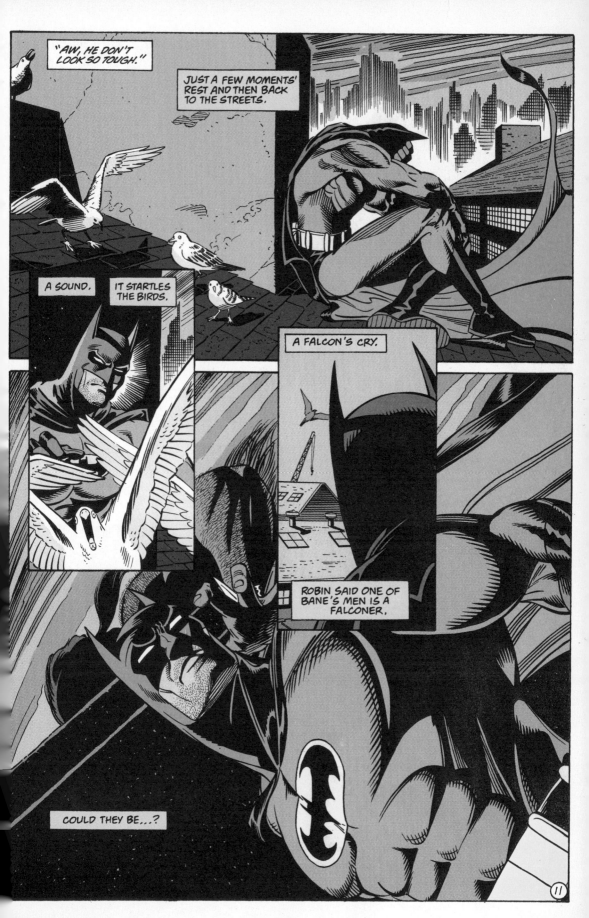

"AW, HE DON'T LOOK SO TOUGH."

JUST A FEW MOMENTS' REST AND THEN BACK TO THE STREETS.

A SOUND. IT STARTLES THE BIRDS.

A FALCON'S CRY.

ROBIN SAID ONE OF BANE'S MEN IS A FALCONER.

COULD THEY BE...?

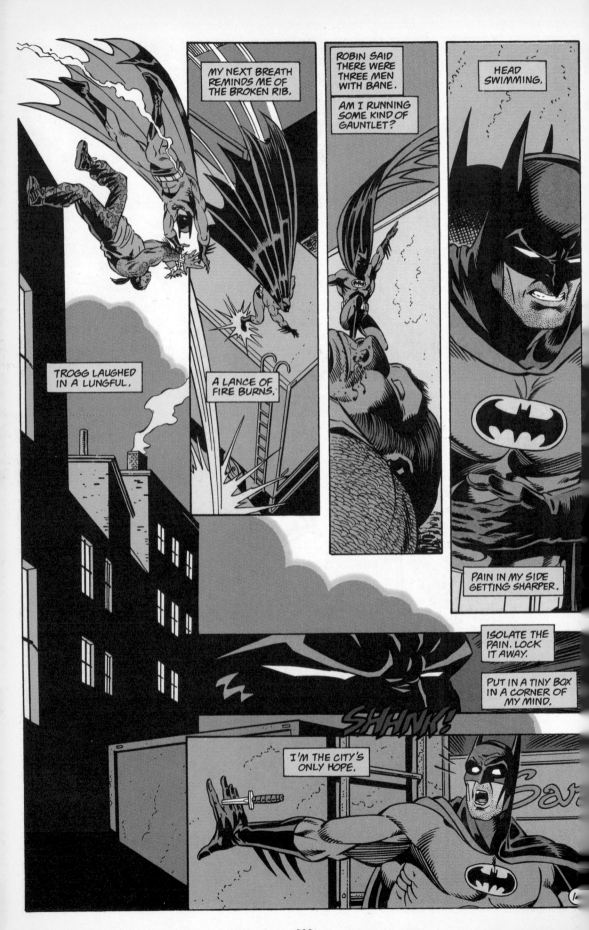

I'M ALL THAT STANDS BETWEEN THESE MONSTERS AND GOTHAM.

IT TAKES AN EXCELLENT EYE TO *MISS* THAT ACCURATELY.

I JUST WANTED YOU TO KNOW THAT I DO NOT RELY ON BRUTE STRENGTH.

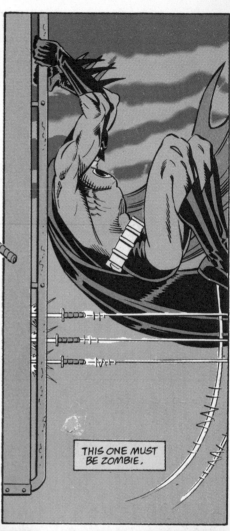

THIS ONE MUST BE ZOMBIE.

SO IT'S ANOTHER TEST.

LIKE BREAKING THE INMATES OUT OF ARKHAM.

ALL TO TEST MY ABILITIES AND ENDURANCE.

AS THOUGH BANE WERE STUDYING ME.

TO WHAT END?

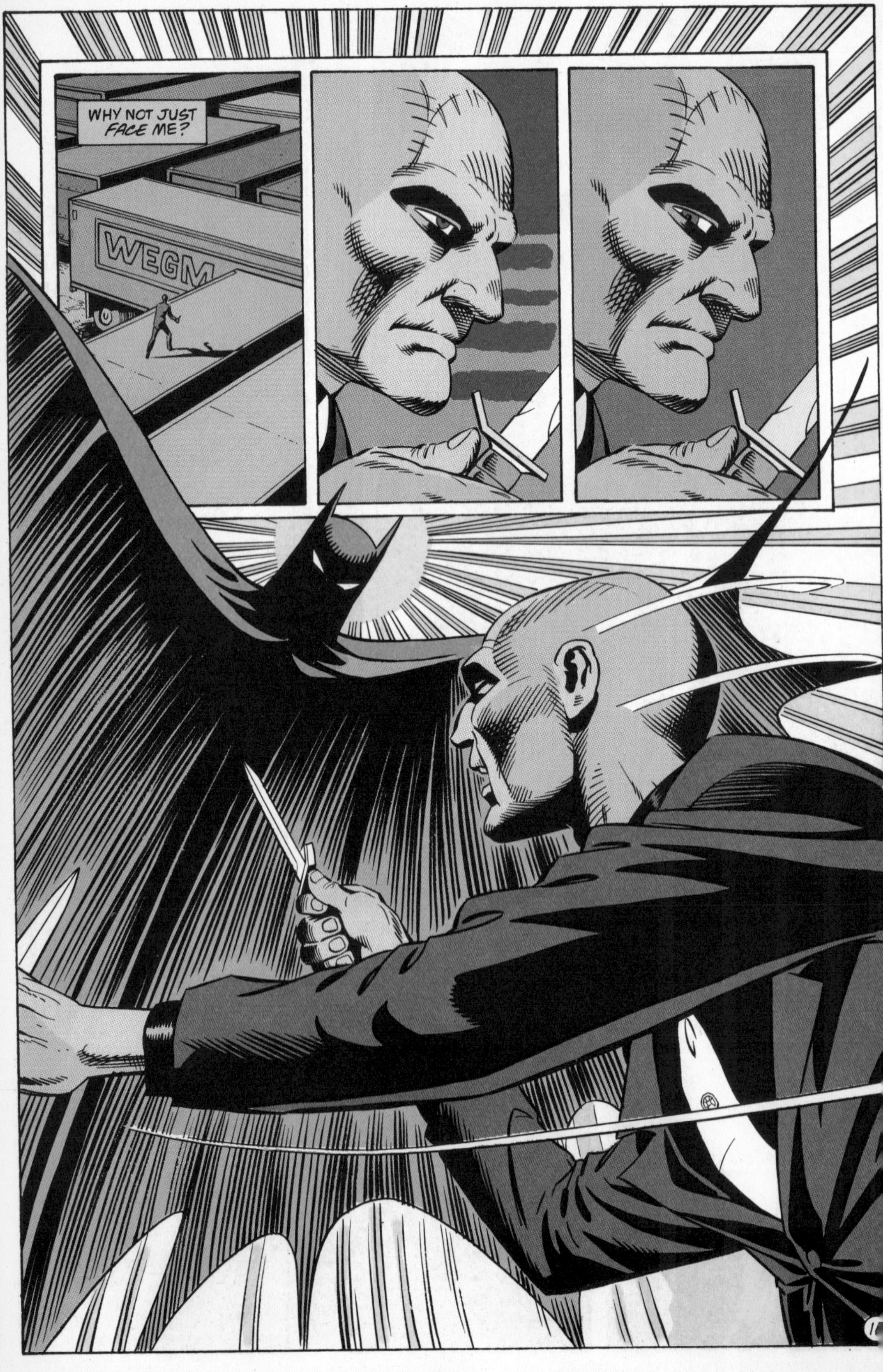
WHY NOT JUST FACE ME?
WEGM

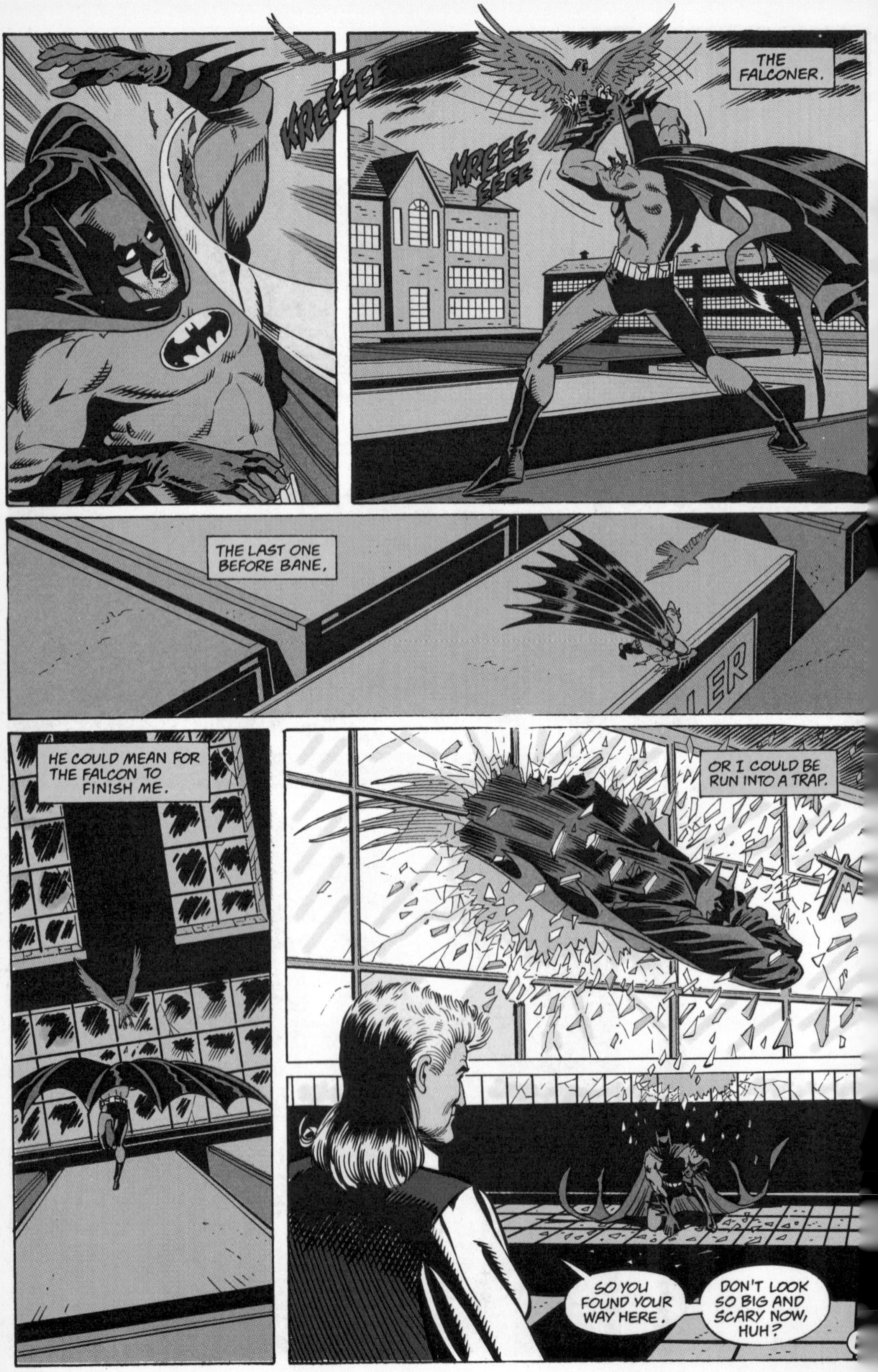

KREEEEE
KREEE-EEEE
THE FALCONER.
THE LAST ONE BEFORE BANE.
HE COULD MEAN FOR THE FALCON TO FINISH ME.
OR I COULD BE RUN INTO A TRAP.
SO YOU FOUND YOUR WAY HERE.
DON'T LOOK SO BIG AND SCARY NOW, HUH?

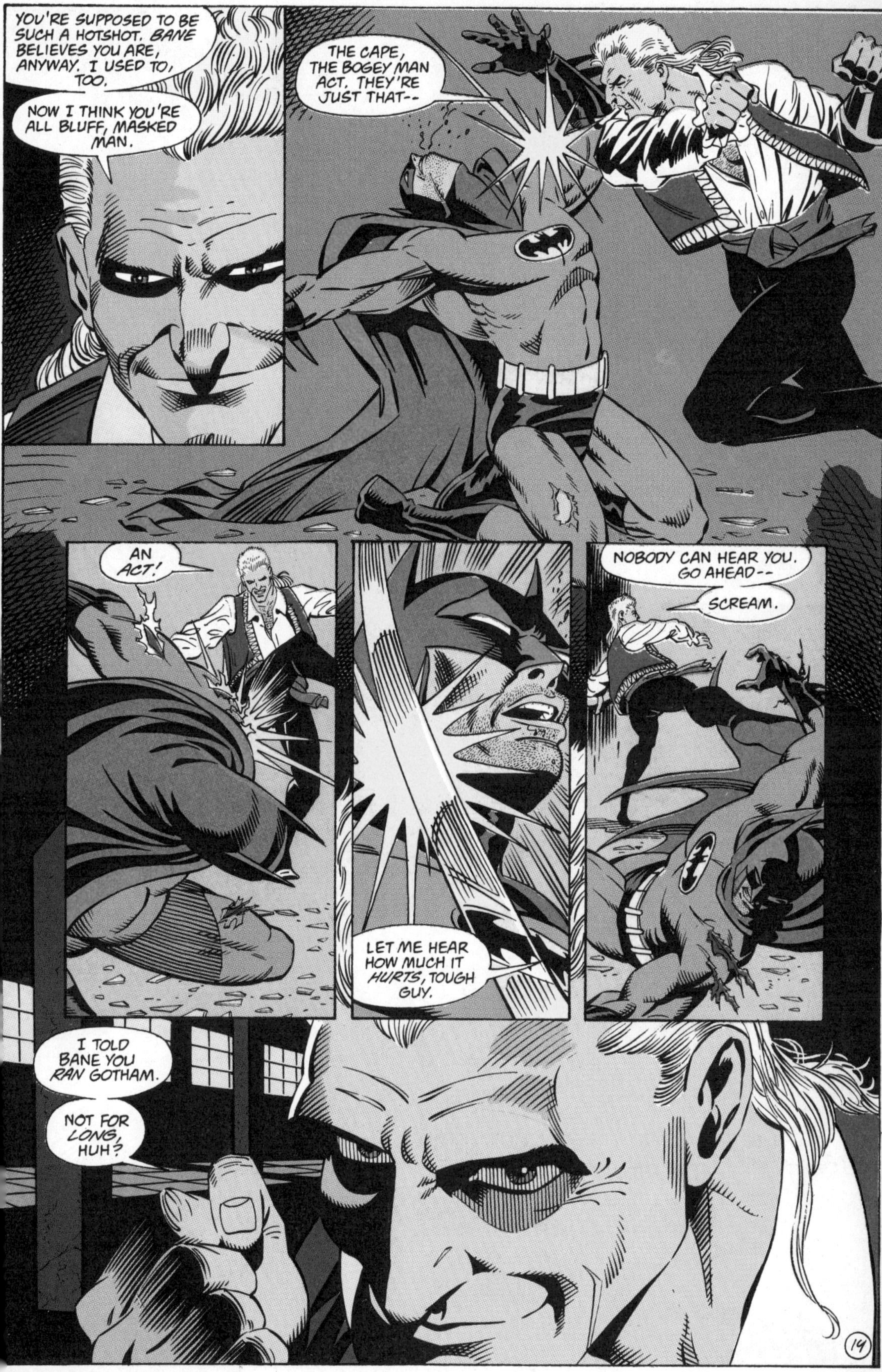
YOU'RE SUPPOSED TO BE SUCH A HOTSHOT. BANE BELIEVES YOU ARE, ANYWAY. I USED TO, TOO.
NOW I THINK YOU'RE ALL BLUFF, MASKED MAN.
THE CAPE, THE BOGEY MAN ACT. THEY'RE JUST THAT--
AN ACT!
NOBODY CAN HEAR YOU. GO AHEAD--
SCREAM.
LET ME HEAR HOW MUCH IT HURTS, TOUGH GUY.
I TOLD BANE YOU RAN GOTHAM.
NOT FOR LONG, HUH?
14

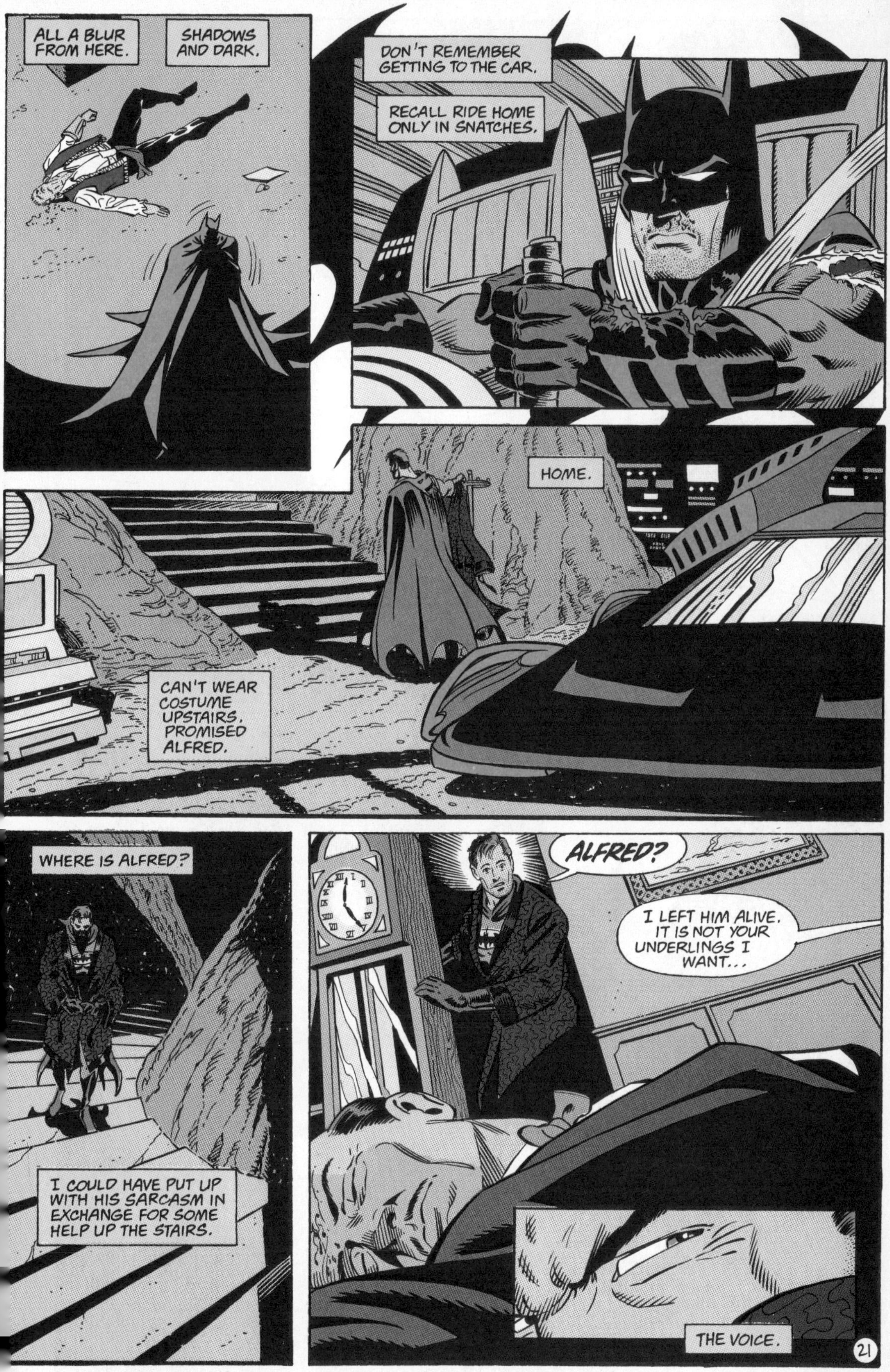
ALL A BLUR FROM HERE.
SHADOWS AND DARK.
DON'T REMEMBER GETTING TO THE CAR.
RECALL RIDE HOME ONLY IN SNATCHES.
HOME.
CAN'T WEAR COSTUME UPSTAIRS. PROMISED ALFRED.
WHERE IS ALFRED?
I COULD HAVE PUT UP WITH HIS SARCASM IN EXCHANGE FOR SOME HELP UP THE STAIRS.
ALFRED?
I LEFT HIM ALIVE. IT IS NOT YOUR UNDERLINGS I WANT...
THE VOICE.
21

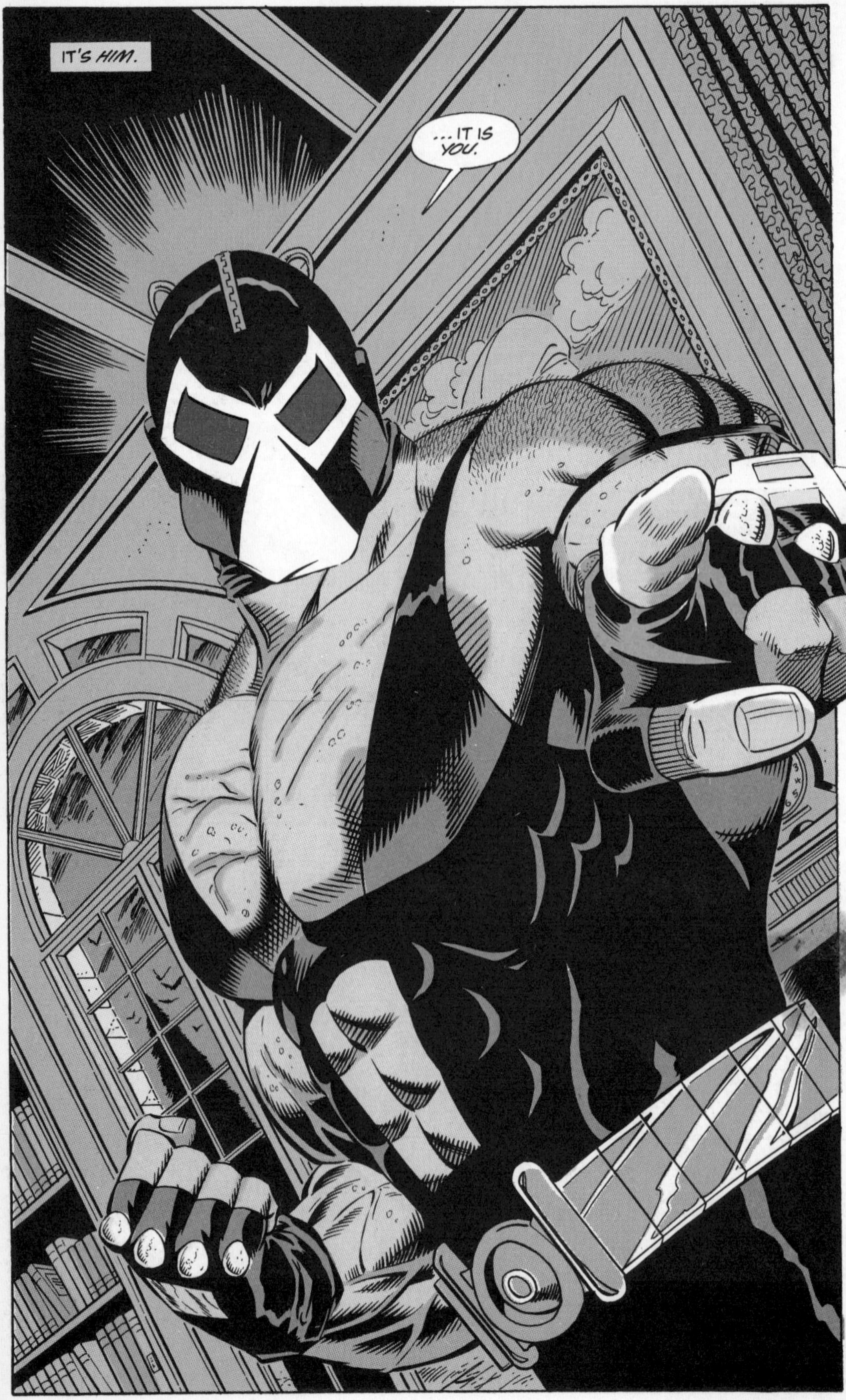
IT'S HIM.
...IT IS YOU.

VENOM, YES -- YOU *FOUND* SOME, NO DOUBT, PUMPED INTO THE *RIDDLER*.

AND YOU ARE... *FAMILIAR* WITH VENOM?

YES.

THEN YOU *KNOW* WHAT IT CAN *DO*?

ALL TOO *WELL*.

YOU *THINK SO*? I THINK *NOT*.

I WAS ONCE MADE A *GUINEA PIG* FOR AN EXPERIMENTAL "*IMPROVED CONCENTRATE*" OF VENOM.

TRUST ME, NO MATTER *WHAT* YOUR PRIOR EXPERIENCE, YOU KNOW *NOTHING* OF *MY* VENOM.

THE SHEER STRENGTH AND *FEROCITY* NOW COURSING THROUGH ME IS ENOUGH TO *BREAK* A MAN -- *ANY* MAN -- LIKE A *DEAD STICK*.

HOW DID YOU KNOW --

I'VE *KNOWN* YOU SINCE I LIVED IN THE HELL OF A *DARK HOLE THOUSANDS OF MILES* FROM HERE.

I'VE KNOWN YOU IN MY *DREAMS*.

3

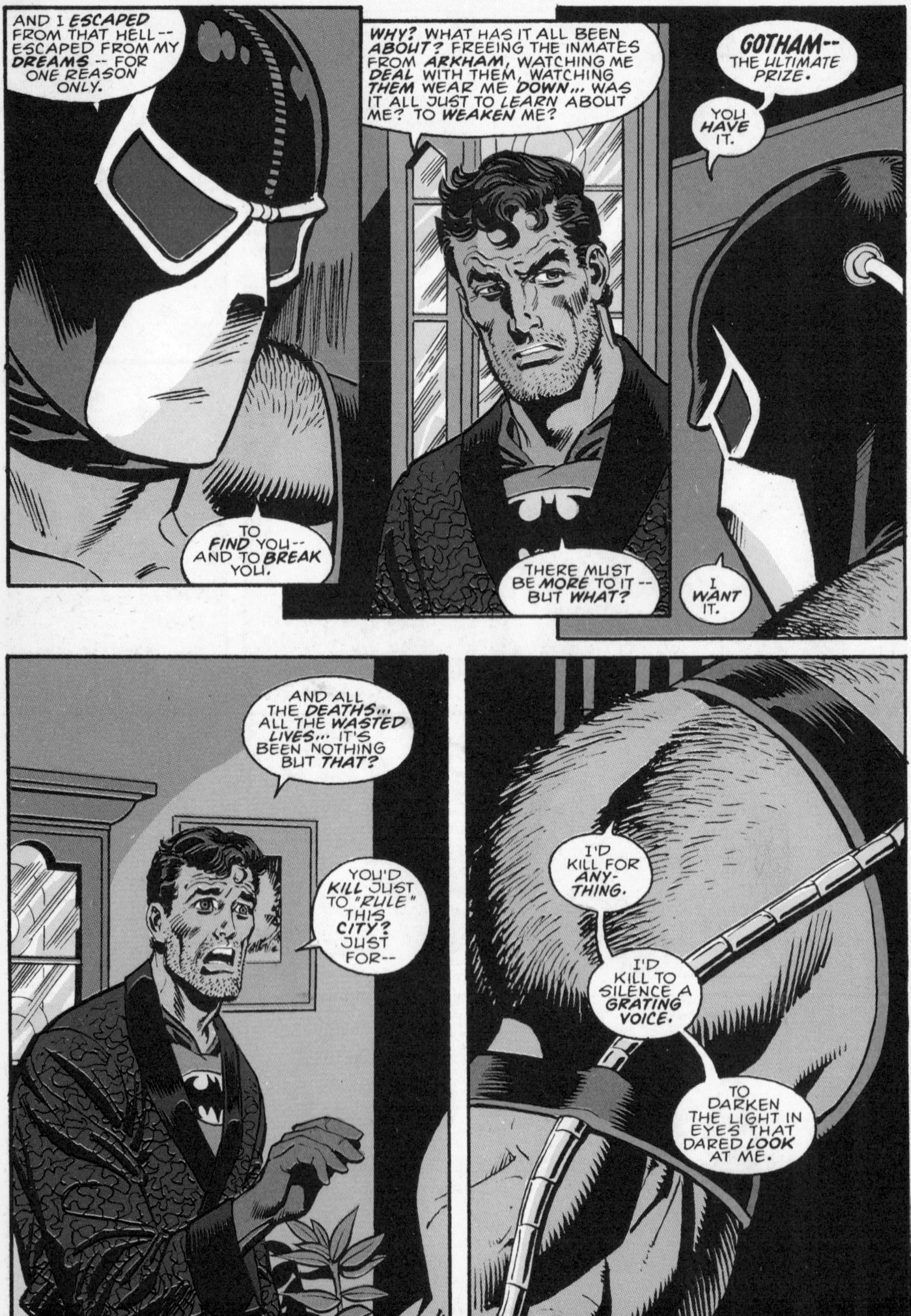
AND I ESCAPED FROM THAT HELL -- ESCAPED FROM MY DREAMS -- FOR ONE REASON ONLY.
TO FIND YOU-- AND TO BREAK YOU.
WHY? WHAT HAS IT ALL BEEN ABOUT? FREEING THE INMATES FROM ARKHAM, WATCHING ME DEAL WITH THEM, WATCHING THEM WEAR ME DOWN... WAS IT ALL JUST TO LEARN ABOUT ME? TO WEAKEN ME?
THERE MUST BE MORE TO IT -- BUT WHAT?
GOTHAM-- THE ULTIMATE PRIZE.
YOU HAVE IT.
I WANT IT.
AND ALL THE DEATHS... ALL THE WASTED LIVES... IT'S BEEN NOTHING BUT THAT?
YOU'D KILL JUST TO "RULE" THIS CITY? JUST FOR--
I'D KILL FOR ANY-THING.
I'D KILL TO SILENCE A GRATING VOICE.
TO DARKEN THE LIGHT IN EYES THAT DARED LOOK AT ME.
4

THEN WHILE YOU *REVEL* IN IT, BANE, I'M *SICK* OF DEATH -- SICK OF *BLOOD* -- SICK OF THE CHAOS AND HORROR YOU'VE BROUGHT TO GOTHAM --

--AND RIGHT INTO MY *HOME.*

I'VE SPENT MY *LIFE* FIGHTING YOUR KIND OF MADNESS AND EVIL --

-- AND NOW THAT LIFELONG FIGHT HAS BROUGHT ME TO DEATH'S *DOOR,* MY *OWN* DOOR...

I WOULD NOT *BE* HERE WERE IT *OTHER-WISE.*

I REALIZE THAT -- AND I REALIZE YOU MAY WELL BE THE *SINGLE GREATEST* SOURCE OF MADNESS AND EVIL I'VE EVER FACED...

EASILY.

AND IN *THAT* CASE...

...ONE *MORE* TIME.

BUT *THIS* TIME IS DIFFERENT.

5

251

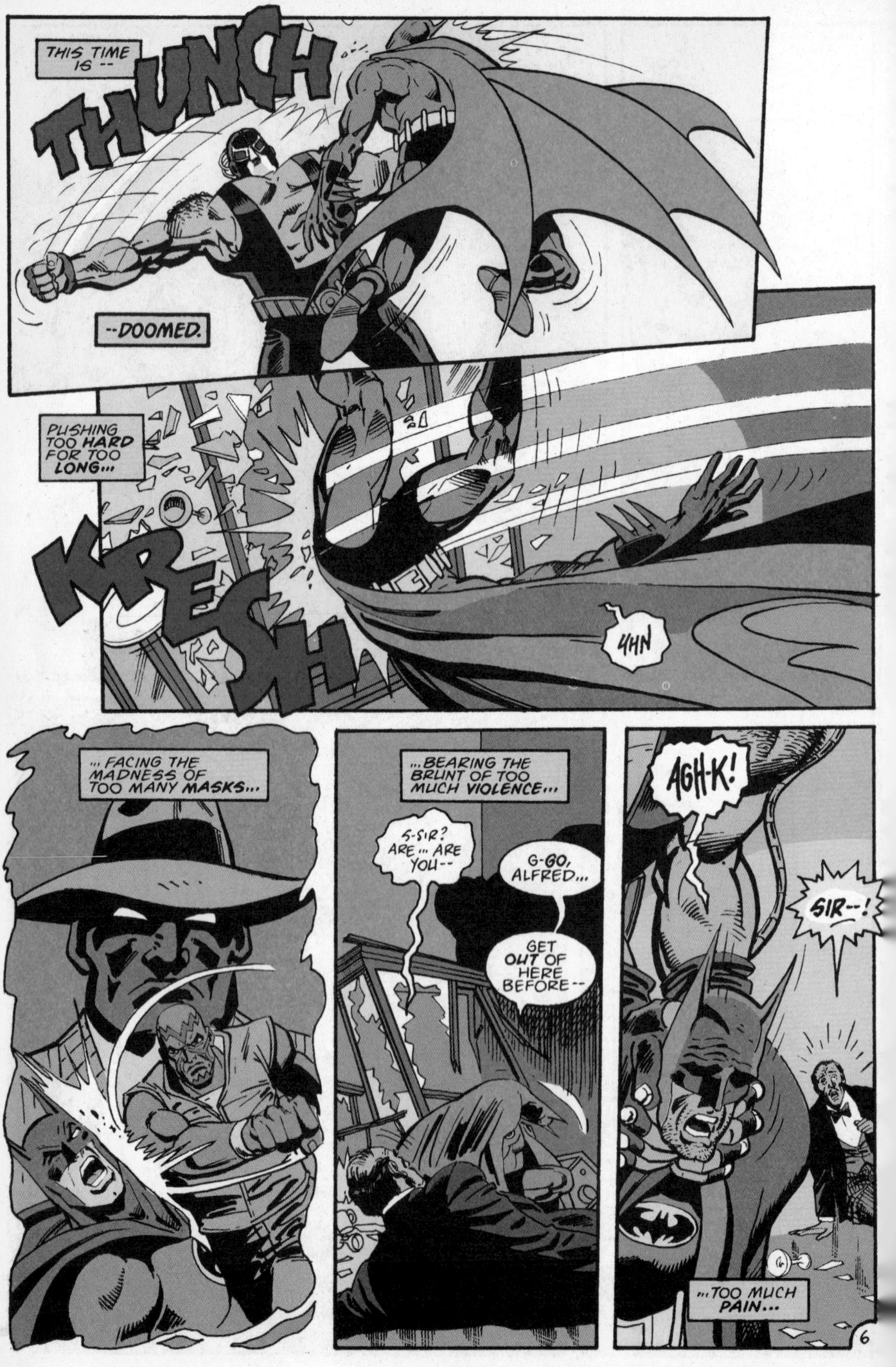

THIS TIME IS --
THUNCH
--DOOMED.
PUSHING TOO HARD FOR TOO LONG...
KRESSH
UHN
...FACING THE MADNESS OF TOO MANY MASKS...
...BEARING THE BRUNT OF TOO MUCH VIOLENCE...
S-SIR? ARE... ARE YOU--
G-GO, ALFRED...
GET OUT OF HERE BEFORE--
AGH-K!
SIR--!
...TOO MUCH PAIN...
6

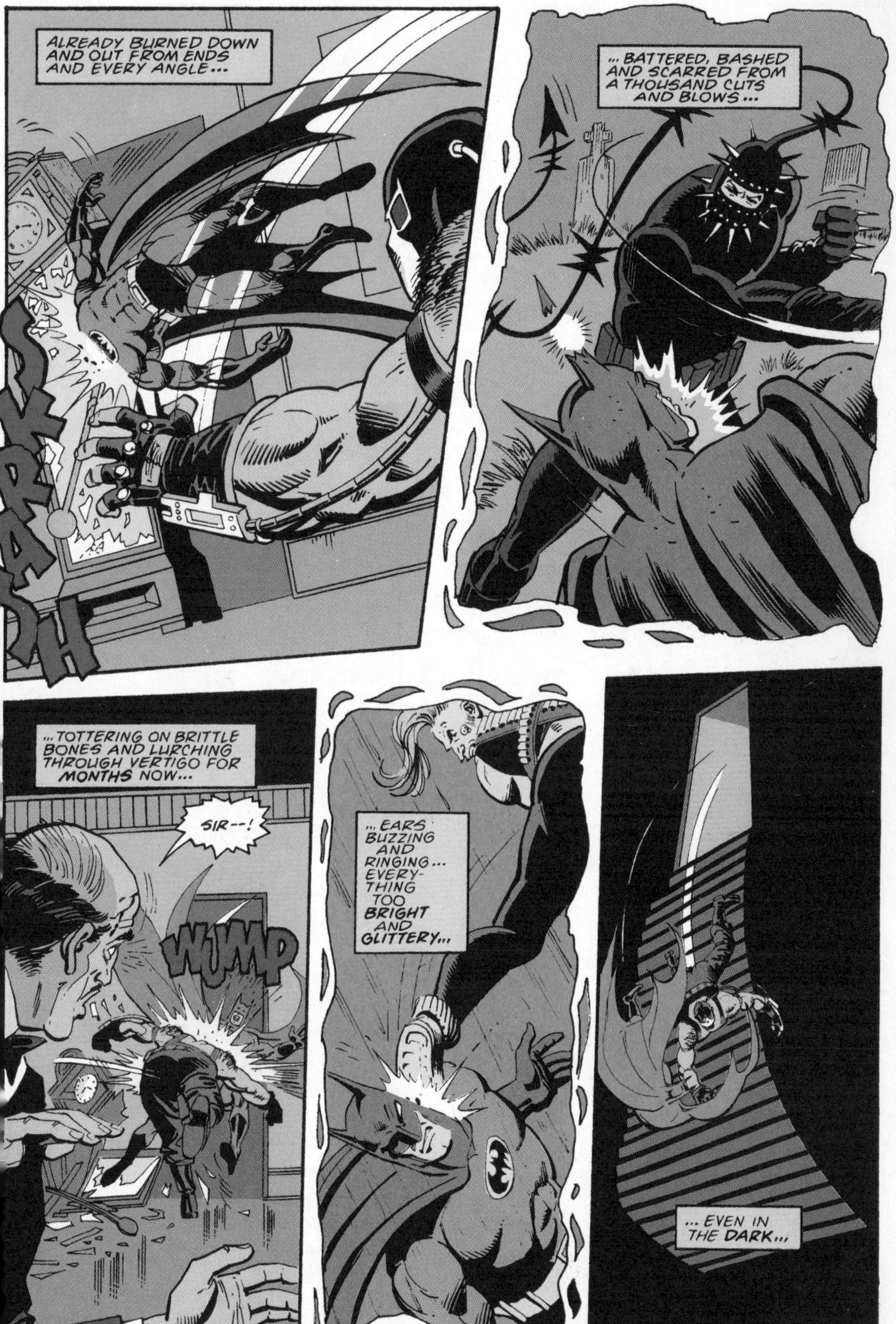
ALREADY BURNED DOWN AND OUT FROM ENDS AND EVERY ANGLE...
...BATTERED, BASHED AND SCARRED FROM A THOUSAND CUTS AND BLOWS...
...TOTTERING ON BRITTLE BONES AND LURCHING THROUGH VERTIGO FOR MONTHS NOW...
SIR--!
WUMP
...EARS BUZZING AND RINGING... EVERY-THING TOO BRIGHT AND GLITTERY...
...EVEN IN THE DARK...

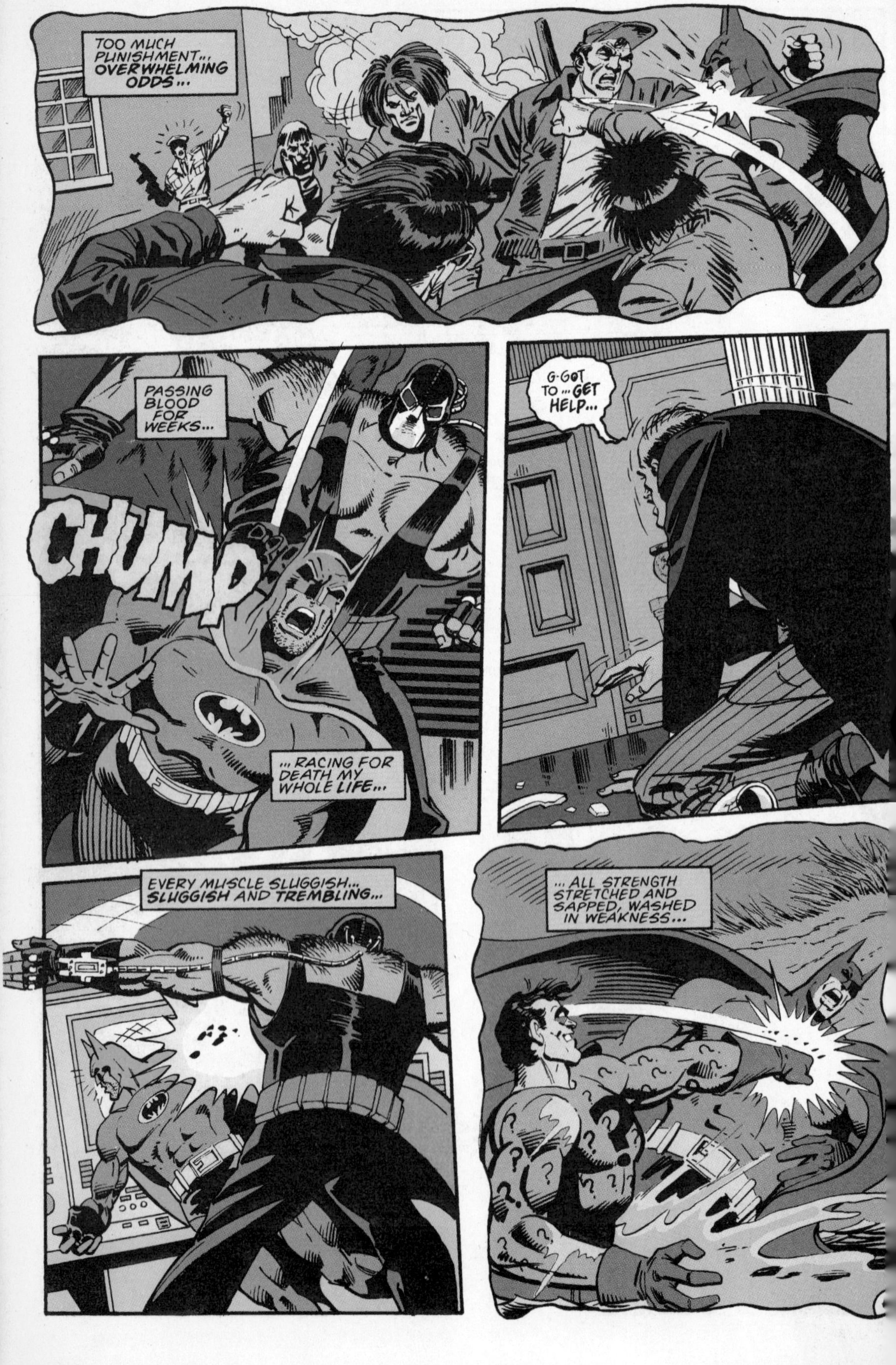
TOO MUCH PUNISHMENT... OVERWHELMING ODDS...
PASSING BLOOD FOR WEEKS...
CHUMP
...RACING FOR DEATH MY WHOLE LIFE...
G-GOT TO ... GET HELP...
EVERY MUSCLE SLUGGISH... SLUGGISH AND TREMBLING...
...ALL STRENGTH STRETCHED AND SAPPED, WASHED IN WEAKNESS...

KRUNCH

... MIRED IN A SLOW-MOTION PANIC OF HELPLESSNESS...

... AND THROUGH IT ALL, NO SLEEP, NO REST...

... EVEN WHEN MOVEMENT ITSELF WAS IMPOSSIBLE...

... NOTHING BUT THE MIND'S DESPERATE URGE TO GET OFF THE FLOOR AND STRIKE BACK.

... EVEN WHEN EVERY UPHILL EFFORT IS WASTED AND FUTILE...

YOU ARE ALREADY BROKEN.

CHFT

... REALITY ITSELF SMASHED AND SPLINTERED, LIKE THE RUDE DEATH OF AN IMPOSSIBLE DREAM...

9

BUT STILL THEY LOOMED AND LUNGED FROM THE DARK...

...LAUGHING DEMONS WITH BAD INTENT...

...BEARING PAIN AND NOTHING MORE...

SHUMP

...CHIPPING AWAY AT WHATEVER WAS LEFT...

WUMP

...WEARING ME DOWN TOWARD NOTHING...

BRIING BRIING

STILL NOT HOME...

...EVEN AT NIGHT.

DR. SHONDRA KINSO

...AND NOWHERE.

THWOK

12

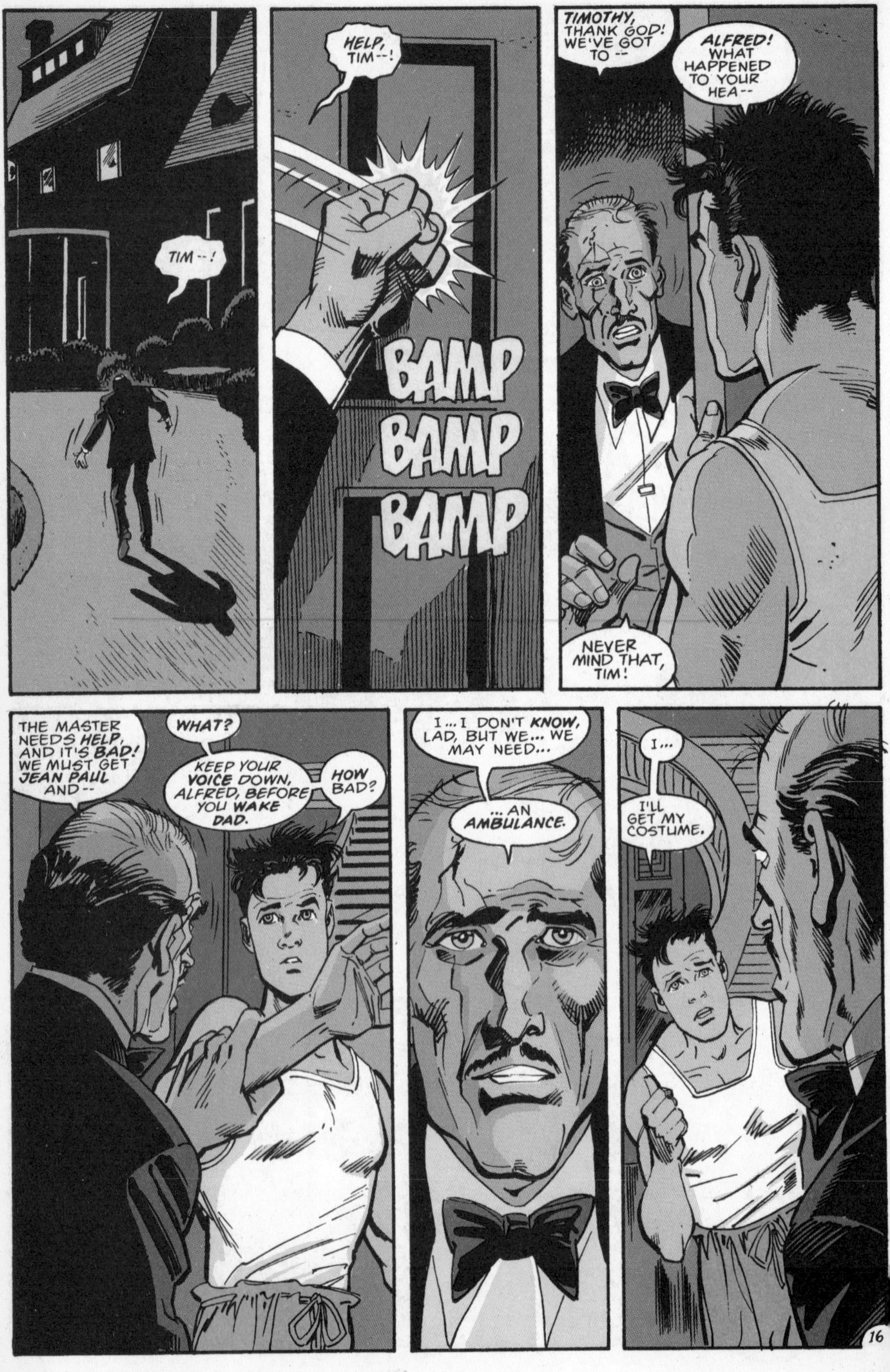
TIM--!
HELP, TIM--!
BAMP BAMP BAMP
TIMOTHY, THANK GOD! WE'VE GOT TO --
ALFRED! WHAT HAPPENED TO YOUR HEA--
NEVER MIND THAT, TIM!
THE MASTER NEEDS HELP, AND IT'S BAD! WE MUST GET JEAN PAUL AND--
WHAT?
KEEP YOUR VOICE DOWN, ALFRED, BEFORE YOU WAKE DAD.
HOW BAD?
I... I DON'T KNOW, LAD, BUT WE... WE MAY NEED...
... AN AMBULANCE.
I...
I'LL GET MY COSTUME.
16

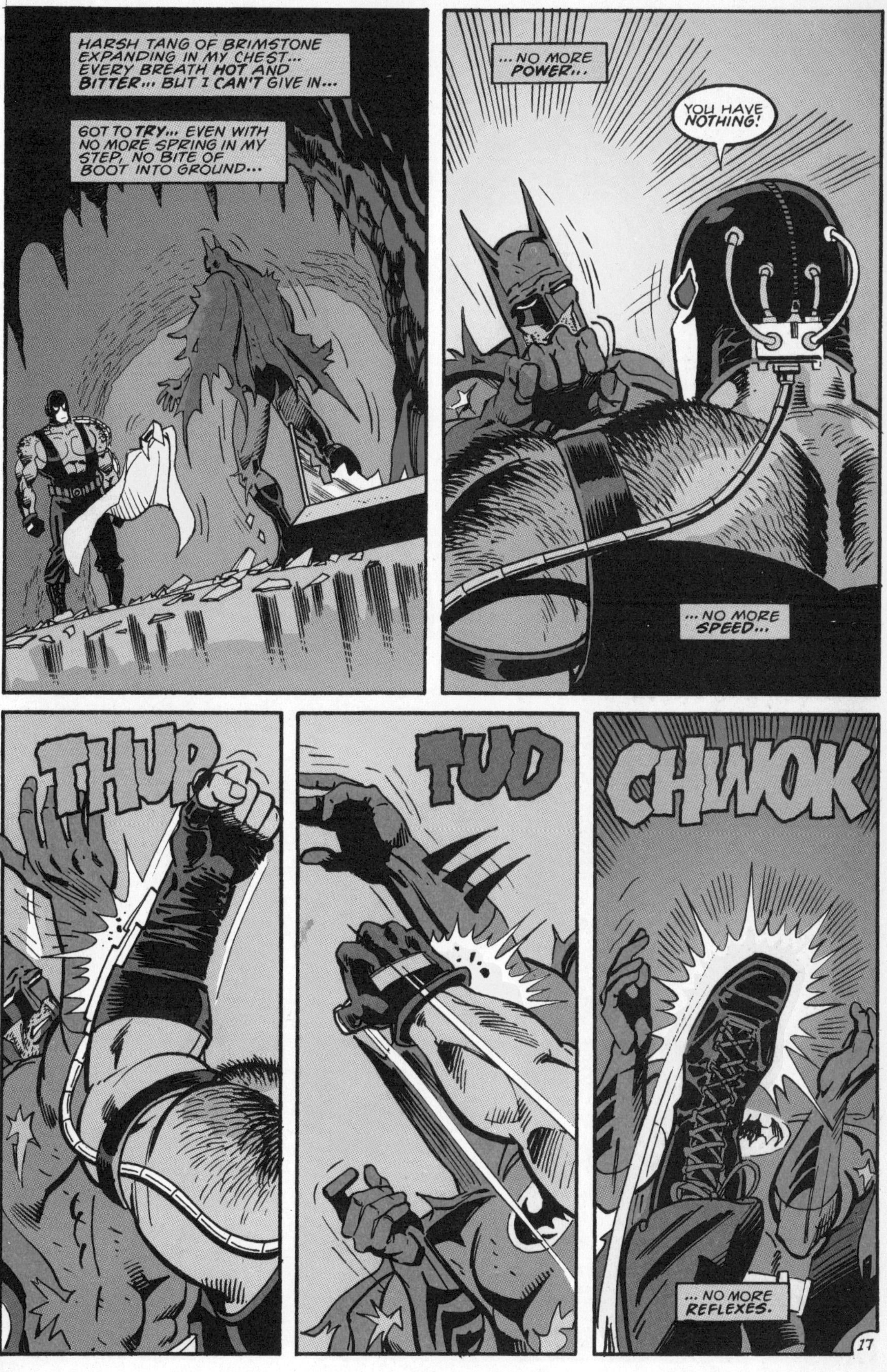
HARSH TANG OF BRIMSTONE EXPANDING IN MY CHEST... EVERY BREATH HOT AND BITTER... BUT I CAN'T GIVE IN...
GOT TO TRY... EVEN WITH NO MORE SPRING IN MY STEP, NO BITE OF BOOT INTO GROUND...
...NO MORE POWER...
YOU HAVE NOTHING!
...NO MORE SPEED...
THUP
TUD
CHWOK
...NO MORE REFLEXES.
17

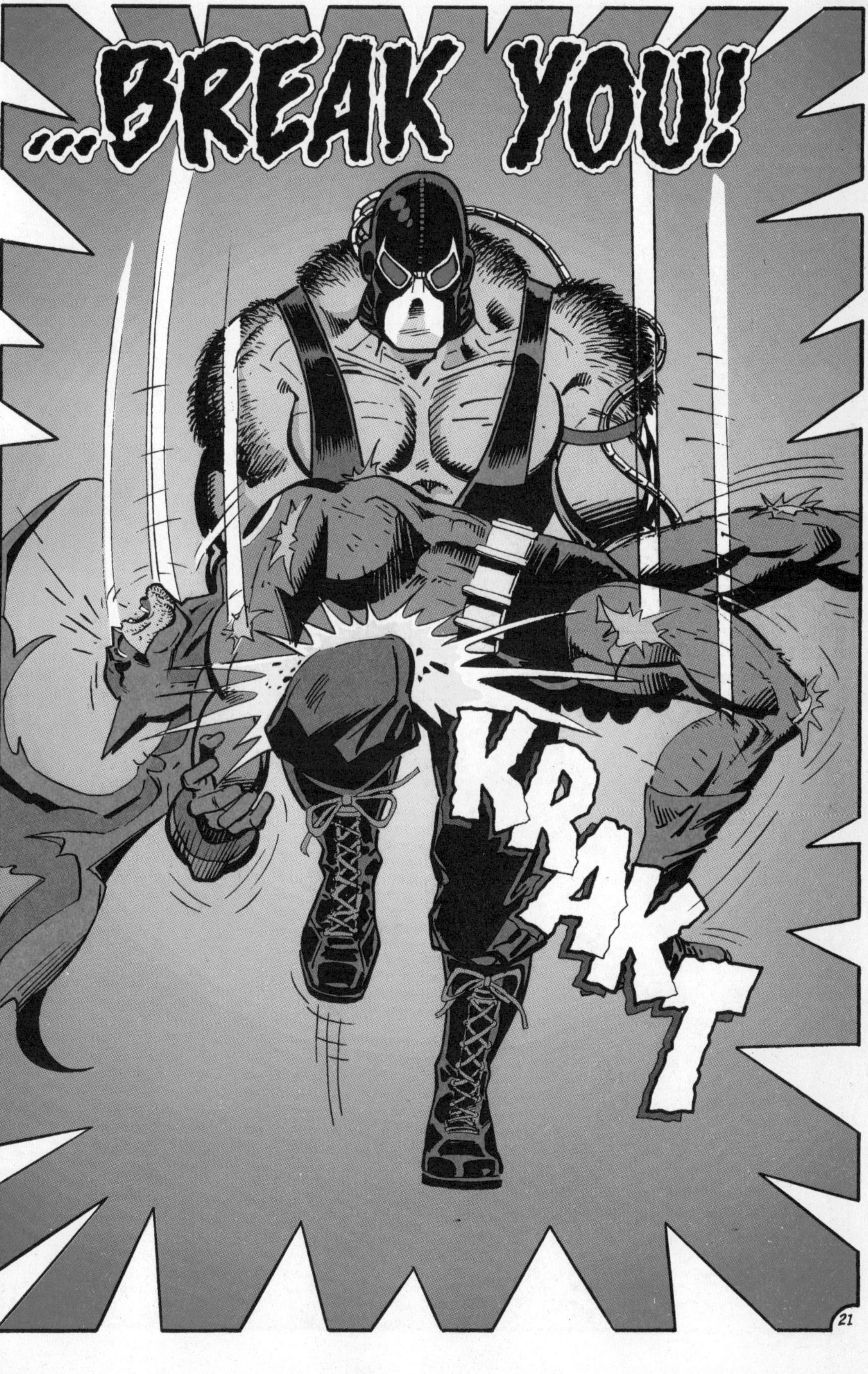
...BREAK YOU!
KRAKT
21

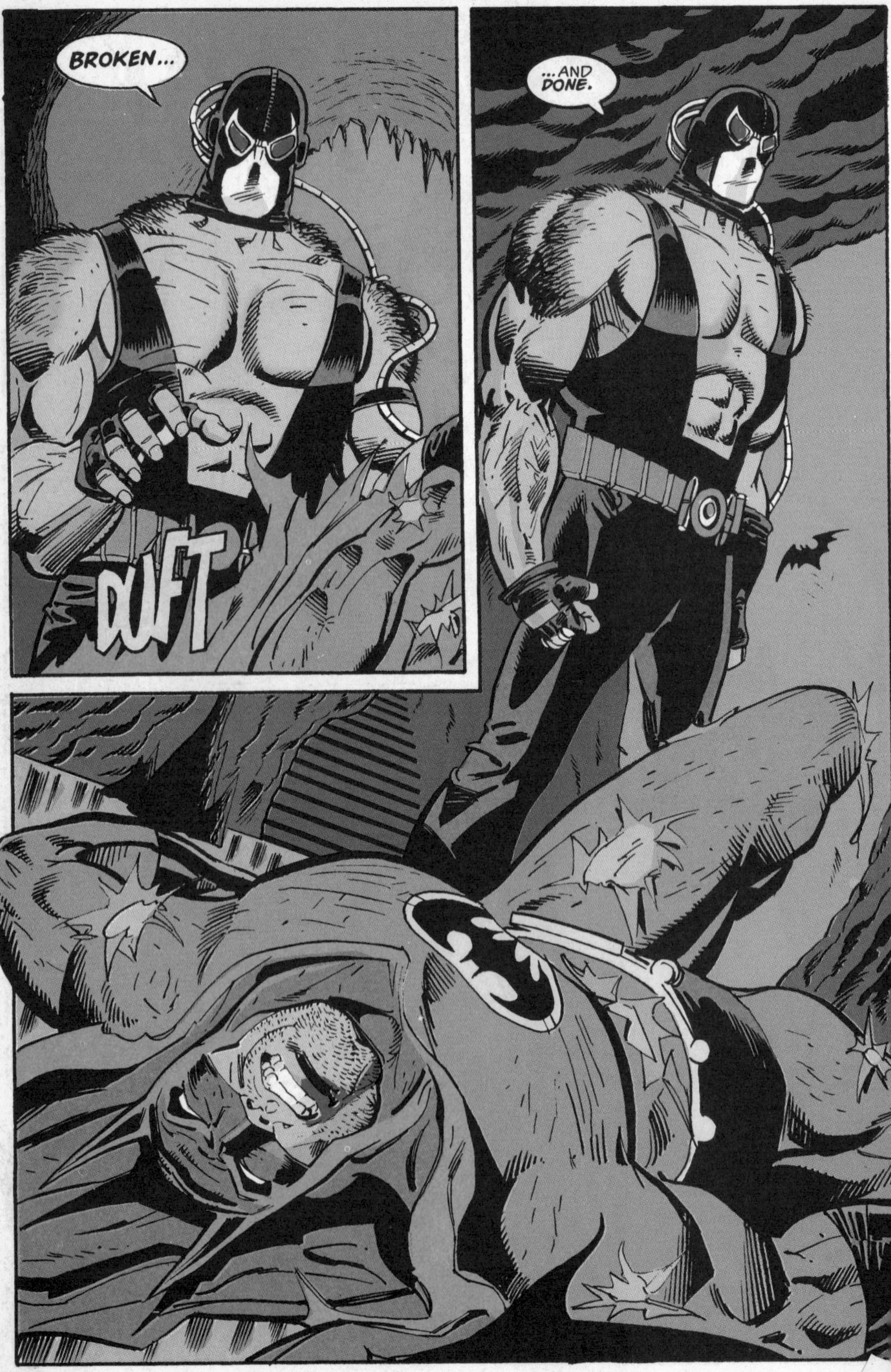
BROKEN...
...AND DONE.
DUFT

BATMAN:
THE LONG HALLOWEEN

JEPH LOEB TIM SALE
BATMAN
THE LONG HALLOWEEN

JEPH LOEB/TIM SALE

BATMAN:
DARK VICTORY

JEPH LOEB TIM SALE
BATMAN
Dark Victory

JEPH LOEB/TIM SALE

BATMAN:
HAUNTED KNIGHT

From the Eisner Award-winning creators
JEPH LOEB TIM SALE
BATMAN
HAUNTED KNIGHT

JEPH LOEB/TIM SALE

BATMAN:
SCARECROW TALES

BATMAN
SCARECROW TALES

VARIOUS

BATMAN:
BLIND JUSTICE

BATMAN
BLIND JUSTICE
SAM HAMM
DENYS COWAN
DICK GIORDANO

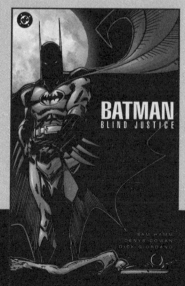

SAM HAMM/DENYS COWAN/
DICK GIORDANO

BATMAN:
TALES OF THE DEMON

BATMAN
TALES OF THE DEMON
Featuring
BATMAN'S
Deadliest Opponent
RA'S AL GHUL!

DENNIS O'NEIL/
NEAL ADAMS/VARIOUS

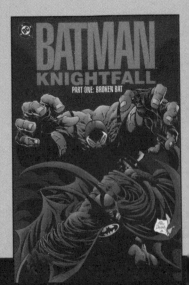